An Accident of Birth

by

T. Alex Blum

UnCollected Press

An Accident of Birth

Cover Art / Design:

Calvin Lyte, Sr.
Rebecca Whitney

Back Cover Portrait:

Suzanne Strong

Book Design by:

UnCollected Press
8320 Main Street, 2nd Floor
Ellicott City, MD 21043

For more books by UnCollected Press:
www.therawartreview.com

First Edition 2026
ISBN: 979-8-9938987-1-1

For my brothers, Hank, Pete, and Bill, and of course, for Andrea

“We live two lives. The one we learn with, and the life we live after that.”

Bernard Malamud

there is only one sin
beyond forgiveness, and
that is fear of a code. To
fail someone who needs
you, to starve someone
of love, because you fear
to offend against a code -
that's a mortal sin —

you, [illegible]
come to terms
with yourself
again — never

Prologue

I find myself on the Amtrak Acela with Andrea, my wife, traveling from New York to Baltimore to meet my brother Hank for the first time. He is two years younger than I am, and the eldest of my three younger brothers. Eventually, we will meet Pete, the middle brother, and Bill, the youngest, but this will be the first in-person meeting we have had with any of my birth family since we were connected on 23andMe. The ride has become uncomfortable for me. The only seats we could find are facing backwards, and I am fighting uneasiness, motion sickness, watching the scenery go by in the wrong direction, things appearing suddenly in the foreground and then racing into the distance, as memories do, receding at high speed even as I try to hold onto them long enough to make some sense of them.

We are making this trip to Baltimore because unexpectedly, I am reinterpreting my past, adding a parallel narrative to my life story and filling in the gaps. I have always known I was adopted, but now the blank spaces in my history are filling in, like words appearing on a blank page, revealing some of the mysteries of that adoption. Who was I, how does that knowledge affect who I am now? What have I inherited, good, bad, or indifferent? Unexpectedly, I have three full brothers; what can they tell me, and what questions can I answer for them? And how does it affect the person I am today, this new perspective, as inevitably it pulls me back into the past? Can it tell me anything about the life I have lived and the decisions I have made?

We enjoy a wonderful dinner at the Sagamore Pendry Hotel with Hank and his wife Jen. It doesn't feel like meeting for the first time, it feels like being reunited with old friends. We share stories from the past, but they are not exactly shared experiences, they are parallel stories; it's like comparing notes, orienting ourselves, something that will happen again when we meet Peter and Bill and their wives a few months later in Florida. It was funny at that first meeting how similar we look, Hank and I, and if you see the four of us together, it's obvious we are brothers, but it's not just our appearance, it's also our mannerisms that are strikingly similar, and the way we communicate with each other is seamless and unselfconscious. There are people I have known for decades that I am less comfortable with than I was with my brothers in the first hour I knew them. From the first time we spoke on the phone, it has been strangely as if we have known each other our whole lives, and we are just filling in the blank spaces between us, random events we have missed.

Of course it's common to assign ourselves powers of prescience, to experience premonitions, to invent connections, to find fate in coincidence, to see patterns in the universe, where there is only randomness. Daniel Kahneman, in his book *Thinking Fast and Slow* draws on his extensive research to show instead how massively we underestimate the significance of luck and coincidence in the major events of our lives.

James Gleick, in his book *The Information*, describes in an equally compelling fashion the foundational power of DNA in human experience, noting, as Samuel Butler said, "A hen is just an egg's way of making another egg."

It's not an argument you can resolve, it's a dilemma with no resolution, and in my experience, they are both right. My innate connection to my brothers was compelling and visceral from the very first, and the whole thing happened because of pure luck and coincidence. Welcome to the universe.

My brother Pete has two daughters, who both play key roles in this story. Brook, Pete's younger daughter, sent away to 23andMe for a kit for her husband. Amazon sent her an extra one by mistake. She could have just thrown it away, or forgotten about it, but instead she decided to go ahead and send in a sample, and that simple decision, really just a flip of a coin, sparked the connection between me and my brothers, proving Kahneman correct that the most important things that happen in life are often the product of pure luck. I had been on 23andMe for years and discovered almost nothing, but that one decision Brook made changed everything.

Jamie, Pete's older daughter, filled in the family history for me. No one asked her to; she just did it. There was a locked chest of what was assumed to be family papers and pictures and stuff in Bill's attic in New Jersey. Jamie and her boyfriend Nick took the initiative to go and retrieve that box. They, literally, broke it open and indeed there were photographs and papers in it, but they also made a discovery that was essential to my understanding of the story, my story, and my brothers' story as well.

My birth mother died in the late nineties, and my adopted mother died in 2001, a few years later, so there was never going to be an opportunity to peel away the years and address the history with either one of them, there was never going to be a dramatic moment of revelation, a scene for the cameras. But my birth mother did leave me one brief message, not directly addressed to me, perhaps, but still a message. I don't think she ever expected to find me, but she left a note, unsigned and unaddressed, which is the only direct expression of her feelings that exists, so far as any of us know.

The note is written in pencil on two sides of a faded scrap of yellow lined paper in loopy pencil script that Jamie found at the bottom of the box that she and Nick found in Bill's attic.

On one side it says:

There is only one sin beyond forgiveness and that is fear of a code. To fail someone who needs you, to starve someone of love because you fear to offend against a code, that's a mortal sin.

On the other:

You never come to terms with yourself again – never.

And that is the origin story of my life.

Chapter One: Just the Facts

As far as I can tell, a dysfunctional family is any family with more than one person in it... (Mary Karr)

The young woman who wrote that note, my birth mother, barely twenty years old, pregnant and unmarried, gave me up, and four months later, I became part of a family that was not hers, or, from the perspective of DNA, mine either, a family she would never know.

At that moment, my life began with a mystery, a question, and since then, the world has always seemed to me like a Chinese box, a problem to solve, a puzzle, a search for somewhere to belong, a life story without history or context.

I was given up for adoption in 1955, when adoption was largely anonymous, confidential, and essentially firewalled, with no exchange of information permitted between any of the parties for any reason. Until recently, I knew nothing about my birth mother; I had no idea what she went through, or why she gave me up. I didn't know even the simple facts – that she had an affair in her early twenties with a married man close to twice her age, a man she probably met at work, she got pregnant, and she was forced by circumstances, and her family, to give up her child. Then, a short time later, he left his wife, and they were married. I wonder, did it feel strange to her to start a family barely a year later with the father of her first child, the child she had given up? Did it affect the family she did have, the three boys, Hank, Pete, and Bill, her sons, my brothers, born after she married our father? And then, ten years later, how did she feel when her husband died, in yet another reversal of fortune, leaving her with three boys under the age of ten to raise? Did she feel anger at the unfairness of it? Despair?

Those three boys, Hank, Pete, and Bill, and I, four brothers, connected after almost a lifetime apart, have pieced the basic story together, their story and mine, filling in the blanks as best we can, building bridges to each other across decades of parallel lives.

Our father was a global executive for a soft drink company, and they were expatriates, living in Johannesburg for a while, then moving to Bad Homburg, Germany. In Africa, the boys had a Zulu nanny; in Germany they went to Frankfurt International School. They vacationed all over Europe, visiting castles in the Alps and spending weekends in Paris. Then on vacation at a spa in Italy, their father (no longer mine) suddenly falls ill, is taken to the hospital, and dies overnight of meningitis. His wife finds herself a single mother of three boys, returning to the States, scraping to get by, selling real estate in Darien, Connecticut and sending her boys to public school.

I can only guess at the challenges she faced. I think the note clearly suggests the trauma and guilt she felt about giving up her child. I have some knowledge of the experiences of my brothers from their stories - losing their father, sticking together to survive the parenting of an erratic, unpredictable alcoholic mother, torturing them over the older brother she "lost in childbirth", repeatedly reminding them about her disappointments. In some sense, as Aldous Huxley and others have said, everyone is ultimately unknowable, and certainly that is true of her for me, but in a sense also to the three boys she raised. Ultimately, we can put the pieces of her story together, but the truth of it, how she thought and felt, why she became what she became, how she could have been different, if she could have been different, we will never really know. Her name was Emily; most people called her Lee, and I am the son she lost, and the older brother Hank and Pete and Bill never had, until now.

In the 50's, adopted children were discouraged from even raising the question of their history or birth family. It was strictly off limits. That was the prevailing wisdom about how adoption should be managed, and the laws of practically every state required a court order to allow an adoptee to access any information about the circumstances of their birth.

I'm not certain when I first learned that I was adopted, but I do remember a conversation about it when I was very young that was probably the first one. I have a vision of my adopted parents' bedroom in the Upper East Side brownstone where I grew up, in midtown Manhattan. My parents, Nancy and John, had twin beds with polished wood headboards and there was a marble fireplace with an upholstered chaise longue in front of it, and I think my adopted older brother, Jonathan, and I were sitting together on the chaise longue. It was evening, probably not summer or we would have been at our country home, in Connecticut, where my mother grew up. This was probably the first time the subject was ever discussed, but for some reason, I felt as a child as if it was something I had always known, that I had never experienced learning about it as an event, it was taken for granted. I just knew my brother and I were adopted, and we were given to understand that it was no big deal, just something we shared, like hair color, but the opposite, a matter-of-fact explanation of the absence of common DNA, something that explained why we didn't look alike. I suppose my parents would have had to explain what it meant to be adopted, but I'm guessing they cut to the chase and kept the discussion of birth parents and related subjects to a minimum. They would almost certainly have been instructed by the adoption agency to be matter of fact and keep it simple, and they would have leaned right into that, because they were that way by nature, very disinclined to explore the emotional landscape of anything. This is how I remember the conversation, and in retrospect it's consistent with their style of communication, which tended towards telling us what to think without much explanation or receptiveness to questions, and they certainly didn't veer into any discussion of anyone's feelings. As kids, we really didn't even know what questions to ask, and adoption stories, and particularly reconnection stories, were virtually nonexistent at that time, so we had little reason to question anything or imagine that there was more to know or understand.

I had a few experiences growing up with people who found it shocking, or surprising, that I was adopted. I remember one kid at school, not someone I knew well, getting all twisted about it like it was a problem, "Wow, you're adopted? That's weird!" but that was rare, and, in fact, it made me feel special, I wasn't embarrassed about it or anything. It did confuse me, though, if anyone asked me how I felt about it, because I really didn't know, it had all been presented to me in such a dispassionate way. My mom didn't react well if anyone made a fuss about it, she was thin-skinned, that was obvious, so there was a message there which I took to heart, even though it didn't occur to me to wonder why it was okay for her to be sensitive about it, but we were supposed to shrug it off as if it was unimportant.

That one conversation in my parents' bedroom is the only one I remember having with either of my parents about adoption until years later when my brother's wife Liz was working at the Sheltering Arms, the adoption agency my brother and I were adopted from, and in one of those unimaginably strange coincidences, she discovered she was working with the individual who had managed the placements for both my adopted brother Jonathan and me. To think that we were that close to both my story and my brother's story, which he is only now in the process of discovering as well, because the files were locked and it has taken another 40 plus years to uncover our stories because of the firewalls around adoption that the journalist Steve Inskeep outlines so well in his Atlantic article *No One's Child*. At that point, both my birth mother, and my adopted brother Jonathan's birth mother, were still alive. It's hard to fathom all the different doors that might have opened, good and bad, if we had been able to access that information then.

Nancy, my adopted mother, was simply annoyed; she took a dim view of people trying to connect to their birth parents, and she acted as if my sister-in-law was in some way to blame, as if she was meddling in something that was none of her business. Obviously, my mom felt threatened by it, perhaps understandably for someone who adopted in the fifties, and she apparently never thought that this could be an opportunity to collect some information that might be important, if not life-changing, for me or my brother later. Somehow, it seems as if it never occurred to her, or my father, that there might be some value in discussing the emotional landscape of adoption, in exploring the meaning of it, or the context. At the time, in fact, although she didn't say it out loud, she made it clear that if I took an interest in my birth parents or my history it would be an act of disloyalty to her and my father, my adopted parents, who took me in and gave me a home.

I assumed my parents chose to adopt because they couldn't have kids, but I don't remember ever getting a specific explanation. They were both 40 when I was born, so they were older parents by 1950's standards, noticeably so. I had a girlfriend in high school whose grandmother was the same age as my parents, which felt a bit strange, although today, I don't think anyone would even remark on it, except maybe in terms of IVF and risk factors and so on. My mother had a long scar like a necklace that ran around her throat from one collar bone to the other, like a piece of jewelry; I think when she was younger, she'd had her thyroid removed, so maybe she couldn't have kids because of that, but I don't know for sure if that was the reason, it was never really made clear.

"We just wanted so much to have kids, and we couldn't, so we decided to adopt, and that's how we got you boys, and we were so happy, etc." was the kind of narrative you never heard from my parents. There were just a few anecdotes, my father forgetting to shave when he left for work the day after they brought my brother home, stuff like that, but no emotional context.

There was, however, a strange story they loved and frequently told about taking my brother to the adoption agency and letting him "pick me out". I have this picture in my mind of the three of them walking him around this big room full of cribs, all of them identical, like a hospital ward in an old movie, each one containing an orphan baby, and him coming to my crib and saying, "This one! I want this one!" In something that feels like a dream, I picture my mother in a tailored suit, her hair up in a bun, as always, like Kathryn Hepburn, and my father in a suit and crisp white shirt and knit tie, with his customary fedora, looking like Humphrey Bogart. I imagine them walking around a big institutional nursery reading the tags hanging off the sides of the cribs, as if it was the furniture department at Macy's, or a canine rescue facility, checking off the features, baby after baby, until they come to me – blond hair, blue eyes, white skin, had all his shots, check, we'll take this one, thank you. When I think about it now, I see a shadowy version of the dream, or perhaps the reality underpinning it, where the true picture coming into focus is not so appealing - go to the baby store, pick out a baby, take it home, cut to happy ending.

My adopted brother and I are almost exactly three years apart and I was four months old when I was adopted, so the whole concept of him "picking me out" is ludicrous. It was a story they presumably developed for his benefit, perhaps to make the adjustment of having a little brother easier for him, and if you repeat something enough times, it starts to sound like it's true. I know my brother bought into it at the time, he was a child repeating a story his parents told him; I heard him repeat the story many times, as if he could remember it even though he was barely three years old when it was supposed to have happened. In retrospect, I think it gave him a feeling of ownership over me, which I used to experience as meddling and resent, until years later when I realized that he was trying to take responsibility for me, to act like a big brother, and I learned to appreciate it, having someone who cares about you without expecting something in return.

Lots of people have children, and many of them do it for all the wrong reasons, which is unfortunate but it's a fact. This probably keeps a lot of psychotherapists in business. I think there is a tendency for people to assume that this is not true of adoptive parents, because there is so much intention involved in adoption, but the fact of the matter is that the same thing is also true of adoptive parents. Many of them are ill-equipped, and many of them do it for all the wrong reasons, and they are unprepared for the challenges that follow. I often wonder about adoptive parents, whether in the throes of a crisis, discovering a congenital defect or a disability, for instance, or a severe mental illness of some kind, something they wasn't part of the picture, they ask themselves if it was all a mistake, if they wish they could un-ring the bell, rewind the tape and start over. I wonder about my parents, whether they ever asked themselves that question when I started being difficult as a teenager, did they regret their decision to adopt?

My parents didn't make the classically big mistake some adoptive parents make of not telling us we were adopted, or waiting until we were teenagers to tell us, which never turns out well. There was, however, a subtle underside; because they just disclosed the basic facts, dispassionately, and revealed almost nothing about the meaning of it, about the emotional stakes, about why they did it, why they wanted kids, how they felt about it, who our parents might have been, why they might have given us up, we felt like we didn't know anything. We knew the bare facts, but not the story. And most of all, we didn't know how to feel, and that gap, that void, lived in my subconscious, like a suitcase you get so used to carrying, you're no longer conscious of its weight, knowing that you grew up in someone else's tribe, but not exactly knowing why, and wondering if some day some stranger is going to show up and claim you, like Natalie Wood, in The Searchers, when John Wayne shows up to take her away from the Indian tribe that raised her and she isn't happy, or relieved, she's terrified.

Lots of people obfuscate with drama, or disguise painful realities with lies, or prevaricate, but sometimes full disclosure is, ironically, the best way to avoid discussing something challenging or painful. That's it, now you have the facts, time to move on. It's just like taking the blame for something when you're not responsible or expecting someone with depression to just snap out of it – it turns the tables and ends the conversation. "Okay, it's my fault, let's just drop it, okay?"

It turns out that my birth mother, Lee, was a classic unreliable narrator, constantly telling made up stories and half-truths to my brothers, possibly to protect herself from her guilt by revealing at least a small part of her painful truth. She told them they had an older brother, which was part of the truth, but her story was that I had died in childbirth, rather than that she had given me up.

My adoptive parents, Nancy and John, on the other hand, minimized their story with bare facts and silence. For most of my life I never considered the idea that there was a real live person out there, hardly more than a young girl, who went through some sort of private hell, not hard to imagine given the moral code of the fifties, which caused my life to start the way it did, that the privilege I grew up with was in some way tangentially associated with someone else's pain and loss, or that my presence in the family I grew up in was collateral, the result of a crisis in someone else's life.

Nancy and John weren't kid people, not the kind that are just dying to hold someone's baby or get down on the floor and play games, they weren't fun. My mom was not the kind of woman who feels like her life just won't be complete unless she gets to conceive. She used to say this thing about women forgetting the pain of childbirth like she knew what she was talking about, but even at a young age, I knew it was baloney, she had no idea what it was like, she had never actually had a kid. They liked to have cocktails and tell stories and go to restaurants and the theatre; it seemed like they were always dressing up in black tie to go somewhere, to a play, to Lincoln Center, or to a party, or a dinner. They weren't the type to stay home and watch TV or play games with the kids. I used to hang out in their room and watch them get dressed to go out, that was something I was intrigued by, but it also made me a little nervous. Being physically close to them felt strange, and there was something about the way they smelled that didn't appeal to me, and I didn't even know how strange that was until I had my own kids, and I learned how everyone loves the smell of their own kids, at least until they become teenagers.

My dad had racks of tailored suits and jackets, everything from pinstripes to tweeds, from shiny black to suede, summer tux, winter tux, morning coat, tails, all hanging in his closet in perfect order. They went to a lot of black-tie events, and I used to sit on the chaise longue watching my dad fit his 18K gold studs and matching cufflinks into his crisp white starched tux shirt while my mother put on her makeup at the bathroom mirror.

My mom had a distinctive style, kind of upper class boho. She liked Indian silks, and Asian Mao jackets. I never knew her to get a manicure, and she wouldn't have been caught dead in a beauty parlor. She wore interesting quirky jewelry, she wasn't into diamonds or furs; her style was very uncharacteristic of Manhattan society in the late fifties and sixties. She was striking, in a Kathryn Hepburn sort of way, though not as beautiful as Kathryn Hepburn. Her features were not as sculpted and fine and her hands were like men's hands, strong from gardening and country stuff, I guess, not dainty female hands with perfectly polished nails.

I called my parents Nancy and John when I was little until my brother decided, perhaps from a desire to be more like other families, that we had to start calling them Mom and Dad, which was something I found hard to get used to at first. They were into parallel play, which mostly meant I'll read the newspaper, and you go read a book. Once we went to Bermuda for spring vacation and it rained practically the whole time. My brother Jonathan was old enough to get a rented motorbike, so he was gone, off to the disco at Elbow Beach, but I was stuck with them, just the three of us, and we had a rented house, so I didn't even have a hotel to wander around in and there was no TV. I read 14 books in two weeks; once I ran out of the ones I brought with me, I just started picking them randomly off the shelves in the house, books by writers like Mary Stewart and J.B. Priestley and Rumer Godden, books that were left behind there, books nobody reads anymore. I never knew either of my parents to play Go Fish or Monopoly, or even Chess or Backgammon. They would have died rather than set foot in Disneyland, or frankly the entire states of Florida and California; we were led to believe those places were insubstantial and lowbrow. We went to Old Sturbridge Village and Historic Deerfield instead, smaller versions of Colonial Williamsburg, amusement parks for WASPs and

Daughters of the American Revolution. I thought I was going to faint from boredom. I think they were believers in the British model; they expected my brother and me to just amuse ourselves until we got old enough to go away to boarding school, and they used to refer wistfully to the British practice of sending the boys away to school at seven or eight years old. It was a far cry from the way people think of raising their children today. When we were younger, we had live-in nannies, so my parents were insulated from having to give their full attention to small children. Then, once we got old enough to amuse ourselves, it was just a question for them of waiting for us to grow up and become "useful" as my dad used to say.

My brother and I both went to St. Bernard's, the quintessential upper east side boys' school, certainly one of the very best in New York City, which is saying a lot. I believe that the education I received there carried me through the rest of my academic career, but the social context of it was anachronistic and tone deaf, seriously out of touch with the changes that were taking place in the society at large. I doubt if there was even one black kid in the whole school, which was mostly populated with a lot of old money high-class New York families, as well as a sprinkling of recognizable names and media personalities. I remember going to the Hamptons for the weekend with one of the kids in my class and being confused because we were going across the bridge to New Jersey, until I discovered that we were boarding a private jet at Teterboro airport that was flying us to Easthampton. One of my friends was the grandson of Diana Vreeland, one was the son of the writer, John Gunther, who lived on Sutton Place and was friends with Greta Garbo, and another one was the son of Michael Burke, of OSS fame during the war, and at that time part owner of the New York Yankees, as well as sons of Walter Cronkite and Nan Kempner. Most of the teachers were either

English, or Canadians pretending to be English, like the headmaster, who had an affinity for small time corporal punishment of the kind that was common in English boarding schools ("hold your hand out, boy, so I can crack you across the knuckles with this ruler" type stuff). There were some great teachers there, and we were given to understand that excellence was expected, mediocrity was not, and failure was not tolerated. If we misbehaved, teachers would throw chalk at us, or board erasers, or they would grab us by our ears. We took standardized tests and essay exams to get into boarding schools. We were told that anything less than the 99th percentile was mediocre, because public schools were included in the curve, and they were assumed to be substandard. We wore jackets and ties to school starting in second grade, and it was clear to us that our world was altogether different from the kids who grew up in the projects a few blocks uptown in Harlem, although we couldn't possibly know just how different it was.

Everyone was expected to go to one of the top boarding schools – Choate, Hotchkiss, Exeter, Andover, Lawrenceville, Groton, Deerfield, Taft, and so on, and then on to the Ivy League, essentially following the same path as generations of privileged East Coast kids before us. My family had all gone to Choate, my parents were married during WWII in the Choate chapel, and the headmaster was my father's roommate at Yale, so there was never much question where I was going, and no question of asking my opinion about it either.

But there was change on the horizon, rumbling and flashing in the distance like thunder and heat lightning. Johnson was president, Vietnam was on the TV news every night. Both JFK and Bobby Kennedy had been assassinated, along with Malcolm X and Martin Luther King, Jr. Under the surface, a power structure that had been stable since before

WWI, turning out the country's leaders and its officers, its managers, its men in gray flannel suits, was starting to crumble, like chunks of stone and concrete dust falling off a building in an earthquake. I joined a nascent little cell of grade school kids modelled after the Students for a Democratic Society, and we went to meetings and talked politics and went out and collected signatures on petitions. Unfortunately, one formative experience I had as a result was being out in the crowds on East 86th street collecting signatures and being approached, stalked, and circled by a pervert mumbling about the things he wanted to do to me and assuring me that it wouldn't hurt at all.

Who did I tell? No one, because in our generation, you didn't share these things, no matter how terrifying they might have been, with the adults in your life because somehow it would go sideways. Instinctively, even at that age, I just knew that my parents would end up turning it into something I had to answer for and explain, that I would somehow end up feeling like I was at fault. The phrase "don't trust anyone over thirty" was coined in the free speech movement of the sixties and often quoted by people like John Lennon and others and it had the ring of truth because of the behavior of a lot of parents. Nowadays people may think of it as quaint, or funny, but for us, it wasn't really a joke. It was a warning, and words to live by.

Hank:

After my mother told us our father had died, I was dazed. I was walking around not really living with the reality of what had happened, sort of floating almost like underwater. Everything seemed muffled and distant. We were at the spa resort with my parents' closest friends, the Starks, though this may be the friends I chose to act this role in the drama. I know they had friends with this name, but I can't be sure they were the ones actually there. Mrs. Stark had taken me with her I think to help give Mom a break. We were returning in an elevator and some stranger said something about me in German and Mrs. Stark's response included the phrase "hat seinen Vater verloren ". I remember thinking - they're talking about my father's death, and I speak German and they don't know I know they are talking about me" I felt a little embarrassed and in a weird, removed way felt intense pity for myself, and for Pete and Bill.

Later, we were standing in the neighbors' driveway, in Bad Homburg, Germany, saying goodbye. I was ten years old. Dad had only been dead for two weeks, but mom had already packed up everything and shut down our life in Germany, and we were going back to the United States. Bill and Pete were probably around somewhere, maybe with the neighbors' kids; I'm not sure if they really understood what was going on, so I was there in the driveway, alone with the adults, with Mom and Mrs. Stark. My attention was laser focused on Mom; she was melting down, it was pure emotional wreckage, she was sobbing ferociously, flushed, blubbering. Somehow, even at the age of ten, I just knew from my experience of the two weeks since dad died, from her behavior, that she was coming unglued, and it wasn't just sadness, it was anger as well.

I guess it's understandable – she's lost her husband, her dreams for her life have evaporated in one horrific twenty-four-hour period, from the time he goes to the hospital, to the next morning, and she is abandoned with three boys under the age of ten, but she had come totally unglued. She's not close to her family, she doesn't want to go back to them, it is the last place she wants to go, but already she feels that she has no options. I can label it now, I know that it was surreal, but at ten years old, it's not surreal, it's reality, I was freaked out, and I remember vividly, thinking, "holy shit, she can't handle this" and I thought, at ten years old, I'm the oldest boy, I have to take over, we can't count on her, I have to take care of my brothers, we are on our own.

It's crazy that I thought this at ten, but I did.

And in the end, she took us back to Connecticut, she never remarried, and in a way, it all turned out to be true.

Chapter Two: Colebrook

The Berkshires seemed dream-like on account of that frosting with ten miles behind me, and ten thousand more to go
(James Taylor)

There was an unspoken narrative about why my adoptive parents wanted kids, one that they wouldn't have denied. In fact, they would have endorsed it as sort of an outmoded concept of heredity, like primogenitor or droit de seigneur. They adopted us because of a place they called The Farm (capital T, capital F) which was my mother's family home in Northwestern Connecticut. It was not actually a farm at all, although it had been at one time, but a sort of compound, with several houses and barns and about six hundred acres of land. Over the years, it had remained in the Phelps family, for hundreds of years, in fact, from before the Revolutionary War. My mother's Phelps ancestors fought in the Revolutionary and the Civil Wars; her great grandfather was a general in the Connecticut Militia. After the war, in 1787, Arah Phelps built an Inn on what was then the Hartford Albany Turnpike, and it grew into a farm and a sawmill and a lumbering operation, a prosperous going concern on land that had been surveyed by his ancestors when they came down from the Massachusetts colony in the late 17th century to Connecticut. The family fell on hard times after the Civil War, when my mother's grandfather went off to Minnesota and got wiped out in a bank failure, which was quite common in those days before all the banking laws were written after the Depression. He mortgaged the whole place to save himself and came back to Connecticut. After that, over time, the place kind of fell apart. In 1912, he was forced, in financial desperation, to sell off the last virgin pine forest in the state of Connecticut for lumber, and those mortgages didn't get paid off until my mother married my father. My mother often referred to herself as the last surviving member of the Phelps family, so she was carrying the weight, or perhaps the torch, for all those generations on that land, and the place was her dream and ultimately, her obsession.

When my son was born, my first child, I called them in the middle of the night in Connecticut from New York Hospital to tell them the news, and my dad rolled over in bed, and said, "It will be good for the farm" which kind of illustrates how my brother and I were positioned in the whole scenario.

My mother was obsessed with her family history. It is unusual in this country to have roots in a place for so many generations; there were literally nails that had stories attached to them. My father, on the other hand, came from a rich New York family, wealthy Jews who emigrated from France to this country and started a textile dyeing business in Lodi, New Jersey, one of the largest in the country at that time. Today, I think people have forgotten that there were wealthy European Jews for whom assimilation was a value, and though they didn't deny it, they chose not to primarily self- identify in terms of being Jewish and had little or no interest in any faith or religion. My dad had family money, and he was successful as well. He invested a lot of money in fixing up the place in Connecticut, particularly restoring the house, a beautiful two-story hip-roofed gray clapboard building surrounded by fields and pine forests, a registered historic landmark that was originally built as an Inn, the A. Phelps Lion and Eagle Inn. My mother's worst fear before she met him was always that she would lose the place, she literally had nightmares about it, and she used to love to tell the story that when he asked her to marry him, she told him she couldn't say yes until he had seen The Farm. For some reason, I always felt a flash of anger whenever she would tell that story, it just felt so precious and cute to me.

We spent weekends and summers there, hanging out with other friends with summer houses or "camps", as they sometimes liked to call them, on Doolittle Lake, beautiful and secluded, where the houses were set back from the shore and hidden in the trees and the sound of engines never broke the silence, which was only disturbed occasionally by voices of kids laughing, splashing in the water, or the clink of rigging against the metal mast of a Sunfish, or faint music from a radio somewhere. We had a tennis court in the field behind our house, and a farmer who looked like a Quaker who came and mowed the fields twice a year for the hay. We spent months in the summer at camp in Maine; we climbed Old Speck and Mount Katahdin and learned to sail in the saltwater bays of the Kennebec River. When my parents came up for their one visit of the summer, we had fried clams at the end of a pier, and there was drinking and genteel grownup conversation. In my childhood, the sound of ice clinking in a cocktail glass was never far away. We didn't wear sneakers; we wore moccasins from LL Bean. When Ralph Lauren first appeared on the scene, I remember thinking he must have been hiding in the bushes when I was growing up, because all the stuff he was "designing" and selling at outrageous prices, was the style we grew up wearing without even thinking of it as a style, the stuff they sold at Brooks Brothers and LL Bean. Nobody thought to take credit for designing it.

When James Taylor sings about the snow that dusts the turnpike from Stockbridge to Boston, or Paul Simon about heading down the turnpike from the Maritimes, I see those roads etched in my memory, from repetition, Sandisfield to Lenox to Stockbridge to Boston, and on up to Maine. But it's more than the roads, it's the stories, the *Suzanne the plans they made put an end to you* stories, the suicides and the privileged, rudderless, brilliant, messed up kids, the kids who go off to Yale or Dartmouth or Harvard and come back twitchy and strange and get packed off to McLean to recover from "nervous breakdowns". It's my world, the high-class world of the East Coast, of WASP society, with its unspoken rules and closets full of skeletons, the world of cocktail parties and sarcasm, of prep school kids who consider "Hey shithead" to be an appropriate greeting for a friend. The lyrics of those songs are often conflicted, and usually sad, about leaving it, or rejecting it, unlike now when everyone is trying to acquire it instead, to buy it, as if it's about the wardrobe, or the house, or the perfect vintage sports car. It's what my mother used to call nouveau riche, like the rich heiresses in the Gilded Age, social climbing, trading money for class.

My mother would happily spend all day in the garden, tending to perennials her mother and grandmother had planted generations before. Despite the Opium Control Act of 1942, we had opium poppies growing all over the place, brilliant orange flowers with furry gray green stems and strange crinkly leaves and generations-old peonies and orange double lilies that were like a flower within a flower, something I've never seen anywhere else. She wanted us to help her with the weeding, since she loved gardening, and she expected us to love it too. My dad talked about doing "chores", which seemed somehow pretentious, or at least phony, coming from someone who drove a Jaguar and wore a tie even on weekends. Apparently neither of them was ever a kid, because they seemed not to know that gardening and chores are not things that real kids actually like to do. He grew up with servants, and a butler. He played polo and hung out at a country club, but he turned into a country squire with the common touch, play-acting the farmer, and we were supporting actors, like Eddie Albert on Green Acres, all countrified and simple. We had to do chores with him, and mow the lawn with a push lawnmower, and act like we enjoyed it. Even as a kid, I felt like they had something to prove, they could have paid other people to do this stuff, but they felt like we would get spoiled if they didn't make us do it. They were very proud of being all down to earth and unpretentious, that's how they saw themselves. My mother had grown up there, so she had known the local people since she was a kid, real country people, farmers and stuff, people with rusty vehicles on blocks in their front yards, friendly people who knew about nature and machines and how things work. Once I got over being afraid of them, and believe me, they were nothing like my parents, I found there was a lot of interesting stuff you could learn from people who did things with their hands.

My grandparents were different; they didn't fit any standard script at all. My grandfather, Carrington Phelps, was a pulp fiction writer and wrote for the WPA during the Depression. He looked like Eugene O'Neill, white-haired and tall and weathered, and he drank like him too, although I just thought it was something adults did. He was a character (with a capital C) and he had a bit of a reputation all over town, but it wasn't clear to me for what exactly, people just kind of smiled knowingly when they mentioned his name. I didn't find out until later that he had apparently had affairs with some of the women in town. When I was a little kid, he took me to Lime Rock racetrack, and we were sitting on the hill overlooking the track watching the cars and I said to him,

"Granddaddy, what race is this?"

And he said to me, "It's the human race..."

I was four years old when he died but I remember that moment clearly. Years later, long after he died, out of the blue, I suddenly realized what he had said, and it made me laugh. I guess he taught me the difference between wit and humor that day. It was a gift, kind of a time-released joke or a message, just between the two of us, that I carried with me unaware, lurking in my subconscious, until I grew up. I didn't have him for very long, unfortunately, I'm thinking he might have helped me make sense of it all since he had clearly seen a lot and led a pretty untraditional life. One time in English class in grade school we were reading short stories from a collection, and I turned the page and there was a short story that he had written, The Spider, by C. A. Phelps. I was excited and I went home and showed my mother, and she was nonplussed, she had never read it.

My Phelps grandparents mostly didn't have any money, thanks to the Minnesota bank failure and all, and the place was mortgaged to the hilt and literally falling down. The beautiful old Inn had been partially burned in a fire in 1942. My grandfather was one of those people who liked to follow the fire engines, and he followed them home to his own burning house, blazing from a gas stove he left burning by mistake when he went to the store. When I was a kid, it sat empty, like a hulk, waiting, hoping, abandoned. My mom was always talking about how they hid from the bill collectors when she was a kid, and it was always feast or famine depending on whether my grandfather had sold anything, and then his publisher died, and things really dried up after that. Her mother, Marion Pierce Phelps, was half Parsee, her mother had emigrated from India, which was a problem for her Phelps in-laws because that meant she wasn't really white, or at least not white enough. She had been an actress in San Francisco when she was young and I have some beautiful photographs of her taken by Arnold Genthe, the California photographer who did the famous study of the Chinese in California in the early 1900's, documenting the conditions in the Chinese slums of San Francisco. She was there for the great earthquake of 1904 when the whole city burned down. I think she and my grandfather were a little suspicious of my dad, or maybe they didn't think they needed to be saved after all the things they had survived, but I guess they warmed up to him after a while. There's a picture of the four of them sitting on the terrace drinking Bloody Mary's together so obviously they had that in common.

We called my grandmother Nana. I remember her very well, she was warm and loving, I remember her as a presence I felt safe with. I remember playing with her out in the long grass in the hay field in Connecticut, I remember her voice and her jet-black hair, I remember her tucking me into bed at night. She died in 1959, a few months after my grandfather, when I was four years old. My mother told me that often older people die close to each other in time because one loses their desire to live after they lose the other one, which was an interesting story, perhaps a kind of fantasy, as the truth turned out to be a lot more complicated, as it always is.

One night, my mother was putting me and my brother to bed in our bunk beds on the third floor of our townhouse in New York, when suddenly she said, "Nana died…. of old age, in her sleep. Your father and I are going to her funeral in Colebrook. There's no reason for you to go."

It was another one of those matter-of-fact statements, delivered with a complete absence of emotion or even the anticipation of it. That was that. We were kind of mystified, and we didn't really know what to do. She didn't seem to feel anything, although I'm sure she must have. My parents just didn't provide any kind of a model for dealing with emotions of any kind. My dad, of course, had nothing to offer but suck it up and be a man, that kind of thing, useless information that you think you should take seriously as a child. When I was little, if I cried, he would tell me to grit my teeth and tighten up my stomach muscles so I could stop crying. I missed my grandmother after she died, but I didn't really know how to process it, and there was no one to talk to about it so there was no closure. Once again, it was over, close the door, just move on. It seemed to me that my brother was a little oblivious, but

I couldn't connect to my own feelings either; it wasn't something people did in my family. I just drew a blank, I didn't know what to do with it, I felt invisible.

My mother mostly grew up poor, feast when my grandfather sold something, and famine when he didn't, but mostly they had nothing. When there was money, she went away to a fancy girls boarding school called Wyckham Rise, and then the money would run out and she would be home again, back at the Colebrook School. She was always talking about how hard it was growing up, how they hid from the bill collectors, how they almost lost the place, but there was a distinct hint of nostalgia and romance in the depiction as well. When she was eighteen, during the Depression, she went to New York and worked at Wanamaker's, the department store, and sent home half her salary, which was eight dollars a week, to help support her parents. She and her roommate had only one nice dress, so they couldn't both go out on a date on the same night.

Once my dad paid off all the mortgages and started fixing everything, she was released from the nightmare she had lived with all her life, the fear of losing the place, which must have been wonderful for her, but unfortunately, she lost all sense of perspective. There were pictures of the place in magazines, and historical societies came to see it, and we opened the house and gave tours on holidays. She trained me to be a tour guide, shepherding people around the house showing them all the antiques and telling them all the stories. Small towns in New England always used to have these old women who were like the corporal memory of the town, sort of like the Queen Mother, and she became that sort of a celebrity, everybody knew her.

Most upper-class Manhattan families had a city home and a country house, that was considered normal, whether it was in the Hamptons, or the Berkshires, somewhere away from the city, quiet and beautiful. We grew up in this New York, New England world of city and country, cabin on the lake, dad drives a Jaguar, cocktails before dinner, tennis court in the hayfield behind the house, but the Phelps family history started to permeate the whole experience, to become something to be worshiped as much as enjoyed. Eventually, we gave about three hundred acres of forest land to The Nature Conservancy to be part of an eleven-hundred-acre nature preserve, The Phelps Research Area, and I thought that was great, I was proud of that, but then it started getting out of control. My parents started putting restrictions on the remaining land and then the buildings as well, more and more easements and covenants controlling how the land and the houses had to be treated. Every time they added more restrictions, they would promise that was it, and every time they would go back on those promises, even when it got to the point my brother and I were begging them to stop. They would talk to us constantly about how we were inheriting it, and they wanted to be reassured that we cared about it as much as they did, but it was like people who have too much cosmetic surgery, it becomes like an addiction, and they keep doing it, and they can't see that they are turning themselves into freaks. After a while we started to feel like maybe they were really protecting it from us, not for us. By this time, my brother had gotten divorced from his first wife, who he was only married to for four or five years, and they used to use that as an excuse, that something like that could happen and he would have to sell his share of the property, and some developer would buy it and subdivide it into house lots. They didn't say that to him, they said it to me about him, which was a divisive characteristic of theirs that I started noticing more and more. In the end, they put so many easements and restrictions on it that by the time my brother and I inherited it you could barely move an ashtray without getting permission from some historic preservation organization in Boston or somewhere. Try too hard to hold on to something and we all know what happens; the thing you are most afraid of is the thing that ends up happening. The place was so restricted and overvalued and over appraised that by the time we paid all the taxes, we had to sell it anyway, and by then, it was a relief. I didn't even have any resiliency left to feel sad about it, it was all so annoying.

I do miss the actual land, the feeling of being surrounded by a world that is yours, that has been in your family for generations. I miss the overgrown logging trails in the woods, which I knew like the back of my hand, winter or summer, the swamps and the wildlife, the beavers and their busy compulsive dam-building. I miss the woods, making the first cross country ski path when the snow is deep and untouched, pushing through waist high fresh snow, laughing at the beauty of it, voices echoing in the quiet of the woods after the snowstorm. I miss the feeling of pulling into the driveway on a Friday night, after driving up from New York, and just listening to the silence, feeling it, in the total darkness, looking at the stars, amazingly bright in the sky, in the absence of any other light. I do miss the land, but the other stuff, all the family dynamics, and all the talk, all the self-importance that was associated with it became noise and static, something I just wanted to turn off.

All the antiques and the books and all the objects with all the stories attached to them, when someone dies, you discover its objective worth, you discover that it's just stuff, which can come as a shock. Very few of us own things that are objectively valuable because value is about the marketplace, it's not about history or sentimental value, which has a dollar value of exactly nothing. It's like a child's stuffed animal; it's not that it has intrinsic value, it has life because it is loved. I learned that all this valuable stuff, all this historical stuff, wasn't worth anything like my mother thought it was because the market only values things that are perfect, and that is just transactional value, it's just about money, what it's worth today if someone buys it. There was a big book collection in our house, probably ten thousand books, and I brought in a book dealer to see if the $300,000 insurance appraisal they had on those books was accurate, and he said, betraying his disappointment, "To tell you the truth, this is a readers collection" and what that means is it's just a bunch of used books, and the value probably wasn't even five percent of the appraisal, so I had to sell the collection or pay the taxes based on the appraisal, and that's how it went with most of the antiques as well.

So, my brother lives in North Carolina, and I have been in California for over twenty-five years, and all that New England family history is just that, history, because its ability to evolve was strangled by my mother's pathological compulsion to control it from the grave.

Pete:

When Grandpa died, I remember mom just said, "grandpa died" and we really didn't talk about it... I don't remember crying or her crying but maybe I missed it. The next morning, we all packed up and drove to NJ to be with Grandma... we got there late... evening. We were all put to bed and then mom and grandma stayed up all night talking about grandpa... which felt weird to me - since we never really talked like that as a family but here mom and grandma were just talking on and on and on - and on ... about him. It was weird, I don't think I could have verbalized it then, but I think it made me feel like we were sort of invisible.

I believe I was 14 when grandpa (mom's dad) died... when we visited, I remember there being 2 single beds in one room so 2 of us were there... mom was in another room with a double or queen and we kind of alternated sleeping with her...

although I think by this time (me 14 and Hank 16) that wasn't happening anymore. I remember us competing for who got to sleep in the big bed with mom... but then she would read with the light on which made it impossible to sleep. I also remember sleeping bags, couches, etc.

As far as talking about it – we didn't really. Grandpa died and, as when dad had died, it just kind of happened and we kept moving on. Same thing happened when mom's mom died when I was 24 or so...

Chapter Three: So That's Why

Somebody put orange juice in my orange juice.
(W.C. Fields)

Pretty much every day, when I came downstairs to have breakfast before going to school, my mother was angry. We lived in a brownstone on the Upper East Side of Manhattan, and you had to come down two flights of stairs to get to the kitchen - bedroom, parlor floor, ground floor, where the kitchen was. I used to dread breakfast. I could hear her banging around down there as I came down the stairs, making eggs and bacon for breakfast, which frankly I didn't want. As a child, I was not a morning person, it literally made me want to gag, but she would not compromise or relent, and substitutions were not allowed – no Frosted Flakes for us, ever. It was like a pitched battle every morning, and sometimes she would undercook the eggs and the white was all runny like snot, and it was just so gross. I used to wonder how she could be mad at me already when I hadn't had a chance to do anything yet. I couldn't work it out, and I was a kid who wanted to understand things, to know what the rules were, to figure it all out, so it was frustrating, disconcerting, I felt like I was doing something wrong, but I didn't know what. She would get mad if we complained, and throw the eggs back in the pan, indignant, like we were being difficult or spoiled, like it wasn't actually totally gross. My brother used to do this thing where he would gag and run into the bathroom, it was hilarious, although it scared me a little, he would get all red in the face and everything.

In my twenties, early in my marriage to Mary Ann, my first wife, we were watching a Spencer Tracy/ Katherine Hepburn movie. It was black and white with lots of clever dialogue, of course. Tracy and Hepburn are in a glamorous apartment or a hotel in a city somewhere, and they roll out of bed in the morning but it's obvious they both got up on the wrong side of the bed. They haven't had coffee, and they can't even have a conversation. Don't talk to me, just make the damn coffee, and get me some aspirin is the gist of the whole thing. They're both wearing those ironed cotton pajamas with the baggy tops and bottoms; monogrammed pockets, just like my parents used to wear. And it's funny and witty and everything, and the source of the humor, of course, what's driving the scene, is that they're hungover, because they drank too much the night before, as everyone always seems to be doing in those movies. At first, I didn't really take note of it since it's kind of a comedic trope anyway, until I realized how familiar it was, not just from seeing it in movies, but from real life. It takes me back to all the talk about drinking in our house - hangovers, if it's cocktail hour yet, is the sun over the yardarm, whether this person or that one is an alcoholic, how you define alcoholism, and so on. My parents taught me to make a pitcher of martinis for them every night when I was in grade school, they were what an alcoholic friend of mine called professionals. And suddenly the picture came into focus, and I realized that the problem with my mother was that she was hungover pretty much every morning when I was growing up. That's why she was in a bad mood and cranky and out of sorts. And my dad as well, I guess, but he was disagreeable in the mornings anyway and he just sat there and read the paper, so it was hard to tell, unless you bothered him and then he would snap at you. And, of course, it's all consistent with the societal attitude about drinking that characterized that generation – unconditional positive regard, nobody thought they drank too much, and people who admitted to alcoholism were considered damaged or weak.

It was an epiphany, but somehow, I failed to recognize it. Instead, I filed it away in my subconscious without really taking it in or drawing any conclusions from it. I used to feel a lot of uneasiness and stress all the time as a kid that I couldn't characterize or find a reason for, but I couldn't find a way to let go of it or connect the dots about what it was coming from. I hadn't done anything to make her angry, that was a revelation, but at the same time, it wasn't liberating, I didn't feel released from anything. I asked myself, should I be relieved because it wasn't about me, that I wasn't responsible for it? But I didn't feel relieved at all, I felt sort of empty. It took me another twenty years to accept it, to get some distance from it and label it, to take in the fact that she was hung over every morning, to stop imagining it was normal, to drink so much that you're hung over practically every single day, to make the jump to accepting that my parents and most of their friends were alcoholics, and frankly I had to work my way through several more alcoholic relationships before I got there. They told me they weren't alcoholics, so that's what I believed, they told me that people are only alcoholics if it impairs their ability to function in day-to-day life, whatever that means. I guess they didn't think it included terrifying your kids.

I tended to get excessively attached to other people in my life if they filled the emotional vacuum, substitute mothers you could call them. Janice, our English nanny, was one of them. I remember literally experiencing surprise as a small child because I was upset about something and she asked me why, like she really cared about it, which she did. She was from a small town in England, in Northamptonshire, near London. My mom and dad went to Europe once and we all flew to London together, but we went with Janice to stay with her mom, in Weekley, the town where they lived. We had fun, we did kid things, we went to amusement parks and ate weird English chocolate bars; her mom couldn't have been nicer, she was so happy to have us there, we felt special and welcome.

Janice was lovely, I think of her still with tremendous fondness. After five years with us she left to go have a life of her own, to get married and have kids. I had settled into a real sense of security with her around, so it came as a shock to me when she left. I'm sure my parents had plenty of advance notice, but I had none. One day, suddenly, my parents told me she was leaving; there was no discussion, no getting used to the idea; literally the way I remember it was that I found out the day she left, although I am sure in my memory it is compressed into a singular event. It felt the same as when my grandmother died. I didn't see it coming. Things would happen that I didn't expect, and it was always like I was being silly, well, what did you think, she was going to live with us forever? Well, yes, I guess I did, I didn't realize that in life people die, and leave, and it makes you sad, or surprised, and you grieve because you feel the loss. But there was no baseline, nothing to fall back on. I remember when my brother left for boarding school I felt the same way. People I trusted tended to disappear, leaving me to fall back on my parents, who consistently made up their own arbitrary rules and often moved the goalposts as well, without warning, anytime they felt like it.

We had a housekeeper, Maude, who was from South Carolina, who was one of thirteen children, and her husband had been killed in a car crash when they were young. Their car was hit by a train, but she survived. She never had any children of her own, so she thought of me as her child, which was fine with me. She was someone I felt I could trust and depend on, but of course she wasn't in control of anything. She used to sing spirituals while she was doing the ironing, my mom used to call them "Negro Spirituals"; I used to sit with her and watch her iron. I was into Marvin Gaye, and the Temptations and the Supremes, but she was all about Sam Cooke. Her ironing was like a science, I've never seen anyone who could iron like that. Later, when I got in trouble at boarding school, she took my side.

She told my mom, "That's my child, you leave him alone, I'll deal with him, I'll straighten him out, that's my child."

She didn't have to do that. For all I know she could have lost her job, and she worked for my parents practically her whole life. This is the kind of thing people do out of love, things they don't have to do, things that may cost them something. Screenwriters call that character. I think my mom was relieved, she had no idea what to do with me, anyway. I understand it's a stereotype, the privileged white kid raised by a black woman, but it bothers me to see it reduced to a stereotype, and after all, it's in the nature of stereotypes that they share the same universe with truth. She eventually died of cancer, but she lived long enough to hold my son before she died. He doesn't remember it, of course, but I still picture that little towhead blond kid sitting in her lap, an eerie echo of his father at the same age.

In 1963, when I was eight years old, I came home from school one day, and Janice and Maude were crying. JFK had been assassinated. That was the real beginning of the sixties. I could see that it was a big deal, but assassination – it was a concept I wasn't familiar with at eight years old, except in relation to Abraham Lincoln, who I knew was assassinated by John Wilkes Booth, but that was history. I had never thought of it as something that could happen in the present. Who knew it was just the beginning, that the world was starting to get sideways on its axis, and everything was going to change? All the talk was about Lincoln and Kennedy, so it seemed as if only two presidents had ever been assassinated, and they had been elevated practically to the status of saints, and nobody mentioned McKinley or Garfield all that much. At moments like that, people want to say that only the good die young, and write songs about it, and manufacture sainthood, but I'm sure plenty of bad people die young as well, the world is far more random than we want to believe. We watched the funeral on black and white TV. I remember the black horse with the empty stirrups and the boots backwards and the caisson with the coffin. It was dramatic and somber and meaningful, but I had no frame of reference at that age, so I didn't realize how truly shocking it was. Everybody connects it with Bobby Kennedy, for obvious reasons, as if he was next, but it was Malcolm X, and then Martin Luther King, Jr, and then Bobby Kennedy.

The Christmas after JFK's assassination in 1963, Janice gave us Meet the Beatles for Christmas and we got Beatle wigs, these funny black wigs that were supposed to make you look like a Beatle, a Mop Top. They came to America in 1964 and appeared on the Ed Sullivan Show. It was life changing in a completely different way. Suddenly folk singers, Peter, Paul, and Mary and Tim Hardin were out, Herman's Hermits were out, and Petula Clark, and in came the Beatles, followed by the Byrds, Jefferson Airplane, Buffalo Springfield, Cream, and The Doors. It was the Sixties now, for real.

What I didn't understand, like most white kids, was that there was another America, and another music scene, the world of Miles, and Coltrane, Lee Morgan, and Monk. In that world, in 1959, the year Kind of Blue was recorded, Miles Davis was arrested and beaten outside of Birdland by New York cops, beaten so badly he had to be hospitalized. He was already a huge star, a cultural icon, the coolest man in America, and Kind of Blue was already considered to be one of the greatest recordings of all time, but he was smoking a cigarette between sets hailing a cab for a white woman and he refused to "move along", so to them he was just another black guy to be taught a lesson. This was the America I didn't yet understand. The Beatles and the Stones were recording songs by black artists, they were talking about Chuck Berry and Muddy Waters and the Isley Brothers and Little Richard; guys like Brian Jones and John Mayall and Peter Green were students of American blues, trying to evangelize black artists to white kids, but we were just starting to grasp that rock and roll was not invented by white people, that the Beatles didn't write Roll Over Beethoven. There was just so much to learn, and so much bogus history to unlearn. To this day, I'm still discovering new facts, many of them tragic and shocking, about the entirely different version of American History that didn't, and in many cases still doesn't, appear in our history books. I don't know why they call it Critical Race Theory; it's critical American history.

Around this time, in another separate universe, three boys, my brothers, the oldest of whom is ten years old, lose their father to meningitis. He is a big international executive for an American soft drink company, and they live in Germany, but they are at a spa in Italy on vacation when he is taken ill. He goes to the hospital with an earache and a sore neck and never comes back, dying that night of meningitis. The first news is that he has died; they are almost too young to appreciate the gravity of it, and certainly too young to imagine how their life is going to change.

Hank:

Before dad died, I remember them arguing, I remember yelling coming from behind closed doors. I'm not really sure if dad's death was the singular event that irretrievably knocked the train of our life off the tracks, that otherwise things would have been "normal". I don't know if it was a simple tragedy, a bolt of misfortune, unexpected, that plunged her into a resentful, angry mess, or if some of the seeds of what came later were already there. I suspect that maybe they were.

I tried to parent Bill, probably to the point of neglecting Peter. Because Peter was close to my age and Bill was a baby when we lost our father, I think I felt he was the one in greater need. I coached little league teams with Jim Jespersen and went to almost every game and to many of the games and meets. I helped Bill develop as a soccer player, helped him with his schoolwork, and did my best to protect him from the pain of being a kid in that household. I attended events at school often.

Pete:

There was a period when Bill was in probably 9th or 10th grade when I picked up that he and Hank were "spending more time together" ... for example, Bill had tried smoking pot at some point and Hank knew all about it, and I had no idea. It wasn't a problem or anything, it just felt strange, like I was sort of out of the loop... which now learning that Hank was, at the time, feeling like he was neglecting me is kind of interesting ...

Hank:

Peter said in an email that I was the primary target of Mom's abuse because I was the oldest. I think that is partly true. I also think it is true that there was an aspect of my personality that exacerbated Mom's anger.

And I did actively and with knowledge (even as a teenager) try to engage her away from my brothers. This sounds like a hero story, and I am sure there is some revisionist history involved, but in my mind, there is no question that I felt I should try and deflect her abuse away from them, and I made attempts to do that. Sometimes I blurted out something that pissed her off, without any real conscious awareness of what I was starting, but sometimes I actively thought – well this will get her going and focused on me. It's muddled and mixed up – but I am sure I am not making this up to make myself feel better about those years. My behavior was of course affected by my own dependence on drugs, alcohol, and other forms of escape as well as a coping mechanism.

I spent years taking the bulk of the abuse until the time I left. I'd like to think that perhaps we can true-up some of our destructive family histories, as it's more than a little painful to be remembered as the one who fled. I think the idea that I abandoned everybody was cultivated by Mom and should be reformed into the real story.

Chapter Four: In Microcosm

When the truth is found, to be lies, and all the joy within you dies.... (Darby Slick, with a little help from her sister and the Jefferson Airplane)

It seems as if the significance of the Sixties is boiled down today into a lifestyle choice or a fashion statement. Like flappers dancing the Charleston in the 20's, or people in shabby clothes waiting on bread lines or at soup kitchens in the 30's, that time is frozen in photographs of long-haired kids writhing around in the mud at Woodstock, flashing peace signs at the camera. Peace signs have become a fashion accessory, along with tie-dying and bell bottoms and flower power, stuff you buy at Free People, or in diamond studded versions from Tiffany's, baubles whose original meaning has been drained out of them. It's important to understand that it's misleading, it's a trivialization of a serious sociopolitical phenomenon, something exceptional that has not occurred all that often in our history, a grassroots movement that changed the country and, in some ways, changed the world. Everybody talks about Woodstock and peace and love and all that, but the real driving force of the era was that kids were getting drafted and sent to die in Vietnam and people started asking why, refusing to accept the vague conceptual rationalizations about why we needed to be there, killing our own children and ultimately millions of Vietnamese citizens as well. We lived in fear of growing up. We saw the war on TV every night, and we were afraid. Nobody wanted to go halfway around the world to die in a jungle somewhere, and we didn't have to imagine it. There was nothing theoretical about it. They were assigning new draft numbers every year, and we had older brothers, and camp counselors, and sons of family friends, and even teachers who were getting drafted and going to Vietnam, and some of them weren't coming back.

It's not an accident that today, despite social media and the internet, you don't see war on TV the way we did in the Sixties, live. The Pentagon learned a lesson from Vietnam, from the fact that people were watching the war on network news every night, the reporters went wherever they wanted, and they were broadcasting stories that were deeply embarrassing to the government, which was lying to the country about the war. This is one of the reasons why journalists are "embedded" today; embedded journalists can be controlled and what the public sees can be managed. You see stuff blowing up, but you don't see people bleeding and dying the way you did in Vietnam, you don't see young American kids in uniform getting killed the way you did then. Imagine if kids were being drafted to go to Iraq or Afghanistan, privileged white kids, and you were seeing them getting killed on TV every night; you would see people getting politicized in a hurry, and all this red state, blue state stuff would vanish overnight.

The idea of peace was revolutionary, it wasn't something people easily believed could actually happen. The country had transitioned directly from World War II to Korea to Vietnam with basically no time in between, so people were used to the idea that being at war somewhere was a common state of affairs, it was the norm. The war was rationalized as being about preserving freedom around the world, containing the spread of totalitarianism, containing Communism, as if we were defending something, and the justification for it was presented as self-evident. The problem with that, when you start being sure that history is on your side, is that it becomes a very short step from there to letting yourself believe that the ends justify the means, and by the time the Sixties came around, that kind of thinking had already gotten way out of control. The CIA had destabilized and overthrown governments all over the world, but particularly in Central and South America and in Iran, where they overthrew the democratically elected government of Mohammad Mossadegh and installed the Shah. From there, it was a logical step to meddling in Vietnam, trading in nation building and "regime change".

The anti-war movement was about active resistance to a war that many people thought was immoral, pointless, and a stain on the conscience of this country. We weren't anywhere near as naïve as our parents wanted to believe. We were teenagers, and we were asking questions, and mostly, our parents didn't have answers, they weren't used to hearing these things questioned.

There was a kind of radical canon, books you had to read – *Soul on Ice*; *Be Here Now*; *Manchild in the Promised Land*; *The Autobiography of Malcolm X*; *Invisible Man*; *Another Country*; *Black Like Me*; *The Wretched of the Earth*; *Stranger in a Strange Land*; I read Richard Wright and W.E.B. Dubois and Frantz Fanon. You could buy the Black Panther Party newspaper on street corners in New York. To me it seemed like the Anti-War Movement and the Civil Rights Movement, and later the Women's Movement, were about the same thing, which was the failure of the country to live up to its promises.

I think the trouble really started when I began to understand that the idealistic myths that they taught us in school were actually just revisionist history, that there were big gaps in the story, troubling things that I was hearing and reading, sometimes from more adventurous teachers, but most often in books I was reading and things I was hearing from other people. I started to understand the compromises that Jefferson and Adams and the other framers of the Constitution made, what "all men are created equal" really meant, what the three fifths compromise was; the true nature of slavery and its economic value to the Southern states, why it inevitably caused the Civil War, about the moral vacuity of

Andrew Johnson, the contested election of 1876 and the compromise that killed Reconstruction, about Andrew Jackson and the Trail of Tears, about Jim Crow and the Ku Klux Klan, about the Japanese American Internment Camps during World War II and all the promises broken and the genocide perpetrated against Native Americans, about the virulent strain of racism and xenophobia that runs through the DNA of this country, which is stamped out and reborn every generation.

Vietnam was the tip of that iceberg, the proof that nothing had really changed, that our leaders believed it was a good idea to go half way around the world to a small country in Asia and kill a few million of their people over a socio-political theory, a policy, containment, when the Vietnamese would have been no more likely to tolerate the Russians or the Chinese than they were to tolerate us or the French before us.

Basically, we felt we had been lied to, that the bedtime stories of our childhoods were all lies, and now the mess was being dumped into our laps. We didn't know whether to feel guilty, or angry, or both. We were naïve and idealistic, and we had been sold a picture of our country that was ridiculously inaccurate and misleading, so of course we were disillusioned and resentful and rebellious, which is probably a good description of most budding revolutionaries, and it's important to remember that revolutions are generally not started by poor people, they are started by intellectuals, and they are populated by a wide spectrum of people, often with widely diverging interests. The proletariat don't lead themselves; someone has to light the match.

Ultimately, the protest movement created by the Vietnam War and the Civil Rights movement started to be intermeshed, to meet in the middle. People like Martin Luther King, Jr. and Malcolm X, and Fred Hampton and Muhammad Ali were saying, why should black kids get drafted and sent halfway around the world to kill brown kids in another country? For what? We are an oppressed population in our own country! And there wasn't actually a very good answer for that, and even though we were white and privileged, we were receptive to it, we understood that it made sense. And if you had asked us whether our primary self-identifier was white, or young, we would have said young.

We may have been just kids, but we were paying attention, and there wasn't any Adderall or Xanax, or Wellbutrin or Zoloft or video games to dull our senses, to anesthetize us to reality, to make us apathetic and manageable.

These issues, these arguments, this anger and frustration was all being aired out in privileged New England boarding schools, and that's what I found when I showed up as a freshman at Choate, in the fall of 1969, and it fit me like a glove. These schools liked to think of themselves as a microcosm of society, they believed in the authority of in loco parentis, which essentially meant they saw themselves as having substitute parental authority, so unwittingly they set themselves up as the perfect target of our anger, our frustration, our disillusionment. The people who ran these institutions were used to a presumption of respect and authority derived from the privileged role they had played in the educational system for decades, and they had long ago stopped questioning, or even examining their own behavior or the basis of their relevance. Needless to say, they were ill-equipped to respond to change.

They had embraced the idea for years that their mission was turning out the country's leaders, channeling them into the Ivy League to take their rightful places at the top of the American capitalist pyramid. No one had ever questioned it, but now questions were being raised about the relevance of this kind of education, whether this kind of elitism was appropriate or even fair, whether institutions like Choate should even exist at all. One way they tried to address it, to be more relevant, was by bringing in minority students, which mostly meant black kids, but they were smart too, and the schools got themselves all twisted about what they were trying to achieve. They couldn't understand why the black kids weren't more "grateful" for the chance they were being given, why they were being troublesome and they struggled with some of the younger teachers as well, who were inclined to be a little resistant to the party line, and often were smoking dope on the sly, especially at schools like Putney, or Barlow, which were more permissive than Choate.

It's hard to believe that this is who we were in high school, in ninth grade no less, but it was. Put a bunch of brainy privileged kids together at a time like that and things happened. We were overeducated and intellectual and we took it, and ourselves, all very seriously. Emotionally, I don't think we were particularly mature, but we were smart. We were perhaps the first generation that cared more about its principles than the privileges we were born into, and our parents had no idea what to make of it.

"Do you have any idea how fortunate you are?" they would say, incredulously. They had lived through the Depression and the War, and they couldn't believe their children were throwing it all back in their faces. We really didn't care, we didn't value our privilege, we weren't proud of it the way people are today. People didn't brag about "flying private", they didn't imagine that they were in some way better people just because they were lucky enough to be rich. We were embarrassed by it, and we felt responsible for the injustice of it, and we may have been naïve and self-indulgent, but we felt it was time for it to change.

JFK went to Choate, as did Adlai Stevenson, and John Dos Passos, and Edward Albee, and many other famous and influential people. My dad used to tell a story from when he was a senior about making the future president run laps around the track in the middle of the night because he and his freshman friends were making noise in the dorms. In addition to my dad, my uncle, my brother, and my cousin went to Choate, and the headmaster was my dad's roommate at Yale. Actually, I wasn't totally down with the Choate plan, I had friends at Hotchkiss, and I wanted to go there, but my dad wasn't having any of it. He was very comfortable laying down the law, and he didn't expect any resistance. Choate was a tradition in my family; my parents were married there in 1942, in the chapel on the campus, with my dad in his Navy uniform, and my mom in a tailored suit, no frills, very businesslike, no white wedding dress for her. Under the circumstances, nobody was expecting me to come to Choate and be rebellious and difficult. I remember a trip back to school from Connecticut during my freshman year with my dad, driving along the parkway in his beautiful grey convertible Jaguar XK150 with the top down, when he decided that was the time to set me straight, he was apparently feeling like I was embarrassing him. His exact words, over the rushing wind noise and the sound of the tires singing on the concrete road surface, were "don't dishonor my name" which he delivered entirely without irony. I remember wondering in a disconnected sort of way what he actually meant by that, what was in his head, how he thought that statement was going to affect my behavior and decision-making.

In the spring of 1970, when Nixon invaded Cambodia, we shut down the school; I say we, but I don't really know who was responsible, it seemed to just happen. Somebody invited John Froines, who was one of the Chicago Seven, to come and speak, and he came. He was under a gag order from the court, but nobody cared, especially not him. There was a huge crowd of kids there to see him speak, and it was inspiring, full-on left-wing radicalism, and no one went to class or showed up for anything, and there weren't a lot of teachers in evidence, and no one from the administration showed their faces.

I was elected president of the freshman class, and the first thing I figured out when I got into the student council meetings was that there were two groups - the rebellious, radical side, which was all about the rhetoric of revolution, and the preppy side, which was all about "college suck", which was basically anything you did to look more appealing to college admissions people. Nowadays, privileged people in the entertainment business are getting indicted because they're bribing people and actively buying college suck for their kids, but back then that kind of thing was treated with a certain amount of disdain. People cared about what college they got into, but it was considered a bit desperate to try too hard, and people who did it were referred to as "strivers", which was not a compliment. There were four or five of us in the Student Council on the radical side of the fence, led by the head of the Afro-American society, who was a brilliant kid named Denis Orton. He had the major afro, and heavy black frame glasses, which gave him an air of seriousness, and he wore a black leather jacket, like a Black Panther, and he was an intellectual. It was like having Huey Newton, or Bobby Seale or Fred Hampton in the room, he was that impressive to me. The guy who was the actual head of the student council was a guy named Rob, who was a perfectly nice guy, but he hadn't the first idea of what we were on about or how he should handle it. We were just questioning everything, we had hold of a thread, and we were trying to pull the whole sweater apart.

They had a tradition at Choate that every year the board of trustees would have a meeting with the student council, to give them a preview of what the leaders of tomorrow were looking like, the standout students in the school. There were serious money people on the board,

Mosbacher (the America's Cup sailboat guy), and Bill Talbert, the famous tennis player, and a bunch of other bigwigs. We waltzed in there, we called ourselves the Minority Council because by the numbers we were a minority faction in the student council, and we immediately got the board on their heels questioning school policy, political issues, racism, and the Vietnam War. It was mostly Denis, who, as I said, had some serious oratorical chops when he got going. The board was not happy, and neither was Seymour, the headmaster, or the Dean, whose name was McFarlane, who was a dick. Their displeasure was writ large all over their faces, kind of like the scene at the end of The Graduate where everyone in the church is swearing at Benjamin Braddock but you can't hear them because they are on the other side of the glass doors. I could see they would have loved to just expel us all on the spot. It was awesome, a huge adrenaline rush, I thought we really got them on their heels, but, of course, it wasn't that easy. By the beginning of the following year, my friend Jon Lee, who had also been a speaker and a leader, was not asked back, and Denis had graduated, and things were just not the same, which probably should have been my first life lesson about what happens when you have backlash from the powers that be, they don't just roll over and let you win.

I was in New York for the weekend at the end of my first semester and, consistent with family tradition, we went out to dinner at PJ Moriarty's, which was kind of the family spot, a few blocks from home, the classic New York shrimp cocktail and steak kind of restaurant. It was dark and wood paneled, with white tablecloths, lamps on the tables with little white cloth shades, and an electric train that ran all the way around the restaurant at the top of the paneling near the ceiling. Tim Moriarty, PJ's brother, used to run the train for me and my brother when we were kids; he would always come by the table and make nice with his Irish charm, kiss the ring with my dad, flatter my mom.

It was my first extended visit home since going away to school, and it was around Christmas time, the four of us, my parents, me, and my brother. I think we were still at the cocktails phase of the program, and the subject of drugs, specifically marijuana, came up, because a family friends' kid had gotten busted in a stop and search in upstate New York. My parents had always told us that we should be honest, that things always turn out better when you are honest, that this was an important value in life, so when they asked if I had smoked pot, I thought for a second, and I said yes. Given the time and the circumstances, they should not have been surprised by the answer, every kid was smoking pot, but they were unprepared, and they did not shine. This is when I learned a basic principle of parenting that was valuable to me later in life when I was raising my own kids: Don't ask direct questions if you are not prepared for a response you don't like. If there is a right answer, and a wrong answer, then it's not a conversation, it's an interrogation. At that moment, I learned that they were the kind of parents that you lie to, that as long as they got the answer they wanted, they were fine, even if it was a lie, the most important thing was not to scare them or surprise them. So, when they asked if I had experimented with LSD, I was at least smart enough to say no. I don't remember what my brother did; perhaps he was smart enough when they went nuclear to mumble and let them focus on me. I wouldn't blame him at all, he was the oldest and he internalized a lot of their bullshit, which must have been worse, so it's fine if I took the bullet for him that one time.

I have a picture in my mind of the Christmas decorations in the restaurant as their angry voices fade into wordless noise, the flocking and the cheesy tinsel and the happy oblivious Christmas lights, blinking away as I lose interest in the conversation, in the subject, in the restaurant, in them.

Hank:

Mom loved Christmas, she used to go crazy with the presents, just ripping through everything; sometimes by the time Christmas Day came, there would be none left. She would just tear one open, and then another one and another one, and so on. So, I remember one Christmas Eve in Darien, we had already developed this code between us about what was going on with mom, and it was whether she was going to be the good witch, or the bad witch. We had learned to recognize it, when she drank we could see the transformation, her self-control would drain away, and so would the joy, and then we knew, we dreaded it, when we saw the bad witch coming, we could see the devil in her eyes. So, we were still holding out hope for Christmas Mom, the good witch, but we were seeing the transformation, so we knew the bad witch was coming.

Among the decorations, there is a nativity arrangement - Jesus, Mary, Joseph, and the Wise Men. It's familiar, it comes out every Christmas, the figures each time a bit more worn and fragile. This is classic New England Christmas, the decorations are more tattered every year, but they are treated like treasures and never replaced; each year they go gingerly back into the box and up to the attic. She is sitting on the floor in front of the tree, fooling around with the plaster figures as she drinks, holding them in her hands, rolling them back and forth from one hand to the other. We were watching her, watching her face, wondering how the night is going to go; it's like her anger and pain takes over, and suddenly we see that she is literally crushing one of the figures in her hand. It is crumbling, breaking into little pieces, turning to dust.

We see it's already too late to stop her or distract her or anything. We don't even have to look at each other to know what we are all thinking. She is distracted; she drops the crumbs and pieces of the figure that she has crushed and stares off at nothing. We look to see which one it is, and of course, it is Joseph, the father.

Already they are a million miles from Germany, or Italy, or Johannesburg, the first foreign city they lived in as children, and everything has changed. That life of privilege has evaporated; they are living in Darien, their father is gone, and already they suspect they are on the wrong side of the tracks.

Pete:

I think growing up I kept deluding myself that we were a normal family... sure dad died but normal. But none of what any of us had to deal with was normal.

Mom abused Hank more than any kid should have been abused. It is like she was hurting that she lost her husband but had no realization and concern that we lost a father... which was hardest on Hank because as the oldest he knew dad better than me or Bill...

Bill:

Both of my older brothers were always trying to keep things together and I loved them for that. Both Pete and Hank always worried about me and made sure I was ok. It felt a bit unfair. They seemed to worry more about me than each other sometimes. Maybe because they were closer in age and more peers while I was the baby.

I remember when I flubbed the end of a baseball game, I made an error in the last inning, and we lost. Mom wouldn't speak to me. Pete came over to me and said that it was really cool the way I threw my mitt after missing the ball. It was the perfect thing he could have said to me.

I have weirdly remembered that comment the rest of my life. After I totally fucked something up, I did something cool.....that life is not over just because you fuck something up.

Hank:

Bill was actually a superstar athlete in so many ways. I can't believe that he has one particular memory about losing one game on an error when he won so many with dazzling play at first base. He was an exceptionally fine fielder at first base. He dug out so many errant throws, more than once in the bottom of the ninth. It was a joy to experience as an older brother. I remember being so proud of him.

I remember Jim Jespersen used to pull the entire little league team into the bench and hit Bill screaming ground balls to show the rest of the team "how it is done". We were all really good athletes and had certain sports in which we excelled. Bill was an excellent soccer and hockey player and also a very good baseball player. To Mom's credit, she did try to support us in our athletic endeavors – though the "buck-up" routine was excessive, abusive, and frankly bizarre.

Chapter Five: Wheels Up

Excuse me, while I kiss the sky. (Jimi Hendrix)

The first time I smoked pot, we were down in the basement of one of the dorm buildings at Choate, me and my friend Chris, and the first time I tried LSD, we were at his house in Long Island. In both cases he offered, and I said yes before the words were barely out of his mouth. The first time I smoked pot I remember I kept trying to check myself (am I stoned, really?), but with LSD it wasn't too hard to figure out. I didn't necessarily have the kind of "wow, the walls are melting!" experience with LSD that people talk about. It was more like an extremely intense version of real life with some key elements dramatically altered. We went down to the North Shore to Chris's mother's house. That night, she dropped us off at the movie theatre in town and just about the time that we saw the huge line in front of the theatre and found out the movie was sold out, the plane kind of took off, and there we were, wheels up, in the middle of Northport, L.I. tripped out on acid with nowhere to go. It was a little like the part in the horror movie where the teenagers decide to go into the scary-looking haunted house to get out of the rain even though they should be going in the opposite direction and fast. Instead of calling his mom or his brother to pick us up, we decided to walk home, at night, on the deserted two-lane road that his house was on. I had no idea how far it was, and I had no idea where his house was, and he wasn't making any sense, so I was having some doubts about the whole program, and I was somewhat concerned that he was going to wander out into the road and maybe get hit by a car. Luckily there wasn't too much traffic, but I felt I needed to make sure nothing bad happened, which is a bit challenging to act on when you are tripping on LSD. I remember looking down the road, and noticing that around every streetlight there was a crinkly blueish purple halo, so very strange and beautiful, and I thought, wow, where did those come from? I saw those halos every night for years after that, like a reminder from another reality, residue of a dream state, until after a few years, they finally faded away.

This was about when the cop car pulled up, and the cop leaned out the window and suggested we get into the car.

We climb into the back and the cop says, "Watch out for that shit in the back seat", but I had no idea what I was sitting on or what he's talking about, except there is definitely some stuff on the seat, some equipment or something.

Then we start driving and he says to Chris, "Why didn't you steal your mother's car this time?" and I think wow, this can't be good.

And Chris, who hasn't said a single coherent thing since we left Northport, says, "That was my brother." I had no idea whatsoever what any of them were talking about, so I thought just fasten your seatbelt and see where this is going. I didn't know if we were going to jail, if they were going to take us to the hospital and drug test us, I didn't know what was going on.

I've been lucky. There have been times in my life where bad things could have happened, that didn't happen. Imagine, for instance, if we had been two black kids, walking down the street at night, in suburban Long Island.

The cops drove us home, dropped us off, and drove away. I was stunned, I felt as if I was made of Jello. I couldn't believe that was it. My imagination was running wild, and I was still totally confused about the conversation in the car. I later found out that at some point, his older brother took his mother's car, and she reported it stolen, and the cops picked him up, and they must have confused Chris with his brother.

I remember lying on the bed in his brother's room, listening to the song ***Time Has Come Today*** by the Chambers

Brothers, and there is a ticking clock effect in the middle of the song where the music stops, and they chant the word TIME! over and over but successively slower each time and there is this tick tock effect. I just can't describe what that sounded like. The sound was ringing in my brain, only that sound, as if my head was an empty metal barrel and someone was banging on it with words made of steel. Chris and I were laughing uncontrollably, and his brother was laughing at us, and then his mom came into the bedroom to talk to us, and we just couldn't stop laughing. I thought, once again, now we're screwed, but miraculously, she didn't seem to get it. She was a very nice woman, kind of lonely, I think. I guess she was divorced and unhappy and she was glad just to have us there with her for the weekend, so she wasn't going to find fault with a little foolishness.

We stumbled outside in the back of the house, and it was winter, so there was snow on the beach, and we were tripping over things and falling down and goofing around. I remember the texture of the snow, and the sand, how similar they were, yet different, out there in the dark in the cold of winter. I thought one of these things is about summer and one is about winter, and here they are together, what's up with that? The sand is cold when it's supposed to be hot, but the texture is the same. I didn't feel the cold, I'm sure we could have stayed out there long enough to get frostbite and never noticed.

These experiences change you - you're not just going to come down after five or six hours and everything's going to go back to normal, and the fact is you don't want them to. You know it, even though you're young, you can feel that you are somehow different for the experience and for me that was exactly what I was looking for. I wanted to hold on to it, I wanted things to be different, I wanted to be expanded, broken open, I wanted to understand. It's not just recreation, it's re-creation, ecdysis, shedding the old skin and growing a new one. Watch a snake or a lizard do it sometime, it's not an easy process, the old skin doesn't slide right off, they scratch and squirm. It doesn't look like fun, it looks painful, and they seem kind of dazed when it's over, and that's what it was like. They say the only thing you can really change is yourself, but even that isn't so easy.

My roommate at Choate was a kid from Oxford, Mississippi, Andy Howorth. He was a great kid, very funny, the youngest of five brothers from a really nice family - liberal, left-leaning Southerners, very gracious, educated people. He became a judge, which kind of makes me laugh, because he was so goofy back then. When the jocks who were like RA's or hall monitors used to come and chase him around and beat on him, he used to always yell out, "He's tryin' to cornhole me!" I'm not even sure he knew what he meant by that, but I don't think he was talking about the game you play with the beanbags in your backyard. I went down to Oxford with him, over vacation, and stayed with him and his family, and hung out with all his friends. Oxford has a classic central town square, and we drove around it, fooling around, listening to AM radio, that was an activity, and we went to the drive-in movies, and drove around some more, and hung out in people's backyards. It was something I hadn't really done before, not the sort of thing you do when you're growing up in Manhattan.

I went back several times. Mostly I remember the Southern girls and their suntanned brown legs, the funny expressions they used and the inside jokes.

ABC, easy as 1,2,3, simple as do-re-mi, ABC, that's how easy love can be....

That's what they were playing on the AM radio, that and Karen Carpenter singing ***Close to You***.

We used to drive straight north from Oxford towards Memphis to a lake called Sardis Reservoir, where we would swim and hang out and smoke cigarettes and talk. I remember making out in the back seat of somebody's car at the drive-in and writing letters back and forth with a great girl I met there, a smart girl, a thinker.

Lots of people I know have opinions about the South, and get into all this red state, blue state stuff. This was literally less than a decade after the end of Jim Crow, but it felt different then, it felt like it was all changing. I thought the Civil Rights Movement was going to sweep through there and sort the whole mess out, that the Voting Rights Act and Affirmative Action would fix it once and for all and the people I knew there were all for that. If you had told us then that all this racism and white nationalism would rebirth itself and have another life, we would have thought you were out of your mind. Sometimes, people change when they grow up, but I'd like to think not them.

Towards the end of my first year at Choate, there was a bad vibe, heavy and depressing, that seemed to be taking over, rolling in slowly, like an oil slick polluting the seawater. It was rumored that there were kids getting into heroin, and meth, and kids were getting busted for smoking weed and getting thrown out of school. Three seniors were busted, but the irony was, they had all gotten into good colleges already, and they weren't screwups, they were top students – one of them had split 800's on his SATs, and another one was the son of Patrick Lucey, the governor of Wisconsin. The administration was twitching. It was a classic setup for their hypocrisy to be on full display. There was a no tolerance policy, so they had to throw these guys out, but it made them look ridiculous, because these guys weren't fuckups or troublemakers, they were rock stars. The administration had to make a statement, but they would have rather kept the whole thing under wraps, and they couldn't do both, so they were like Christian Scientists with appendicitis, as Tom Lehrer once said, twitching and in obvious discomfort. Everybody wondered if the colleges would revoke their acceptances, but of course they didn't, they just looked the other way, which shows you how things were at that time.

Choate's preference was to deal with this kind of thing in an entirely different way which was not at all transparent. At the end of the year, after the students left, they scheduled meetings attended by the administration and a group of the more senior teachers, and they rated the whole student body, one by one, identifying the students they thought were problematic, branding the troublemakers. The beauty of it was that technically they didn't expel anyone, the ones they targeted were just "not asked back" with a letter that came at the beginning of summer. It had nothing to do with grades or anything. It was all about something they called negative attitude. In other words, just weed out the troublemakers, make them disappear, and at the beginning of the next year they're gone. It happened to one of my friends from the student council, a super smart kid, but he didn't come from a wealthy family or anything, he may even have been on scholarship, so they just made him disappear. It was tricky, though, because at that time the smart kids, the achievers, were often the outspoken ones, the activists, so the schools were between a rock and a hard place because they wanted to act tough and crack down, but that meant they had to get rid of some of their best kids. At this point it was 1970, everybody was uneasy, everyone was smoking weed and tripping, and there were like five nerds who were straight.

And then some guys pulled an awesome stunt that made the school administration look even more ridiculous. There was a big clock on the face of the Choate Chapel, which was exactly what it sounds like, basically a church where we were required to go to services and special assemblies a couple of times a week. It was extra significant because Seymour, the headmaster, was an ordained Episcopal minister, and he used to get up in his robes and perform the services himself, while at the same time pretending that the service was in some way non-sectarian.

Somehow, some kids figured out how to climb the front of the building in the middle of the night, which was in itself an impressive feat of climbing and engineering. I don't know how they did it without a bucket truck. They had some big cutouts of the head, the body, and the arms and legs of Mickey Mouse and they attached them to the clock on the front of the chapel. We all spilled out of the dorms the next morning to go to breakfast and there it was, the clock tower, transformed into a giant Mickey Mouse watch. Seymour and the deans were furious, and there was a real witch hunt, but they were completely unable to get anyone to fess up to it or rat out the guys who did it. Usually, they could find somebody and scare them into confessing, or informing on someone else, but nobody talked. To this day, I still don't know who the actual perpetrators were, but whoever it was, they deserve a prize. I don't know why, but the maintenance people couldn't figure out how to get it down, so it just stayed up there driving them all crazy. Eventually, there was some kind of storm or something and most of it fell down, and then it looked really ragged and broken, which made the administration even more frustrated.

I had a nasty accident in the dining room at Choate my freshman year. There was a posted calendar, and we were all expected to serve in the dining room on a rotating schedule, which was common in boarding schools then. I was setting tables one afternoon with my friend Wilson Smith and we were pushing these large heavy rolling carts with stacks of plates, four huge stacks to a cart from table to table setting out the plates. The carts were about waist high, and they went down to almost floor level where there was a sharp metal edge. We were pushing two of these carts, and Wilson was behind me, fooling around, telling me to hurry up, and as I stepped forward, he happened to push the cart at the same time and the sharp metal edge sliced right through the back of my heel into my Achilles tendon. I knew right away that it was bad when I tried to stand, even though it hadn't even started bleeding yet, and right away I said, "You better get someone". Wilson was petrified, practically paralyzed, but he ran off, and shortly afterward, came back with another kid, Kevin Phillips, who we used to call Douche Phillips. I used to get laughs from telling the story about how he practically severed my foot from my leg, and when he went for help, the person he came back with was Douche Phillips. Luckily, I didn't have to depend on Wilson or Kevin to deal with the situation because I realized that I was calm and thinking quite clearly and they definitely weren't. By that time, some of the kitchen staff had come out and they took charge of the situation, and I was taken to the infirmary and eventually the hospital, where they reattached the tendon and put my leg in a cast. I remember the fear I felt when the nurse at the infirmary looked at the wound and said to me, "Oh, you're just going to need a few stitches" when I was entirely clear that I was seriously injured, and whatever needed to be done, it was going to be more than a few stitches. In retrospect, it's possible she was trying not to scare me, but it scared me more to think that an adult who should have known better would so completely misunderstand the severity of the situation, and I was worried that they were going to stitch it up and I still wouldn't be able to walk.

One unexpected thing I remember experiencing for perhaps the second time in my life was a feeling of intense clarity and calm, looking around me in the middle of a crisis at people who were paralyzed and unable to act, and thinking okay, I can do this, getting them to focus and act. And what I remember most, was how seductive it was, the feeling of owning the situation, of filling a leadership vacuum, of taking charge. It's a feeling that once I experienced it, I found hard to forget, and something I was inclined to repeat when the opportunity presented itself.

Today, the average wealthy prep school family would probably sue the school and get a nice big insurance settlement, especially if their kid was working in the school dining room, but my parents didn't seem interested in who was responsible or anything. I spent months in a cast and the whole summer doing rehab, stuck in Connecticut with my mom, so I was looking forward to getting back to school at the end of the summer to be with my peers again.

I came back a couple of days early for Student Council meetings the first week of sophomore year and I found that the bad vibe had carried over. The atmosphere around the place was dark. They called a big assembly in the chapel, and all the teachers and the deans were there, looking grim and serious. Seymour gave a speech about how they knew that a lot of people were smoking pot and breaking the rules, and it had to stop. There was a vague "let's wipe the slate clean and start over" vibe to the whole thing, which left us kind of scratching our heads and asking each other if they expected us all to just confess or what. It was very non-specific and didn't totally make sense, which maybe I should have paid more attention to.

The next thing that happened was I got a message to go to the administration building because they wanted to see me over there. I don't really remember if it was Seymour or McFarlane but it must have been in the afternoon because I remember by the time the whole drama was over it was dark outside.

This is the part where I make the same mistake, the honesty mistake, the mistake I made in the restaurant at Christmas, which is someone asks me a direct question, someone I'm supposed to respect, and I tell the truth, without thinking about the consequences. I don't ask myself why they would ask me the question in the first place, or whether they are entitled to the answer, or whether I should lie, or at least keep my mouth shut, because I am still naïve enough to trust adults, even though I know I shouldn't.

I find myself in a dark, wood-paneled office with Seymour, the Headmaster, and McFarlane, the Dean of Students, who was kind of nervous and twitchy, like a tiger who smells blood, and maybe some other people, although I'm not sure about that, and they ask me if I have smoked pot since I came back to school. What flashes through my mind is the assembly, and the clean slate thing, and my thinking is maybe this is what they're talking about, and I should just tell the truth, and everything is going to be fine, especially since they haven't actually caught me doing anything wrong. The smart answer would have been a question, like maybe why do you ask? But I hadn't learned to be that quick on my feet, and I was intimidated. I'm sure they knew what they were going to do before the whole charade got going, but I'm sorry I didn't make them a bit more uncomfortable. I will say that a bunch of adults in positions of authority who get a fifteen-year-old kid in a room, interrogate him, expel him from school, and then justify it based on what he did or didn't admit in a very confusing and ambiguous situation are ethically challenged, and the fact that they tried to make me sleep at the headmaster's house that night showed me that they were desperate to keep the story from getting out around the school. The fact is they never caught me breaking any rules at Choate or doing anything that would justify expulsion, but I'm sure they lied to my parents and said that they caught me smoking pot.

Strangely my parents and I never talked about it. They never asked me what happened or why or showed the slightest interest in my version of the story. I was expelled because of my "negative attitude" and because they saw me as a troublemaker, and smoking pot was an excuse. I'm satisfied with that, I'm not going to apologize for it, at least I was honest, which is more than I can say for everyone else that was involved. A few months later, they encouraged me to reapply and come back, which really mystified me, and I turned them down. Years later, I suspect my father may have had reason to wonder about my experience at Choate because two other kids that he helped get into the school had experiences like mine. I have heard he came to see it a bit differently, but he never admitted that to me, I only heard it from other people.

Hank:

When I was a kid in 8th grade, my friends and I used to break into the garages of wealthy Darien families and steal the liquor stored there - usually beer and wine in refrigerators - but sometimes we would luck out and find hard liquor. I had the bright idea of starting a business and selling the surplus to other kids older and in my own age group. I loved the first few months of the enterprise. I became sort of a celebrity and even some kids much older than me thought I was cool.

And then, during a math test, I dropped the pad that served as my sales ledger on the floor and the math teacher, who was a supercilious and sadistic prick, spent the rest of the class flipping through the ledger and looking up at me with gleeful intent. You can imagine the shit storm that followed though mercifully and unaccountably I was only expelled for 3 days. I guessed they must have believed some part of my lame excuse that it was all just a big joke though I suspect it was more likely the violence of my disintegration and breakdown in the face of their grilling.

After I got caught, we returned to stealing liquor from garages in a matter of weeks until one of my friends was almost killed escaping from a garage. We had entered the garage where we were grabbing boxes of wine and hard liquor. We were laughing and making a racket because the stash was so big, apparently supplies for a party, when a man opened the door to the garage. We took off out the open garage door laughing with cases of liquor in our arms and ran into an adjacent pinewood. My friend stumbled and fell against the trunk of the tree and the jagged broken end of the stick penetrated his skull on the inside of his right eye. I kept running without realizing it was serious and adhering to the keep running code we had established as a basic standard of operation.

Later when I heard he was catastrophically hurt I called him in the hospital, and I couldn't even talk to him because I was sobbing violently. He kept saying "are you crying "in a disdainful way like "what the fuck we don't cry in our tribe."

I want to embrace that stupid kid and say, "yes you fucked up, but you were a kid and desperate and looking somehow for a way out." Not an excuse really but perhaps an understanding.

Chapter Six: Apathy and Boredom

You know the Day destroys the Night, night divides the day, try to run, try to hide, break on through to the other side....
(Jim Morrison)

I had a friend at Pomfret, another New England boarding school, in Northeastern Connecticut, up near Providence, R.I. and he suggested I apply there. I applied, and they let me in, surprisingly quickly, which was fortunate since it was already several weeks into the school year. Maybe they figured I was coming out of Choate with good grades, so it was worth taking a chance on the expulsion, maybe they just liked me in the meeting. Those disciplinary issues, things like that were not taken as seriously then as they are now. There were some interesting kids there, too, and some kids with issues. It was a forgiving place and most of the teachers were pretty great, and I probably should have paid a little more attention to the break that they gave me, but I think I was starting to lose my perspective at that point, failing to learn from my experiences and stumbling into self-destructive situations.

The first friend I made at Pomfret was a kid who roomed across the hall from me. He was a Puerto Rican kid from New York named Walter Soto, who was there on scholarship. We were good friends for a while, and we hung out all the time. Even though he was almost exactly my size, 5'8" and my weight, he was an outstanding athlete, both basketball and football, so he spent a lot of time at practice. Because of that some of the black kids he played with on those teams got on his case and let him know that he shouldn't hang out with me because I was white, which I was completely unprepared for; they didn't even talk to me to determine if I was worth being friends with, they just wrote me off. He was the only Puerto Rican in the school, so the whole thing felt slightly random anyway, but it was upsetting, because I lost a friend, and he didn't seem very happy about the whole thing either. At Choate I was politically aligned with the black kids, and I was friends with most of them as well, and it was a totally different vibe. I could tell he was embarrassed, but there was nothing he could really do about it without making himself into a pariah. It was unpleasant though, because Pomfret was a smaller school than Choate and it made for a weird atmosphere. On the plus side, Pomfret was at least somewhat coed because there were female day students, which worked out okay for me, although I can only imagine what it must have been like to be one of twenty or thirty girls in a boarding school population of several hundred boys.

By the fall of 1970, things in the country had changed completely. Nixon had gotten elected president by stoking the backlash, hammering on about law and order, which was just code for let's take the country back from the blacks and the hippies, and pandering to the "silent majority" which just meant white people who were afraid and felt like the country was out of control. It's incredibly ironic and bizarre that people can say things now in public and on social media that a politician like Nixon would have been afraid to say fifty years ago. The phrase law and order was code and everyone on both sides of the issue knew what it meant. Nixon and his cronies had figured out how to hide racism and a thinly disguised authoritarian agenda behind the law-and-order label, which made it sound like something everyone should agree with. After all, who is against law and order? Only criminals, obviously, and liberals, people who are "soft on crime". J. Edgar Hoover's FBI was mercilessly persecuting every public figure with a left-leaning point of view, and virtually every black leader or celebrity in the country, including not only Martin Luther King, Jr. but even people like Duke Ellington, Nat King Cole, Jimi Hendrix, and Aretha Franklin. The Nixon administration was using the CIA and the NSA to spy on "subversives" like the Weathermen and the Panthers, in violation of the National Security Act of 1947, to the point where Congress had to pass additional legislation outlawing the use of the of intelligence agencies to spy on American citizens, only for it to be once again circumvented by George W. Bush after 911.

The net effect of all this on all of us was apathy, and boredom, which is not a good recipe for managing a group of smart teenagers in an insular environment. Unlike Choate, Pomfret was totally apolitical, and the administration was low key and generally supportive, as were the teachers, so there was really nothing to rebel against. There was a generous helping of generalized teenage malaise, and a fair amount of drug use. We spent a lot of time in the lounge area outside the dining room playing cards and smoking cigarettes which, unbelievably, was allowed. One night a few of us strolled in there and found the room empty, except for several huge stacks of dessert plates, which must have been left over from an event. No one was around, and someone had the bright idea of playing frisbee with the plates, which quickly turned into more of a pitched battle. The result was a lot of noise and practically all the plates got broken, at which point we all looked around, a little bit shocked, and then everyone scattered. But the weird thing was we never heard a thing about it. There was no inquiry, no announcement, no questions, no search for the guilty parties. It was as if it never happened. The next day when everyone showed up for breakfast it was all cleaned up without a trace, and no one said anything about it again. It was a cathartic act of destructiveness, which probably should have resulted in punishment, but it didn't. Nothing happened. If that had happened at Choate, there would have been threats, lectures in Chapel, questions, drama, but at Pomfret, nothing. Live and let live.

In the fall, I went back to Choate for a visit.

I don't remember much about the weekend until the point when I found myself sitting with my friends in a pizza parlor in Wallingford with a handful of downers, little orange Seconals and blue and red Tuinals, trying to figure out whether to listen to my friends who were trying to get me to swallow them to take the edge off an acid trip that had gone wildly out of control. I remember how eerie and far away the pills looked in my hand in the weird fluorescent light of the pizza parlor, strangely color coordinated with the orange and blue Formica benches and cheesy signage. The pills were right there in my hand and yet they seemed to be one hundred miles away at the same time. For some reason, I was the only one who was tripping, which is something you're pretty much not supposed to do, and it definitely would have been wiser to split the LSD between us rather than me just taking it all, but I have no idea how or why that decision was made. Dosing at that time was unscientific, to say the least, but clearly, I would have been better off sharing with the group.

Hallucinogenic experiences alter your worldview and change your life, that's their purpose, that's why they were invented. That's a fact that doctors and clinical psychiatrists and researchers are just starting to embrace again after all these years. That's what Hoffman intended when he invented the stuff. Its original clinical purpose was to cure schizophrenia, something that has yet to be achieved seventy-five years later. And I believe that most people try psychedelic drugs for exactly that reason. It's meant to re-order your thinking process, to interrupt your unconscious thought patterns, to break apart your assumptions, to challenge your habitual perceptions, and for sure it's meant to facilitate non-linear thinking. It's a conscious choice and once chosen it can't be undone. It takes you where you need to go, not where you want to go, or where you think you should go, and it does make a difference.

I did not experiment with LSD and other psychedelic drugs as a form of recreation. I didn't just do it for fun, like smoking pot or getting drunk. I did it because I was looking for something. That half hour or so after you take it is like waiting for a train in a quiet, empty train station. You know it's coming but you can't quite hear it, you strain to listen, maybe the steel tracks glisten and sing a little, and then all of a sudden, it's there, in an explosion of noise and heat and you can't hear yourself think. It's a purposeful decision that takes you from where you are to a place that is entirely different, and you know that place will challenge, and probably scare you. You don't slip into it or do it by mistake. You can't get addicted to it, it's not a narcotic, but you can do it too much or too often, and that's hard to recover from. I'm very sure that if you have underlying issues like schizophrenia or bipolar disorder it can be risky, but there is some evidence that the opposite may also be true. Doing it to someone else, dosing someone without their knowledge, is inexcusable, but I met a woman the other day who had that experience and she chose to trip several more times after that. She is a nice housewife from New Jersey now. She's retired and spends most of her time taking care of her grandchildren. I read an article once that described the acid experience as "punching through to heaven", which is a description that I like, as it suggests acting on a conviction to do whatever it takes to understand your experience in an entirely different way and the effect of it doesn't fade. You can't really build a new self if you're not prepared to tear down the old one.

The next thing I remember after the pizza parlor is waking up from a dream, from a sleep state induced by a powerful dose of whichever barbiturates I had taken. I was in a room in the old house they all lived in, which was a sophomore dorm on the campus. Everyone was asleep, a bunch of us all in the same room. As I awoke, I had that experience common in dreams, of feeling that things are happening in compressed time, very fast. This time, it only took an instant, but the dream I woke up from was my entire life. When I say my entire life, I mean every single thing that ever happened to me in my entire life from the moment of being born, literally, until that moment. And it was not only everything that I had ever experienced, but everything that I had ever learned or known, down to basic facts, like there is a solar system with a sun and planets, there is gravity and evolution, there are birds in the sky and insects in the dirt and worms underground, all of human experience and knowledge. It felt like light speed, or the Doppler effect, where you are on a train, and there is another train coming from the opposite direction on the next track, and as it comes towards you, you can hear the train whistle getting louder and louder, and the noise of the wheels on the tracks, steel screeching against steel, and it explodes with sound and violently displaced air when it comes even with you, in a roar, and then disappears behind you, just as quickly, train whistle wailing off into the distance, and then it's gone.

I had pictures in my mind of common elements of my world, snapshots of very familiar things. One of them was my wallet, which I had been carrying in the same back pocket day after day, for years. It was brown leather, worn and shaped from repetitive use, and in it was my driver's license, among other things, and a card with a picture of the Goodyear Blimp on it. My Dad had arranged for our family to have a flight on the blimp when we were kids. We drove out to the Goodyear airdrome in New Jersey, and they took us up for a flight and then they gave us membership cards. I had saved mine, and in theory, I knew that wallet should be in my pocket with that blue card in it, with a picture of the blimp.

I was entirely open to the possibility that I was encountering a complete re-ordering of reality. It was all very lucid, and I was thinking with total clarity; it was not psychedelic, but it was definitely weird. It seemed as if all reality was a dream I was waking up from, in the same way that you can wake up from any lucid dream and it can seem real for a brief time until you are fully awake. I saw an empty slate stretching out in front of me, an absence of familiar reality, with no indication as to whether anything would turn out to be as I remembered it or understood it or if I had lived through it or only dreamed it. In a sense, I was looking into an abyss, but for some reason, I wasn't afraid.

The whole thing had the exact same quality of being close up and one hundred miles away as the pizza parlor experience. The wallet was my first test. I reached into my back pocket, and pulled it out, holding it in my hand and examining it as you might examine a moon rock or a science project you have never seen before. Visual evidence seemed to indicate that it was, in fact, the same wallet, check. Same stuff in it, check. Everything okay so far, check. Outside the door to the room we had all slept in, there was a stairway that went down to the first floor. I went to the door in the early morning half-light and opened it to see if the stairway was there. Still okay, check. Throughout this process, I don't remember having any emotional attachment to the results, it was like an experiment, and I still remember these things to this day as if they were still photographs, the wallet, the stairs, the room. I was just curious to see how it would turn out. For all I knew, there would be a galaxy full of stars outside the door, or a massive desert, or a moonscape, like something out of *Time Bandits* or *Baron Munchausen*. At this point, the other guys were waking up and they seemed to be concerned, which was not surprising considering what had transpired the night before, and I remember registering their concern, and feeling like I needed to reassure them without really knowing how. Somebody asked me what I was doing.

"Checking to see if it was there," was my response, which most likely didn't help, but for me, same stairway, check, all good.

I wondered whether I had lost my mind, but at the same time, I was thinking clearly. I felt lucid and I felt prepared for what would come next. As the next days and weeks passed, I tried to just accept whatever came, waiting to find out if things were as I had dreamed them or whether reality was going to present something different. The further I went forward, the more confident I became that things were settling back into familiar reality, which on some level was a bit disappointing, and I didn't let go of the possibility that I would open a door or turn a corner, and suddenly, the abyss would be there revealing that, in fact, it was all a dream and all bets were off. I felt like the kid, Kevin, in *Time Bandits*, who keeps pitching up in new situations that are completely unfamiliar and make very little sense. I just wasn't quite sure what was coming next. The minute I started to relax, I started wondering if something weird was about to happen. Truth be told, it might be that I have never quite let go of that feeling, I've just gotten comfortable with it.

Of course, reality does present challenges that we're not prepared for, it's just that the differences, the incongruities, are more subtle and often we don't recognize how deeply strange they really are. It was probably too simple for me to grasp at that point in my life, but over the years it has become familiar and lost its strangeness. One might even call it a friend or a traveling companion. And there are still mornings when I wake up, and I'm just not totally sure what I'm going to find.

Pete:

My experience with drugs was pretty limited... tried Cocaine a few times but mainly because the girl I was with was doing it. Whenever I smoked pot, it just made me tired and stupid, so I didn't do it much... never tried anything else - again, I was just a little too young and missed the 60s. Also, I never could do the hard liquor thing. But I certainly over drank beer and got stupid a ton of times.

Hank:

Drugs and drinking were definitely an escape for me. I was very happy drunk. Everybody was my best friend and closest family member when I was drunk, which was very different than my mother who we came to call Satan when she was drunk.

I loved the adventure of drugs and drinking – the way we could go on a journey of laughter and exploration – risk, radicalism, and perhaps escape. With all the drugs, even LSD, it was more about recreation. I wasn't really mature enough to be doing acid with some kind of vision quest or sacred journey in mind. I was really in a lot of emotional and psychological pain, and using drugs was a way to feel better. For me, drinking, drugs, friendships, and sex were naïve and innocent, in stark contrast to my experience of home, which was tedious and cynical and upsetting, even brutal sometimes.

Chapter Seven: Initiation

Strength is what we gain from the madness we survive.
(James Baldwin)

Somehow, I got back to Pomfret, I'm not sure how, and the first, and perhaps the only person I told was my girlfriend at the time, whose name was Lin. It was a strange story, and it seemed she really didn't know what to say, and honestly, how could she? She seemed to just accept it, so that was reassuring. To her, I'm sure the whole thing was just familiar teenage angst from a familiar source. My relationship with her had started one day when several of us were hanging out on a big grass lawn that was kind of like a common out behind the dorms and some of the other buildings. She had a black bandanna tied to her leg over her (bell bottom) blue jeans, and I asked her what it was for.

"Tribute to Jimi" she said, meaning Hendrix, and I thought, no way.

I was thinking her taste ran more to Cat Stevens or James Taylor, or even Elton John, so I was inclined to call bullshit on that. She didn't seem like much of a *Purple Haze* kind of girl to me, but as it turned out she was pretty much the first girl that I actually had sex with, beyond just making out and stuff like that, and it turned out she was more adventurous than I gave her credit for.

Towards the end of our relationship, the school was having a dance for juniors and seniors. She was a junior and I was a sophomore, so we were hanging out beforehand, but I couldn't attend the dance with her because it was only for juniors and seniors. It got to be time for it to start, so I was supposed to leave, but suddenly she took my hand and I followed her downstairs in the building, where there were some guest rooms which I guess they used for alumni visitors.

One of them was open, and she pulled me in there. She pushed me back on the bed and next thing I knew she was undoing my blue jeans and giving me a blowjob. I remember thinking that if we got caught, it was going to be both easier and more awkward to explain than the whole Choate situation. But we didn't get caught. I have this vivid memory of her, and not much about the relationship after that, which makes me think it might have been a goodbye blowjob.

At this point, I should probably admit that although she may have been the first girl to give me a blowjob, it wasn't my first blowjob. My mother's best friend lived half the year in Tucson, where she went for the winter months, and Vermont, where she spent the summer. She was an extremely competent, funny, and charismatic person who lived with her partner, who was a lovely lady you could have easily assumed was somebody's spinster aunt. Back then the fact that they were lesbians was something a lot of people would have whispered about, but my mother was very direct and matter of fact about it, which was interesting. You could never tell with my parents whether they were going to be cool about something like that or weird, it was completely random. Sometimes, my dad used to talk disparagingly about gay people, referring to them as "homos" or "pansies", but in fact I always thought most of his male friends were gay, and my parents didn't display a lot of judgement about these two women, their lifestyle or their choices. Sylvia was opinionated, in a very entertaining way, and she was the kind of person that knew how things work and how to fix them if they were broken, she had a green four-wheel drive Studebaker pickup truck that was without a doubt one of the coolest vehicles I have ever seen.

In the summer of 1969 before my freshman year at Choate, when I was fourteen, I went up to East Dorset to stay with her and help with some work she was doing around her place. She had a shop where she sold minerals, silver jewelry and American Indian pots and artifacts, all of which she would buy in the winter in Arizona and then transport them up to Vermont to sell in her shop. I enjoyed being with them, and it was a welcome relief from hanging with my mom in Connecticut, which tended to be both tedious and unnerving at the same time, which was not a good combination.

At some point during the week, Sylvia's nephew showed up. He had a small house he had built up the hill behind the shop. He had a wife and kids, or so I understood, but they were not with him. I don't really remember whose idea it was, but I was given to understand that it might be fun for me to hang out with him a bit while he was there. I didn't know him, but I didn't have a reason to refuse his offer, if that's what it was, and he had a nice red Porsche 911, which was cool, so I went along with it. I don't remember if what transpired after that all took place in the course of one day, or over a couple of days, but in my memory, it is compressed into a couple of very memorable scenes. We went to a quarry where the local kids went to swim, probably an old granite or marble quarry like you find in Vermont and elsewhere in New England, which made a really nice swimming hole where you could dive from the stone cliffs and the water was fresh and cold. I remember him touching my leg and complimenting me on my tan lines when we were changing into swimsuits in the bushes. He gave off a vibe that I didn't particularly like that was hard to pin down. It was kind of patronizing in a way that made me feel stupid or naïve, like I needed to try harder to be grown up.

The next thing I remember is I was at his house, and it's later, dark outside, and I've had a couple of beers, which at the age of fourteen I imagine I can handle. Then he's giving me his Playboys to look at, complimenting me on my hard-on, and the next thing I know he's got my dick in his mouth. I'm sure any girl who has given a teenage boy a blowjob knows that it's hardly a long-drawn-out process. For me, it was like an out of body experience; I'm wondering what the hell I'm doing, how I got myself into this, and how I can get out of there, like right now. While I'm zipping my jeans back up, he's telling me to make sure I don't tell anybody, which makes me mad, because I know three things. #1 - of course I'm not going to tell anyone, you idiot #2 - so you obviously know that I'm fourteen years old and this would be a problem for you if anybody found out and, #3 - I know in my heart that if I did tell anybody the person who would end up getting the worst of it would be me.

Somehow, I knew that I couldn't trust anyone, particularly not my parents, to have any understanding for how at the age of fourteen I could have been dragged into this by a man more than twice my age, seduced in fact, and somehow "gone along with it". The narrative would have been about me, and why I didn't put a stop to it, camouflaged as concern but with an accusatory subtext.

I was confused by what happened, and to this day, the whole experience is a mystery to me. Who was this guy, what kind of a person was he? He had a wife and two kids at home, what did he think he was getting himself into? Did he think about the risk he was taking, how this would affect his life if it went sideways? Was it a spur of the moment thing or was this a plan that he had developed somewhere along the way? Was this the first time he had done something like this? Was he a predatory personality, or was he drawn into this by some kind of passion and fell into it without really knowing what he was doing? Was there something about the way I looked or behaved that caused it? I wasn't gay, and frankly this guy wasn't particularly attractive, and I wasn't curious. I felt like I had just drifted into it, without thought. The only way for me to label it was to call it experimentation, but that doesn't explain very much. When you are a teenage boy, your body betrays you constantly. You can have an orgasm just thinking about sex, you can get an erection at the most inconvenient moments for no apparent reason. I wondered if I was just so desperate for sex that I could stumble into any version of it that presented itself, although that felt more like an excuse than an explanation. In the end, I chalked it up to experience and put it into the just part of growing up column, collecting experiences. I used to say I was willing to try anything once, which was a way of rationalizing a lot of bad decisions. I couldn't quite get clear in my mind the chain of decisions, or acquiescence that had led to this experience. Was it a choice or failure to choose? I felt that this guy had taken advantage of my inexperience and naivete, but I didn't have to go along with it. At the same time, I didn't feel like I had done something wrong, like it was immoral or something, I felt like it was my business, and if I had made a bad choice, that was my prerogative, I wasn't damaged in any way. Regrettably perhaps, it wasn't a moment of innocent exploration with someone I was close to, it wasn't a D. H. Lawrence moment. I wasn't ashamed of what happened, exactly, and it didn't scar me psychologically or emotionally, but I knew I should be very careful, more than I had been in the past, about who I shared it with, and when.

In my experience, women are easier to talk to about sensitive subjects than men; these things are-tricky for guys to talk about. They often boil down to details, who did what, how and when. I've noticed people can be very quick to decide that they would have handled a situation differently, when in reality they have no idea what they would have done. To be really honest, I guess it was something I was prepared to submit to, but if his plan had been to stick his dick up my ass, there would have been violence and brute force involved, and that would have been a whole different thing, and I don't know if I would have been able to process that so easily, so I was lucky. In a way, I ended up finding a positive in it, in having an experience that a lot of people would feel shame and fear about and being able to process it and move on, while still understanding that it could have been a lot worse.

I had two teachers try to take me down this road in high school, but I had collected the experience, and I had no reason to repeat it. Maybe these things just happened because I was careless and bored, and I wanted attention. One of them was a young teacher that I met at a class I took outside of Browning. He came from some rich family that was involved with the founding of the Museum of Modern Art, so they were a big deal in the New York art world. He knew some cool people; he would mention parties he was at with Stevie Wonder, who was at the height of his popularity then, and Diana Ross, and other celebrities. He invited me to a screening of Pink Flamingos at the Ziegfeld Theatre, and I met Divine, the famous transvestite provocateur, who was the star of the movie, and Holly Woodlawn, another transvestite who was big in the New York scene and an Andy Warhol protégé, or acolyte, or whatever. Of course, all of that was just another kind of seduction, and when the quid pro quo was introduced with these guys, the thing I remember about them was how annoyed they were when I wouldn't have sex with them, like I was being unreasonable, or difficult, which made me realize that I was just being careless. I was attractive and sexy to them, no more no less, and it wasn't even friendship. I think it gave me a little bit of insight into the experience a lot of girls and women must have on a regular basis, managing unwanted attention from guys who imagine they are getting signals that only exist in their own minds, or making assumptions they have no business making. It was easy to imagine a scene where someone asked me why I didn't just say no, and the only answer I could think of was I was confused, or I felt helpless.

Nowadays, these things blow up into scandals at exclusive private schools, they get teachers fired and destroy careers and lives. They throw around words like molestation, and abuse, but if it had been a woman, as George Carlin says, I would have thought I was just lucky, although I'm sure it wouldn't have been as simple as that. This kind of thing has been going on forever, since ancient Greece at least, so when school administrators, or people in positions of authority, or even parents act all shocked and appalled about it, they're full of it. The first thing I did when the shit hit the fan at Horace Mann and up at Choate a few years ago about something like this was call my brother, Jonathan, and he was like "yeah no shit, big surprise", which is exactly the reaction I expected.

I had a friend in private school in New York and often when we got out of the bars at the end of the night, we would take a detour so that he could piss on the front steps of Loyola, the Catholic school on the east side of Manhattan, in honor of the experience he had there. I never knew the details and I didn't need to. And here's something else, everyone knew about the priests, and I'm not even Catholic. If anyone had cared they could have asked the altar boys. EVERYONE KNEW. If anybody wants to understand why teenagers are so attuned to hypocrisy, it's simple – there's just so much of it around when you're that age, you can't avoid it, every time you turn around it's hitting you in the face, and most of the adults are so obtuse, they think you don't see it, even though it's right there in the open. We all get so busy compromising and explaining everything when we get to be adults we don't notice when we cross the line into hypocrisy, and once you cross it, if you're not careful, it becomes invisible. It's like racism. Nobody thinks they're racist and if you call them out on it, they get offended and angry and who can blame them? They're not even conscious of their own prejudice and they definitely don't want it pointed out to them. It's hard work facing your prejudices and a lot of us want to take a pass and just pay lip service to it.

Pete:

I knew that it sucked. I tried to believe that we had a normal family, maybe I even tried to pretend that we had a normal family, that our father had died, and that was a hard fact of life, but we could just suck it up and move on. Mom was smart and well read; she could be fun, entertaining – she was hurt, she had lost her husband, she was raising us all on her own.

But she was damaged, and the drinking and the crazy behavior just kept on getting worse; by the time we were teenagers, we knew it wasn't going to get better, we were not confused, and as time went by it just got worse and worse.

I remember one night listening to Hank and mom out in the driveway on Clocks Lane and he was arguing with her, "I'm doing the best I can, I'm trying to be a good son" and she was berating him.

"I know I'm the oldest, I'm doing the best I can" he was saying, and I thought, "I know she lost her husband; does she know we lost our father"? I felt bad for Hank, because he knew dad the best, and it was so unfair.

I just tried to keep my head down and keep her off my back, to focus on school, sports, jobs, to avoid the drama and negativity. I just thought, "Why can't everybody just calm the fuck down?"

Everything was a big deal and a big negative to mom - everything. I kept thinking 'what's the big deal" - and "calm down" ... and I think that carried to whatever was going on in the world and the country... I kept thinking that people freak out all the time over anything and everything, so I just decided to stay out of it.

I was focused on what I needed to do - mainly to keep mom off my back - sports, school, jobs to earn money.... I sort of didn't have time to think about anything except getting through the day. Looking back, I was pretty shut down ... happy playing baseball basically...

Chapter Eight: Something Stupid This Way Comes

It's a typical situation in these typical times – too many choices. (Dave Mathews)

So back at Pomfret, I did something stupid, and then I did something really stupid.

The stupid thing was my first bad acid trip, which I think was my last acid trip, although I tried mescaline and MDMA and some other stuff after that without incident. Once again, I did it alone, trusting my sanity in a careless and haphazard fashion to my roommate, Jamie, who entertained me with some fairly convincing Ian Anderson imitations for a while, and then fell asleep. The night stretched out cavernous in front of me, and I'm guessing the acid was cut with a bunch of speed or something because I was wired, with nowhere to go, and no one to talk to. At some point in the middle of the night, I found myself lying on my bed, looking at the upper corner of the room where, up by the ceiling, a lightning bolt would appear, not like literal lightning, but a big cartoony lightning bolt, like a superhero would wear on his outfit. It would take off from the corner, fly across the room and slam into my body and then pass out the other side. Each time this happened my body would convulse from the impact. I have no idea how long this went on, but eventually, it started to get light outside. Soon it was going to be time to go to breakfast, and assembly, and classes and stuff, and I was nowhere near straight. In prep school, if you don't show up for this stuff, they wonder why, and they go looking for you, which in this case would not have been good.

My roommate got up, got dressed, and left. I wasn't particularly bothered about that, because he was a shithead and he wouldn't have been much help anyway, but I was alone without a plan and no confidence that I could handle the random interactions that would inevitably result if I went out into the world. I was pretty much at my wits end, and the clock seemed to be going faster than normal speed, bringing me closer and closer to a reckoning with the implications of my choice of the night before. Suddenly, the door opens, and in walks this kid, I think his name was Paul. I didn't know him very well at all, in fact, I had hardly spent any time with him. I knew he was a nice guy, but that was pretty much it.

"What's up?" he says, "how's it going?"

He seemed to already have a pretty good idea of what was going on, so I'm guessing that my roommate was out there getting mileage out of my predicament with my stupidity as the humorous element in the story. I seriously doubt that he was trying to help. Jamie and his best friend Teddy were "nice kids" from Greenwich or Fairfield or some other Connecticut suburb, and they were two of the most venal, self-absorbed people I have ever encountered in my life. He and his friend managed to make a significant contribution to the erosion of my self-esteem during the time I lived with him that was out of all proportion to anything that made any sense. Their negativity and harassment were just unrelenting. I remember the two of them once telling me a story about essentially raping some girl they knew and feeling simultaneously relieved because I knew they were lying and disgusted that they would brag about something like that. Their absence of morality scared me. I'm sure they both went on to join fraternities at Ivy League colleges and grew up to be hugely successful investment bankers.

Anyway, Paul, who had somehow just appeared as some sort of guardian angel, suggested that we go for a walk, which seemed like a pretty good idea to me. Somehow, he made me feel like he had the whole situation under control, that everything was cool, and I should just play along, and everything would turn out fine. And truth be told, that is exactly what happened. We went for a walk out in the woods near the school. It was winter and there was still a blanket of snow and dead leaves on the ground, but it wasn't that cold. Between the branches of the trees the sky was a sharp shade of blue, partially obscured by the few dried leaves that still rustled in the trees, even though it was almost spring. We walked in the woods and talked a little bit, and soon I started to calm down and feel normal again. There was a huge round concrete reservoir of some kind out there in the woods, with a curved top like a saucepan, and we had no clue what it was.

"Maybe it's a hookah," he says.

And I said, "Yeah, to pick up the world" and he thought that was really funny. In my twisted acid-trip logic I thought he said "hooker", which made no sense, and what connection there is between a large concrete structure and a prostitute is way beyond me. Lucy in the Sky with Diamonds, right? That makes no sense either if you think about it, Tangerine Trees, Marshmallow skies?

He took me in a long circle and led us back to school, where it was just time for everyone to go to assembly. I think we had missed breakfast, but that was manageable. Anything more could have become a problem. We walked into the auditorium and although there were definitely some people looking at me funny, everything was cool, crisis averted. Sometimes I think about Paul and what he did for me. Sometimes bad things happened, and I made some bad choices, but sometimes good things happened as well and that is called luck. I know it's a cliché, but what he did for me was a real act of kindness, certainly nothing he had to do, and nothing I expected. I hope I see him someday and we can have a laugh about it.

The second thing I did was really stupid and I wasn't the only one involved, and it turned out badly for all of us.

I had a friend named Matt and he asked me if I wanted to hitchhike down to New York and stay with him at his mother's apartment for the weekend. Aside from getting picked up by a guy in a station wagon who turned out to be drunk and having to convince him to stop and let us out again, the trip was uneventful. Matt's mother lived alone in a large apartment in a doorman building on the upper east side. The rumor at school was that she was friends with Paul Newman and Joanne Woodward but I had no idea if it was true. I could have just asked Matt, I guess, but that seemed kind of desperate and uncool. She was friendly and vivacious, and she didn't seem to have anywhere to go, so that evening we sat around the kitchen table talking, or really answering questions, mostly, satisfying her curiosity. I remember finding her kind of interesting, and as a teenager, it's always nice when adults are curious about you.

There was also a teenage girl there who was some sort of friend of the family. She was a bit full of herself, like a lot of New York private school girls, but she was cute, so I didn't focus on that very much. She had one of those cute sixties' names, like a flower, or a bird, or an emotion, or a month of the year. Her mother was a society divorcee who had been a well-known actress and "It Girl" in the fifties. She had been on the cover of Look Magazine, but I didn't really know much about her. It wasn't really clear what this girl was doing there, but my suspicion was that his mother had invited her because she was expecting us, and she wanted us to be entertained.

At some point, Matt decided it was time to move on, so he said goodnight to his mom, grabbed a bottle of red wine and three glasses, and the three of us went off to hang out in his bedroom. As we were leaving the kitchen his mother said, "be careful, Matt, she's still a virgin." I couldn't imagine what she thought was going to go on, and frankly, if she was friends with this girl's mother, what she was thinking. I thought it was shocking, but Matt just laughed it off.

Despite what Matt's mother may have been expecting, the three of us did not go off to his bedroom and have an orgy. We drank the wine, listened to Aretha Franklin, and Matt eventually kind of passed out. This girl started telling me about this friend of mine from school she was in love with, and within half an hour, we were making out. At one point, she was kind of singing along to Aretha, to Carole King's lyrics, *you make me feel like a natural woman* and I wondered what that meant to a 15-year-old girl and what I would have to learn in my life to make a woman feel that way about me.

We spent that summer as boyfriend and girlfriend, and frankly, I was never clear what it was about me that she was attracted to, but she kept telling me she was going to get on the pill and we were going to be having sex, so I figured why not just go along with the whole program. But really, she wasn't all that likable. Affluent early 70's parents could be just plain strange. In many ways, they seemed just as confused about themselves as their teenage kids, and we were all experimenting with the same things, which made it doubly strange. I did have occasion to meet her mother later that summer and she wasn't very likable either, so it all made sense.

The next morning, quite early, I woke up and stepped into the hallway that led to the kitchen, and I got a shock. Literally, I thought I was seeing a witch for a moment until I realized it was Matt's mother, but she was completely transformed from the night before, almost unrecognizable. She was a haggard crazy mess. I couldn't imagine what had happened overnight that had caused this transformation, and this is when I learned what songs like *Go Ask Alice*, and *Mother's Little Helper* were all about. Like a lot of women who wanted to lose weight in the sixties, her doctor had given her a prescription for Dexedrine, which was pure speed, and like a lot of women, she had become addicted to it. Why the doctors didn't know that isn't clear to me. The problem was she had to take barbiturates at night to go to sleep and then speed again in the morning to get up and the doses just kept going up and up, which is pretty much the definition of a vicious cycle. I had caught her before she took her morning pills and put her face on and it was not a pretty sight. A little while later, she miraculously turned back into the clever, charming woman I had met the night before. It was like something out of a fairy tale, with magic mirrors and spells and poison fruit.

Not too long after that, we started getting phone calls from school.

I had provided the funds, my friend David (not his real name) had bought a bunch of LSD in New York and brought it back to Pomfret, and another one of my friends, Robert (not his real name), had sold it all over the school while we were in New York. Basically, the school population was small, and I guess a lot of people were bored that weekend, because from what I heard, everybody in the place was tripped out. I think David made the buy on the street, so the acid was not very good. Apparently, a lot of people were showing up at the nurse's office with stomach aches or headaches, so maybe it was cut with something, or it was just sloppy chemistry. The school, or maybe the infirmary, must have contacted the police, so Robert got picked up, and he was sixteen, so they charged him. Any communication about the situation was controlled and we weren't allowed to talk to each other, so I never saw Robert until years later, when I ran into him on the street in New York. Until then, most everything I knew about it from the time I put up the cash was basically gossip or hearsay. Robert told me that he was in jail in New Haven for a short time, but when I saw him, he had gotten his law degree and he was working as a lawyer, so they must have expunged his record or knocked it down to a misdemeanor or something. From what I understand, he could never have become a lawyer with a felony record otherwise. I remember he told me he was in jail with one of the Panthers involved in the Alex Rackley New Haven murder trial, so he came out of it with an interesting story to tell. David, who bought the LSD, was called into the principal, questioned, and expelled as well, but he and I were younger, so the police never got involved.

People had been calling all weekend feeding me the story in dribs and drabs and I was feeling an intense and growing sense of dread. Shortly after I got back to Pomfret, David showed up at my room to tell me that I had to come with him and talk to the administration. Although he didn't admit that he had already told them I was involved, it was obvious that he had, and I couldn't really blame him, I'm sure he didn't know what to do. I could have lied and told the school that I had no idea what they were going to do with the money but once again, it really didn't occur to me to lie about it. The school might have had to accept that story, but I'm just not that person, I don't think I could have lived with myself. At that point, I didn't know the full story about Robert, but I had given them the money to do the deal, so I felt equally responsible for what happened, and I had to face up to the whole thing. The school was nice about it, they couldn't have been more different than Choate, but they really had no choice. My adviser teared up during the conversation. They literally asked me what I thought they should do. I'm sure they felt that they had failed me, and I admired that in them, but they had to throw me out, they really had no options. Wealthy parents today are often very creative about protecting their children from the consequences of their actions, but I think that often turns out to be a bad idea and I had no expectation that my parents would intervene in any way and they didn't.

I could see that I had made some bad choices, thoughtlessly, but it was clear to me that I had no one to blame but myself. My mom, helpful as usual, blamed me for getting my two friends in trouble, which I suppose was a backhanded endorsement of my leadership qualities, but it was hard to see it in that light at the time.

So, there I was at the end of my sophomore year, in 1971, at the age of 16, getting thrown out of my second prep school. I made a funny story out of it, getting thrown out of two schools in one year, and I stuck with that for years, as if I was proud of it, being a rebel and a troublemaker, selling the romance of it. When people ask me where I went to high school, I often say that I went on the East Coast boarding school tour and a surprising number of people seem to know exactly what that means. Really, though, there was nothing funny about it. I was at a point where I felt as if I didn't have agency in my own life, like things were happening to me that I had no control over. I was making choices without thought, drifting into things, even when I knew they were high risk choices. I had no direction and no idea what I wanted. I felt like I didn't belong. I was born, or at least raised, into privilege, but it felt like something was just wrong. The only thing I needed to do was figure out where I wanted to go and get out of my own way, but I couldn't do it. I felt lost with no idea where to turn. I felt like pushing back, rebelling, but I didn't know what I was pushing against. When you feel out of control, the only thing you have agency over is yourself, and that's what you push against, and it doesn't generally go very well.

I had good grades even then and I was an achiever, from an academic point of view, so I was protected by the fact that a lot of kids from backgrounds like mine were having similar problems. So many kids were getting thrown out of school in the early seventies that there was actually a place called New York Tutoring School which did a lot of business administering tests and completing academic requirements for kids like me. Pomfret was accommodating, they turned over all my records, and I took my exams at the Tutoring School and finished sophomore year. I signed up to go to Browning School on East 62nd Street in Manhattan the following year. Browning was founded by John D. Rockefeller, who apparently founded it in 1888 because he didn't think that any of the other private schools in New York met his standards, and the first two students were his son John D Jr. and his nephew. The school had a policy of admitting students primarily based on intelligence tests and academic achievement, so they didn't seem concerned with my extracurricular problems.

My parents were not so philosophical about it. Mercifully, the whole thing was so out of context for them that it completely defied their expectations. They just seemed defeated by the situation, without any tools to address it. They didn't know why I was behaving the way I was, and if they had asked, I'm not sure I could have told them, why the perfect little baby they had adopted with so much promise for a perfect life was turning out this way. They were incapable of seeing it from any perspective other than their own. They experienced it as something I was doing to them, as if it was just patently unfair, after what they had done for me. To them, something had gone unexpectedly wrong, and they just wanted someone to fix it and turn their life back into the fairytale they had signed up for. They wanted their perfect, smart, handsome achiever back, the one they packed off to boarding school, the one that was supposed to go on to Yale, or Harvard, the success story that they had envisioned, or perhaps even expected. I sometimes wonder now if at any point they questioned whether the decision to adopt started them on a path they should never have taken.

In desperation, they sent me to see the family doctor, who was also a family friend and a kind of advisor. He spent about an hour talking to me and immediately told them I should be seeing a therapist. At that time therapy was considered a big deal, not the knee jerk answer to everything that it is now. They jumped at it like passengers on the Titanic discovering a half empty lifeboat. They were not fans of therapy, or psychiatry, and eventually they had second thoughts, but it was too late. I went to therapy twice a week, two hours a session, for the next two years, and even by today's standards that's a lot.

Hank:

I used to fight with her constantly; I think sometimes I was trying to draw her attention to me and away from Pete and Bill, and sometimes I just couldn't help it. And it was so stupid, I just couldn't look the other way, I couldn't let her have the last word, even though I knew it was a mistake. And I think I paid a price for it later, in drugs and drinking and anger: it took me years to offload that burden.

Chapter Nine: The Real World

Not everything that is faced can be changed. But nothing can be changed that is not faced.
(James Baldwin)

The first time I met my therapist, the first words he said were,

"Lots of people will tell you these are the best years of your life, but I'm here to tell you that's horseshit."

I was so relieved I might have cried if I was still capable of it, but the well had pretty much run dry. There were casualties at that time, a lot of smart kids who didn't make it and I could have been one of them, but Walter Slote, my therapist, pulled me through it. That doesn't mean that I sorted out all my issues and everything went smoothly. Not at all, but what he did was deflect me from a path that was most likely going to end in disaster, and that was an accomplishment. He stood up to my parents, he backed them off and made a little head space for me, and that was a big deal, it motivated me to at least survive. I was supposed to go to Vermont for the summer and work in a ski and tennis shop owned by some friends of my dad, but when I got thrown out of Pomfret, he slammed the door on that, for fear, I'm sure, that I would do something to dishonor his name, so I went to work volunteering at a daycare center in Harlem called The Storefront instead.

The Storefront was started by a poet named Ned O'Gorman, who had overseen the Head Start early learning program in New York at one point and grew disenchanted with institutional learning and government programs, so he started the day care center with his own money. It operated on a shoestring, with minimal facilities, but it gave the kids somewhere to go every day, and the people who worked there were mostly from the community, so it provided a little bit of employment as well. When I started there we worked out of the basement of a church, but eventually we moved into an abandoned storefront (hence the name) on Adam Clayton Powell or Lenox Ave, I don't remember which. I didn't particularly like Ned but he wasn't around much, and I felt like he deserved a lot of credit for putting his money and his principles where his mouth was and doing something good in Harlem, which at that time was a wilderness of trashed vacant lots and boarded up buildings, far from the gentrified neighborhood it has since become.

I think the prevailing adult wisdom was that interacting with the "real world" would wake me up to how lucky I was and how my problems were nothing compared to people who had real challenges, as if my parents had any interaction with people in Harlem other than driving past them on Third Avenue on the way to the Willis Avenue Bridge when they left the city for Connecticut. The irony was that I was pretty comfortable with the people I dealt with every day in Harlem, they were nice to me, and in a whole summer of working there, where I saw very few white faces in the course of my day, in what was supposed to be a "bad neighborhood" I don't recall anyone ever bothering me or looking at me sideways. I worked mostly with a woman whose husband was in jail for armed robbery. Her problem was figuring out how to save enough money to buy him a nice suit and some $400 shoes for when he got out, which wasn't going to be easy considering how much money she was making at the daycare center. Most days the kids would eat some sort of meal and then we would take 15 or 20 of them to a playground somewhere and just let them play. I figured my job was just to let them have fun, make sure nobody got hurt, not lose any of them, comfort them if they cried, and get them home in one piece. If we achieved that, I figured I was doing an okay job, with no instruction or guidelines of any kind to work from. Sometimes we would put all the kids on the Fifth Ave. bus and take them downtown to one of the nice playgrounds where the little white kids played, just for the hell of it, to see the expressions on the faces of the nannies and the moms. Perhaps it wasn't that mature, but it was edifying.

One day, a little girl showed up who was very quiet and withdrawn. She didn't speak at all and she didn't really interact with the other kids. I tried to see if I could get her to relax and join in and after a few days, she started to engage a little bit and play with the other kids, and sometimes she would come sit on my lap and talk to me. Her father was a scary-looking guy with a lot of scars on his face, but he seemed perfectly nice when I spoke to him. Then one morning when the parents were dropping off their kids, there was some commotion. Ned was there and he and some of the women who worked there were gathered around and there was some animated discussion going on, but I couldn't tell what it was all about. Then I saw that it was the same little girl, and the commotion was all happening around her. She had shown up with a bunch of small triangular marks on her body. It was pretty clear she had been burned with the tip of a hot iron. I remember it very clearly, looking between the people standing around her and seeing those marks on her body and wondering who could have done that to her, who would do something like that to a child. They took her to the hospital, and I imagine Child Services got involved after that and who knows what happened, but I never saw her again.

If you want to talk about the "real world" that was plenty real enough for me. I had never seen anything like that before. I wondered whether her father, who I had met a few times, had done that to her, whether you could tell by looking at someone that they were capable of something like that, if the scars he had on his face were a clue to the scars she would always have on her body. I never found out any of the details. I do wonder sometimes what happened to that little girl, what came after. If I saw her today, would she remember it? Is she even alive today? Did she survive her childhood?

I remember going home to the Upper East Side, down in white Manhattan, and I didn't tell anybody about it; I just didn't know what to say, I couldn't find the words; I didn't have much capacity for sadness, and it was a story I couldn't bring myself to tell. I know it's complicated, but I just can't understand why people do the things they do to their children, and it has nothing to do with socioeconomic status or genetics or anything else. It's just mystifying. But then again, people do a lot of things to themselves that are hard to understand as well.

It was a summer of the sublime and the ridiculous, the real and the surreal. Often, I went from hot, smelly, garbage-strewn Harlem to cool, air-conditioned West Side coffee shops or restaurants by Lincoln Center to hang with uptown private school girls on summer break with time on their hands. My girlfriend, who had no shortage of self-confidence, went to one of the performing arts high schools and she was studying ballet. She was dancing in the chorus in Petrushka at the American Ballet Theatre over the summer. She was a pretty girl with a great body, and she used to stand, as a lot of them do, naturally in first position with her toes turned out, which I thought was cute and sexy.

She got me in trouble with her mom because we stayed out very late one night, too late, until morning really, simply because she wouldn't go home. We weren't even doing anything all that interesting since the plan with the pill and the sex hadn't materialized yet. Her mother was angry about it and summoned me to their apartment, which was in The Beresford, on Central Park West, to give me a talking-to. It was the first time I had ever set foot in their apartment, and it would be the last. Her mom was sitting at an antique French desk in the living room which was all full of crystal vases and lamps and silver and artwork and expensive fabrics. Behind her, there was a killer view of Central Park and the Museum of Natural History, which frankly kept drawing my attention away from her, even though she was sort of famous and basically beautiful in an uptown sort of way. She looked down her perfect little celebrity nose at me and tried to act parental, which based on my experience of her daughter, she didn't have much talent for, but I didn't feel that intimidated. She reminded me of the people at my grandmother's parties, East Side upper class people, minor celebrities or people with famous names, minor Russian royalty and Eurotrash counts and countesses, fragile people with backstory and the trappings of wealth and status. They all acted very special, but I sometimes felt that if a wind came up, they would all just blow away like dry leaves. I remember thinking your daughter doesn't even care what you think, and she's not even here in the room, why should I let you push me around? I figured I had been thrown out of school twice and I was working all day in Harlem every day for nothing, what exactly was she going to do to me? She threatened to call my parents, and I thought, well, that's going to be interesting, I'm not sure they're going to be all that concerned about you and your little ballet dancer after all I've put them through.

These girls acted sophisticated and urbane and fast, and they had all discovered the power of flirtation, how their bodies and their vivacious cuteness affected boys and men of any age, but like Luke Skywalker and the Force, they hadn't learned to control it yet. They were kind of brittle and a bit silly if you listened to them, but I was easily impressed with teenage female beauty, so it was easy to overlook the silliness. They all seemed desperate to get on with whatever was coming next, and guys like me were mostly clueless and most definitely not in charge, hanging around thinking maybe we were going to get laid. It was common with upper class New York city kids in those days that the girls would often shortcut the process of growing up by finding themselves boyfriends who were much older than they were and had cars and apartments and mobility and could pay for things. We've become serious, self-righteous and judgmental about this sort of thing but back then no one said anything, it was considered normal in certain circles, and the presumption of power imbalances in sexual relationships was a concept that hadn't even been thought of.

It's axiomatic to say now that Roman Polanski is a pedophile, and everyone acts as if it's obvious, but in the seventies, it wasn't that obvious. Back then these girls ended up in these situations with the tacit approval and even participation of their parents, who often knew exactly what was going on and did nothing about it. We used to wonder sometimes what they were thinking or if it was possible that they were oblivious to what was going on with their kids, particularly their girls, but sometimes their boys as well. Things were different then. People talk about the legendary permissiveness of the seventies, but what they don't say is the difference between freedom or "free love" and exploitation was not so obvious, the choices were not so clear, and sometimes the "nuances" were intentionally overlooked. Freedom and lack of boundaries were often confused with each other, since the fact that you are free to do something doesn't mean you have to prove it by going ahead and doing it, especially if it's harmful, or degrading and I think a lot of adults, and parents even, put all the responsibility for making the distinction on the kids. When we were teenagers, we thought we were supposed to be having sex, like we had to make excuses if we weren't, and I don't even think we stopped to think about whether we were enjoying it, or if it was just another box to check, or if we were even comfortable with the choices we were making. .

I remember once meeting after work at a restaurant with my girlfriend and a couple of her friends. Sometimes we would sit at these places for hours and just order coffee, which drove the waiters crazy. After a while, everyone took off, leaving the two of us there, at which point the check came. It turned out I didn't have enough cash to cover it, even though it really wasn't very much. In those days, even rich parents didn't hand out credit cards to high school kids the way they do now, and we paid cash for things. I asked her if she would help me pay the check. She looked me straight in the eye and said no.

So, I say, "Really? No? Don't you have a few bucks?", and she just stared at me.

At this point, the waiter started to get annoyed after coming back the second time to collect the check. I was imagining being marched to the kitchen, the object of ridicule for everyone in the restaurant and washing dishes for the rest of the night, so I asked her again to look in her purse. With a super annoyed expression on her face and kind of a flounce, an indignant head shake, she finally pulled her wallet out of her purse, and lo and behold, there was over $100 in there. She wasn't surprised that it was there, and she didn't try very hard to pretend that she had forgotten about it or anything. I wondered what she thought was going to happen if I had to admit to the waiter that I couldn't pay the check.

If I hadn't already figured it out, that gave me a good idea who I was dealing with. I admit it didn't surprise me, but she was very pretty and sexy and sometimes she was fun, and I didn't have a whole lot else going on that summer for amusement. At some point, we went for the weekend to somebody's house in the Hamptons. It was a beautiful white house with a tennis court and a huge lawn, and everything in the house was white as well, and there were no adults around. We went to some disco on Montauk Highway, and she spent the whole night dancing and flirting with some French guy while his girlfriend and I sat, bored, watching them. Then, we went back to the house, and she had sex with me. Why? Why then? She was nervous and uptight, like it was something she was checking off her list and I'm not sure it was worth the wait. I doubt that she remembers me with fondness.

I ran into her at the SAT's later in the year after we broke up. She had showed up completely unprepared, without the #2 pencils that they used to tell you incessantly over and over to bring, and she decided I should give her one of the two that, as instructed, I had brought with me. To this day it makes me laugh to think of the expression on her face when I said no.

I was starting to recognize that in relationships, you can attribute appealing qualities to people that aren't there and make allowances for unappealing qualities that are there, just because you find someone attractive. A lot of men do this, and women too, although I think women do it because they see potential in a guy that isn't there and think they can make something out of him. It's hard to know which is more pointless. These things I learned without therapy.

When I started therapy with Walter, I had one previous experience with it in a group at Pomfret. I signed up for it simply out of curiosity. I was inclined to try almost anything at least once, which I think is a good thing on balance, even though it has led me a few times into things I might have been better off avoiding.

I don't know what the school's intent was in setting up this therapy group but they made it available to anyone who wanted to sign up, so I did. What transpired was a little bit like the book *Bridge of San Luis Rey*, which asks the question: what are these random people doing together in this place at this time? Why are they here? What do they have in common? In what sense were they chosen? Is there some sort of fate involved or is it just totally random? In this case it was just therapy, but teenagers are tough, and one of the girls basically turned on the therapist and started to pick him apart, session after session. She was the instigator, but others started to join in. To say he lost control of the group is an understatement and they closed it down after a couple of sessions. She just started turning the process upside down by asking him pointed questions, turning the focus back on him, and he kept refusing to answer them, and he didn't seem to know how to deflect the attention. It turned into a power struggle between him and this girl, and he lost. I thought she was a very nice girl, and I was totally curious what it was under the surface that triggered the whole thing, where the anger was coming from. It was like the Stanford Prison Experiment; they just cancelled it early and locked up the lab. It just shows in a different way what a hothouse environment it can be when you put a bunch of smart kids together in one space with time on their hands.

It reminded me of *Lord of the Flies*. Or when you bite your lip and taste the blood in your mouth. It hurts, but you have to admit to yourself that there is nothing that tastes quite as interesting as blood.

You could say that Walter was a stereotypical Upper West Side psychoanalyst. He saw his patients in a book-lined study in his apartment in a beautiful old building on the corner of 65th St and Central Park West with a view of Central Park. His wife was Korean, and she was a classical musician or opera singer or something. Often when I was there, I would hear her practicing off in the distant recesses of their apartment. I met her a few times, and she was lovely. I thought analysts weren't supposed to reveal anything about their personal lives, so I felt privileged to be introduced to her. I don't think I could paraphrase even one hour of the conversations Walter and I had over two years, but it certainly added up to hundreds of hours of talking. I know what it felt like, though. I felt like I was trying to climb out of a hole, continually losing my grip and sliding backwards. I felt like I had a headache that wouldn't go away. I felt like the whole world was grey, drained of color. I had lost the ability to express emotion without feeling like I was being fake, or insincere. I felt like I was on a long exhausting journey with no purpose or destination. I struggled to get comfortable with myself, to re-connect, to relate, to belong. I had no idea who I was and no one I was trying to emulate.

One time I showed up at Walter's office, and I was just furious with my dad because he was trying to force me to go to Connecticut with him and my mom for the weekend. Just the three of us, which was about the worst thing I could imagine, another weekend of chores and cocktails and catching hell for sleeping late. Walter just looked at me, dialed my home phone number and handed me the phone.

My dad answered the phone I said to him,

"You are driving me fucking nuts" and I handed the phone back to Walter, and as he takes the phone, he's laughing, he can't contain himself, and he listens for a moment or two, and then he says,

"Well, he certainly is a precocious young man, isn't he?" and he hangs up the phone, still laughing.

So, my father decided it was time for me to get out of therapy, since it appeared to be helping me more than it was serving him. My mother made it all about herself, like the narcissist she was, worrying that it was all her fault, that she had been a bad mother, at least that's what Walter told me. I found it hard to picture her that way, but I understood that she desperately wanted to be relieved of her self-doubt. I wonder now if she felt more responsibility for her failure because they had adopted me, whether she felt like there was a standard she had to live up to. Walter wasn't having any of it, as I'm sure that solving my parents' problem was not the bar he had set for himself when he took me on as his patient. I was just learning to survive, trying to get out from under a black cloud of self-hatred and detachment and it was hard enough. I couldn't have cared less if my mom wanted to be free of guilt about her parenting skills.

I can't say empirically if therapy works, or it doesn't. It depends on who you are, and what you're trying to achieve. For me, I felt like I was treading water out in the middle of the ocean and suddenly, there was a rubber raft and a paddle. I didn't know where the shore was and a raft doesn't necessarily feel that secure in the middle of the ocean, but even so, it's better than drowning. So, you can sit there, buffeted by the storm and the waves, feeling seasick, or you can start rowing and see where it takes you, and how strong you are. If you want to survive, you can never give up and some days, all you can do is row and don't even bother thinking. If you're lucky, you find that you are stronger than you think, which is a great lesson to learn at a young age. A good therapist can keep the whole thing from spiraling out of control, remind you to keep rowing, warn you if there's a big storm ahead or if you are going in circles. If you're lucky it goes to a good place, or at least it goes somewhere. The challenge is how honest can you be with yourself and how hard are you willing to try. Of course, that struggle is never over, you're never finished, the job is never done, but at that time I didn't know that, luckily, or I might have given up.

Of course, I look back now and think how much easier it could have been, if only I had known at least some of what I know now, which is of course the biggest cliché there is. How long was it going to be before I could have agency in my life, real agency, not just impulsive decision making disguised as decisiveness. How long was it going to be before I had some idea what I wanted my life to be like instead of just trying to get by? I think the best I was able to achieve was a kind of truce with myself, which allowed me to function and get on with it, kind of like when you take a multiple choice exam and you pick out the questions you know the answers for and leave the other ones for later, so that you can go back to them and try to come up with answers if you have time left before the bell rings. What if I had known from the beginning that I was lost, abandoned, living with strangers disguised as parents, people who aren't your tribe, who don't smell right, who can't comfort you just by being themselves. Would that have helped? Would it have been different?

Bill:

She messed with my head all the time. She would constantly criticize me for absolutely anything and everything, whether in sports or school; if my performance wasn't perfect, it was a disaster, she made me feel like a failure. If I made the slightest mistake, like if I would strike out in a baseball game, or make an error in the field, and I was good so I didn't fuck up very often, she would freeze me out, she would refuse to speak to me, sometimes for days.

I have always been anxious and nervous, and I do blame mom for this. She always made me feel like my life depended on my performance on every little thing. Which of course caused me to fuck stuff up all the time!!!

She used to make things up, stupid stuff, but it used to freak me out. She told me that she had an affair with a prince and got pregnant with him and that I was only Hank and Pete's half-brother; intellectually, I knew it was ridiculous, but it was unnerving, and it made me anxious.

Pete:

As the years progressed, mom really seemed to lie more and more, and the lies got weirder. The best example I have is when I was maybe 12 or 13, I asked her if we can or should be reaching out to Uncle Bill – our dad's brother. Mom said he was dead. She actually said that his wife, our Aunt Nancy, found him in bed with "his mistress" and shot and killed him. She further told me that when she and dad were dating, he, Uncle Bill, "hit on her" ... who knows what was true or not but there was definitely deep-rooted feeling keeping us away from any other family. When her mother, our grandmother died, she had a falling out with her sister and never spoke with her again. I remember finding invitations to our cousin's wedding in a drawer years after the marriage ... and then after mom died, I called and spoke with her sister who was very sweet – and sad – that she had never reconciled with her sister and that she tried many times over the years to reconnect, but our mom never responded. I did tell her at the time that we never knew about our cousin's wedding or we, the boys, could have made our own decisions about attending.

Chapter Ten: Roads Unfollowed, Dreams Unfulfilled

So, you want to be a rock and roll star, just listen now, and hear what I say, just get an electric guitar, and take some time, and learn how to play.... (The Byrds)

I started learning to play guitar in grade school like countless kids in my generation, taking lessons from a guy named Bill Knight who was into the Greenwich Village folk music scene at that time of Peter, Paul, and Mary, Dave Van Ronk, Tim Hardin, Dylan, and Joan Baez. I didn't want to be Michael Jordan or Lebron, I wanted to be John Lennon or Eric Clapton. I didn't want to get an MBA and go work for General Foods; I wanted to be a rock star. I saw Cream, the first "supergroup", at Madison Square Garden in 1968, when I was fourteen years old. It was their last US concert, and they were pretty much the coolest, edgiest, thing going at that time. We didn't see these people as just pop stars, they were idols, artists, and role models. We searched the lyrics to know what they were into, whether it was drugs, sex, revolution, or Eastern religion. It was the cutting edge of style and culture - drugs, politics, love, sex, everything that mattered. It was our internet. I was into the Lovin Spoonful, a Greenwich Village band that was big at that time and I remember being devastated when Bill, my guitar teacher, who knew them, told me they were assholes. I went to school the next day and traded all my Lovin Spoonful for a bunch of Herman's Hermits albums (probably the worst record trade in history).

Everywhere I went I took my guitar with me, and I harbored those rock star dreams for a long time. To this day, in most any creative field, when you get on a zoom call there's always somebody with a guitar or two in a stand or hanging on a hook on the wall behind them. I don't think the younger creatives necessarily get the subtext. They don't realize that it's a symbol, a message in a bottle. There was never a shortage of people to jam with, to compare notes, literally, or pick up songs from. In prep school there was always a band and some of them were pretty good. You didn't go on the internet to learn how to play a song, you and your friends listened to the record over and over until you figured out the chords and the fingerings, and then you shared them with your friends. You heard that Keith and Joni Mitchell were using open tunings, you had to find someone that knew how to do it, you couldn't look it up anywhere.

It's tempting to look back at your choices and imagine it could have been different, to think that if you had just done something different, or made different choices, the picture you have in your head of what it could have been, would have been reality. I've tortured myself that way over the years but recently I started to get some perspective on it. I'll walk into a bar, or a restaurant, or go to a block party with friends and there'll be a guy there, doing covers of familiar songs, maybe Crosby, Stills, and Nash, or Jim Croce, or Jackson Browne, or the Eagles, or Joni Mitchell. Sometimes they're good, usually they're just adequate, but I can see from their choices what their history is. They are almost never surprising and lately I have started to realize that the one thing I never think is I wish I could be where they are, that's what my dream of being a musician could have been. If I'm honest with myself, I realize that I probably dodged a bullet and maybe I didn't give up too soon, maybe I gave up at exactly the right time.

During the two years I spent in high school in New York, I had plenty of time on my hands and I could have really studied music. I could have found a teacher, I could have found the time to practice every day. I could have learned to read music, to be a real musician. Admittedly, I did not grow up in a family of musicians. I had no idea what it meant to have a career as a musician, I don't think I even knew any professional musicians. I certainly didn't spend much time imagining just how challenging it can be to make a career as a professional musician in the real world and how many people with real talent try and never really succeed. I don't think I ever even thought about the difference between being some sort of pop star and being an actual musician, and I'm certain I never thought about what it might be like to spend your life on the road, constantly traveling from gig to gig, staying in hotels, eating in restaurants, not making enough money, or what it's like to be someone who once played stadiums for twenty thousand people who is now playing in bars for fifty, or ten.

In the Nineties, when I lived in the suburbs and my kids were young, before I moved to LA, I decided to get serious about playing guitar again, and I found a teacher and studied jazz guitar for several years, which was fantastic. Unfortunately, when I moved to LA, I lost the thread and stopped practicing, but I learned two interesting things. One was that you can appreciate the music so much more when you understand it, when you know what the artists are doing, and the other thing was the world of being a musician, a professional, is a world away from being a pop star. There was a time, certainly, when jazz musicians were pop stars but those days are mostly past. The last jazz musician to be a real rock star was Miles Davis. Jazz is more of an academic discipline now, like classical music, taught in music schools and universities, which sounds unfortunate, but it really isn't. The quality of the music is amazing, there are a lot of good young players and at least we can be certain that the one great art form, the only entirely American art form, will never die.

One day, my teacher handed me the sheet music for Stardust, and he put on the Nat King Cole recording.

"Read along with it", he said.

And what I realized for the first time as I read along with the music was that as distinctive a style as Nat King Cole has, he is singing the song exactly as written, in the same way a conductor can change the interpretation of a great piece of classical music without changing the notes, or a director can change the way you understand a play by how he interprets it and stages it without changing the words on the page. Suddenly, I understood the genius of Frank Sinatra and Ella Fitzgerald and Jon Hendricks and Kurt Elling, what phrasing is, and why I cringe when pop singers record albums of jazz standards, faking their way through the music, losing most of the subtlety that makes it great. Just because it sells and you can do it, doesn't mean you should, and maybe it sounds like the same music, but it is not the same, and yes, the real thing is better, objectively, it's not a matter of opinion.

The business of being an actual musician is a world away from the insanity of pop music, the insatiable machine of the music business, that devours and destroys people in every generation. Think how dependent on random factors like appearance and pure chance success in that world can be and how tortured so many are by their success. Which is not to say that pop music isn't great. It's just different. Don Henley said, "Success is actually so much harder than you realize, and a lot of people can't handle it, and it kills them." Just look at Jim Morrison, or Amy Winehouse. The picture morphs and re-constitutes itself in every generation, before them it was Judy Garland and Billie Holiday, but it's basically the same picture.

It's easy to underestimate the role that your environment plays in the picture you create in your mind of what you can do with your life. It's easy to understand why careers run in families, why people who grow up in LA disproportionately end up in the movie business and kids who grow up in New York end up in finance and what people mean when they talk about structural racism. It's hard to imagine growing up to be a lawyer or a banker when the most successful people you see growing up are drug dealers and half the men in your family are in jail or working as janitors.

I remember my mother used to tell a story about being at a party once with my dad, some business thing, and she was sitting next to this nice man with glasses, and she's telling him a bunch of claptrap about her children and how musical they are, and this man is being nice, and asking questions and stuff like he's really interested. So afterward, when she gets in the cab to go home, she asks my dad who the nice man was she was talking to, and he says, "Benny Goodman." The equivalent today would be talking to Paul McCartney at a party without realizing who he was. That's how close my upbringing was to the music business; geographically proximate, but not close.

Many of us erstwhile musicians talked about going to the Berklee College of Music, in Boston. It had the reputation for being a serious music school, but for contemporary music as opposed to classical. I could say that my parents wouldn't have stood for it if I had told them I wanted to go to music school instead of university and they probably wouldn't have paid for it, but that isn't what stopped me. The bottom line is I didn't think I was good enough, and I was afraid to audition, so I never even broached the subject at home. I also don't know if I would have had the character to support myself by working a menial job in Boston to make money while going to music school full time and I suspect it's just as well I didn't have to face that. Anyone who has ever auditioned for anything knows just how brutal and competitive people can be in that type of creative environment. I had a sense of that and I lacked the self-confidence and the single-mindedness to go through with it. It's easy to harbor ideas, or even regrets about things you think you could have done with your life, but I think it's important to recognize the significance of your own choices and instead of regretting them, accept that in fact they may have been the right choices. So that was at least one thing I didn't have to fight with my parents about, because good or bad, I didn't fail to do it, I chose not to do it, whether I knew it or not.

I applied to Harvard, Yale, Columbia, Wisconsin, and Michigan. Unlike today, we didn't obsess about this stuff very much. If you went to a good East Coast school, you could be pretty sure you were going to get into a good college if you had good grades. I wasn't worried about it. I had lots of AP's and 1500+ SAT scores, so I applied myself to the essays and filled out the paperwork and I figured the process would take care of itself. I didn't waste time going on college tours with my parents and having interviews, that wasn't a special experience we shared. I'm sure at that point they just wanted to get rid of me. Wisconsin had rolling admissions, so I got in there immediately, and Michigan as well. I didn't care that much about the Ivy League, and I was ready to get out of the East Coast anyway, so I never interviewed at the other three. Harvard and Yale turned me down, but I was accepted at Columbia. Although he had always promised that I could go to college anywhere I wanted, my father made it simple for me by letting me know that he didn't want me staying in New York and he wouldn't pay my tuition if I went to Columbia, exemplifying once again the situational nature of his promises, so I accepted Wisconsin. I've never had any reason to regret it.

Pete:

I was very lazy about applying to colleges... I was a straight A student, tri-captain in sports, honors society as well as French and Latin honors societies ... and good enough on SATs so I figured I could get into a good enough school... but again, I was lazy. A friend of mine talked me into taking a weekend to look at a bunch of New England colleges, picking up a bunch of applications. On the Monday drive home, we were going through New Haven, CT and he said "let's go see Yale" ... and my response was "too close to Darien/home and New Haven is a pit of a city, so no..." and he said, "oh c'mon, let's just stop in" so we did. I picked up an application and Yale had an "Early Action" option – not "Early Decision" but instead "Action" ... if you applied by Nov. 1st, you would know by Dec 15th if you're in or not but didn't have to reply until April with all other regular applications/acceptances. It was October 26th, so I went home and banged out the application and was accepted and never applied anywhere else. In all honesty, I think the main reason I was accepted was because the Yale Gymnastics coach, Don Tonry, put me in as his one desired candidate for the year, but either way I got in. When I got in, my mom's reaction was interesting. She was mad at me because I "wasn't excited enough" and that I didn't understand what a big deal this was. The more she spoke about it, it became clear that she was happy because it was a positive reflection on her that I got into Yale. It also surfaced something that was another challenge she had faced in her life... after dad died, evidently a bunch of her "friends" and others told her that her boys were going to grow up to be loser drug addicts because they didn't have a father. This came across a bunch of times over the years when she would say stuff like "don't you dare embarrass me", etc. Well, my getting into Yale was something she could throw in people's faces, proving she didn't fail as a mom. Really quite sad when you think about it...

I spent the summer before I left for college living with my girlfriend, Kim, at her mom's beach house out in Fire Island working in a restaurant in Ocean Beach. It was the first time in my life I had ever actually looked for a job, walking around, going into one place after another, cold, asking for work, and it was the first restaurant job I ever had. I worked six days a week unloading the freight boats at 7:30 and 10:00 AM and then going back to work the lunch shift through closing, after midnight. It was hard work, long hours, but after a while it felt good to be good at something, to work fast, under pressure, to know what you're doing. The night would start slow and suddenly it would get busy and soon you didn't even have time to think and then before you knew it, the night would be over and everybody would be having a beer at the bar.

Kim and her mom were from Great Neck, Long Island, and she was the first Jewish girlfriend I ever had. The family dynamics were very different from what I was used to. There was arguing and carrying on, yelling, slamming doors, and crying. She was argumentative and rude to her mom in a way my brother and I would never have contemplated. Starting when we were very young my father came down on us very aggressively if we talked back to my mom at all, it was scary, so I would have been afraid to talk that way to my parents. Her mother had been divorced multiple times, so that kind of diluted her authority. Kim treated her mom and her boyfriend Al with a total lack of respect.

"If you and Al can share a bedroom, why can't we?"

If she had something to say, she came right out with it, her family didn't traffic in sarcasm over cocktails. And I'm sure she and her mother are incredibly close to this day, so who's to say what works in families. My parents disliked her intensely, but that was nothing unusual. Something I noticed, for the first time, dealing with her family, and often thereafter, was that they just seemed to assume that I was Jewish, even though I never said anything about it one way or the other and my lack of knowledge about Judaism as either a religion or an ethnicity didn't seem to concern them. It seems like being Jewish then didn't carry all the political baggage that it seems to carry now.

In Fire Island in 1973, you couldn't walk down one of the walk streets without hearing *Superstitious*, or *You Are the*

Sunshine of My Life or *Killing Me Softly* coming out of somebody's house. Fire Island was chill back then, mostly moms and kids, hanging out, going to the beach, not much action at night except on the weekends, when all the vampires, the juice bar and Quaaludes house-sharing party crowd would show up. It was easy to forget about politics at the beach and anyway, the country seemed to become apathetic when Nixon was elected and it became clear that the change we all expected was not coming. The war on drugs had been invented, a deeply cynical exercise that was just a smoke screen for crushing any further challenging of the status quo, especially if it was coming out of the black community, like the Black Panthers. Nixon had started his second term as president, and in spite of the bombing of North Vietnam, it seemed inevitable in 1973 that the war was going to end, if only because there was no other plausible outcome. The break-in at the Watergate had taken place in 1972, but it hadn't become clear what it would lead to. The Congressional investigations and the impeachment process were just gathering momentum then and he didn't resign until 1974.

One night Kim and I had a fight and I spent the night on the beach, so I woke up with the sun and walked across the island to Ocean Beach, figuring I would just hang out until 7:30 when I had to unload the freight boat for the Saturday night rush at the restaurant. The morning sun was reflecting painfully bright off the buildings, and the town was deserted. On a bench in front of a bar called the Sandbox on the east end of town there was a girl, sitting by herself in the sun, smoking a cigarette. Even though it was just after dawn, she was dressed like she had just come from a disco. She had long brown hair, layered, and she was wearing platform shoes, a tank top, tons of silver bracelets and jewelry, big blue tinted aviator glasses and really short blue jean shorts. She was very slim and pretty with long suntanned brown legs.

It was as if she had been waiting for someone to talk to and I really had nothing else to do so I sat down with her. She said she had been in some of Andy Warhol's "experimental" movies, which at that point were really no better than amateur porno movies. She said her boyfriend was one of the New York Dolls, which was kind of a glam, pre-punk, CBGB kind of downtown androgynous band that David Johansen was in at that time. Her boyfriend had died of an overdose and I knew the Dolls' drummer had recently OD'd, so the facts fit, but it felt a little off, like she was talking to me about stuff that might be a little bit made up. To look at, she was a very pretty girl. I tried to imagine what she would be like without all the trashy accessories and makeup, but she had what we used to call a real downtown vibe and I knew that the scene at the Factory and CBGB's was pretty degenerate and kind of scary. In spite of all the drugs and the stupid stuff I had done, I was pretty clear that those people were completely out of my league.

She wanted me to go with her to get her friend at the house where they had stayed the night before. I had nothing better to do, so I went. We went up one of the walk streets, her platform shoes clomping loudly on the concrete, to one of those rental houses where people just went to party on the weekend and get trashed. We walked into the house, which was silent, and went upstairs to one of the bedrooms, which was full of sleeping people. This was nothing like a David Hamilton photograph or a Just Jaeckin softcore porn film, with gauzy sunlight playing over beautiful naked bodies. It didn't smell all that special and the bodies were not all that appealing either; my guess was these people had partied very hard and were going to have a rough morning. Amazing that in a few short years, "make love not war" had evolved into this. Take downers and screw a stranger.

She dug around in the flesh pile and woke up her friend, who was completely naked, not at all self-conscious, and objectively a very pretty girl, but she started right in cursing and coughing and sniffling. What with the girlfriend and the fight, it occurred to me that there might be some revenge sex in this scenario, with one or maybe even both of them, but I figured I wouldn't have the nerve to go through with it, even if it was on offer, and the new girl was downright intimidating, kind of what I imagined a hooker might be like.

"What an asshole" she said to her friend, indicating some guy who was still asleep and snoring in the flesh pile, "I fucking barely touched his arm and he came all over me."

At that point, I really knew they were out of my league, and frankly, why would anyone want to wake up in a smelly room after screwing a bunch of strangers, unless they had no other options? I felt naïve and square, like I wasn't cool enough for them, or maybe I wasn't jaded enough, and I walked away and left them there and went to work.

I went back to the girlfriend as well and we made up and all that, but time was pretty much running out on the summer anyway, the whole scene, the girlfriend, New York, all of it.

Next thing you know I was on Interstate 80 going west, in a rented station wagon with my mom, my guitars, my album collection and my clothes, on my way to the University of Wisconsin, in a part of America that at that point, I had never seen. The day after we got there, I unloaded everything at a dorm that was called Ogg Hall (believe it or not), returned the rental car and without drama or regrets I put my mom on a Republic Airlines flight back to New York and turned my focus to Madison, Wisconsin. What I knew was that it was going to be different and that was enough.

Hank:

Mom gave me $2k.

Even though I repeatedly expressed my gratitude, the contribution came laden with a guilt trip, and after that I paid for my education with student loans, scholarships and grants and worked full time.

It got to be too much, and I dropped out of UNH.

When I went back to school at Hopkins, I paid for everything by working full time for the school and taking the free education perk.

This will sound melodramatic, but there was an early 2am morning in Portsmouth New Hampshire where I stood on a bridge and contemplated jumping off. (This was not a lame "cry for help" since the currents in Portsmouth were treacherous.) Instead of escaping by jumping, I realized I had to take responsibility, focus some time and attention on getting my own shit together, recalibrate and refocus. Honestly, we all lived for years in constant crisis mode – although it is wrong to say we did not have times of solace. My trips to the Adirondacks with the Lefferts family for example were very important to me for this reason and for others. Unfortunately, most of our time in the house at Clock's Lane was seldom maybe never a time of solace. It was never a safe place – at least for me. It was a battle ground. I left when I did because I was in crisis and knew that I would probably end up dead (likely from overdose) if I didn't leave. I almost killed myself with alcohol and drugs a couple of times. That was dangerous reality. It became clear to me (though again mixed with confused motives and demands) that I was disintegrating into a state of complete despair. By leaving, I was able to turn inward, begin to understand my own needs and intentions, get a better sense of who I was, and start to heal. I moved to New Hampshire, fell in love with Jennifer and began to become a stable, productive, and much happier person.

Bill:

Hank left for college - He got out of jail, although he still came back for the dreaded hot summers at 33 Clocks Lane. Hank had a business painting houses, and he gave me a job for the summer, and I hated painting houses, and I was really shitty at it. I was a pathetic employee; I really should pay back every cent Hank paid me. Seriously, I was so lazy, and I didn't do shit. I just walked around pretending to do stuff. I really hate that period of my life.

Hank:

Bill has this memory of himself as a pathetic employee but that's not how I remember it. I have zero impression of that. Instead, I remember being glad to have both him and Pete working with me (even during days of frustration and irritation.) I actually feel that the two of them rescued me, because I could count on them – unlike some of the other guys we hired and paid. I wasn't the most organized employer and should have learned early that my CFO/COO skills were and are not the best. Even then, I should have delegated the role of managing the business, getting everyone paid, (as well as keeping your Princess lunchboxes filled). I did my best though. We are all kind of CEO types– so I don't know which one of us could have fit into that role better than I did.

Chapter Eleven: Bars and Cars

Self-discovery is not a linear process.
(anyone who has tried it)

The irony is one of the reasons I went to Madison is that I had heard there was a lot of political activism there. What I found was drinking, a fair amount of recreational drug taking, fraternities, football, and hockey, so obviously, as Rick (Humphrey Bogart) says in Casablanca, I was misinformed.

So instead of demonstrating and striking and changing the world, I hung out with my roommate Peter and his friends, who were from Sheboygan, a biggish town north of Madison which is mostly famous for being the headquarters of the Kohler company, the big manufacturer of premium bathtubs and fixtures, and Sheboygan Bratwurst, which were reputed to be the best in the world outside of Germany. They knew how to party, for real. If you wanted to take a pass, which was frowned upon, if you didn't join in the festivities, you were a "leaker"; if you did, which was encouraged, you knew how to "give'er". The East Coast kids were fine, but why travel a thousand miles to hang around with people you already know? A lot of them were from Long Island but they went around saying they were from New York and hoping people would think they grew up in the city, which was funny because no one from the actual city of New York goes around calling it "the city". I used to correct them sometimes, pointlessly. The West Coast kids were okay, but they were miserable once it started getting cold. They showed up with absolutely no idea what Midwestern winter was really like, and they were in shock. Everyone just figured they wouldn't be around long, which mostly turned out to be true. They thought winter was when you went skiing in Colorado or Utah, where it's beautiful and crisp and sunny and the snow comes down thick and fluffy and piles up on the slopes. They had no idea what five straight months of real winter was like, where the sky could be dull grey for weeks at a time and it could be bitterly cold, day after day, relentlessly, for weeks and everybody's car is always covered with dirt from the road salt and the sand. In my experience, winter recreation for a lot of people was putting on a snowmobile suit and sitting in the middle of a frozen lake ice-fishing. There's no skiing in Wisconsin; there's nothing bigger than a hill in the whole state and frankly back then not a whole lot of cross country either. Mostly recreation involved getting from a warm apartment into a car and ending up in a warm bar somewhere or taking everybody's dogs and going out in the middle of Lake Mendota once it was frozen and running around. We partied hard and not in an East Coast boarding school kind of way, or even a Manhattan underage bar scene kind of way. It was more like a 101 proof Wild Turkey and a pitcher of beer kind of way.

Most of the guys I knew from Sheboygan had worked in the bathtub factory at some point and a lot of them had burn marks on their stomachs from a moment of carelessness pushing a hot bathtub straight out of the kiln on a dolly. A hot bathtub is something you don't want to get too close to and touching one with any part of your body is a mistake you won't make twice. The Wisconsin kids had skills. I remember Pete's friend Dink could put his car in a four-wheel drift on slippery pavement in the winter and slide into a parking space sideways, for real. And you haven't seen how foosball is really played until you've seen it played in a bar in Wisconsin, it's sick. And they were pretty good at playing pool as well. And drinking. And no one gave a thought to not driving after drinking.

I remember coming out of a bar at night with my friend Tim O'Neill. Night had fallen and it had started snowing hard. We got in his yellow Ford Pinto (one of the worst and most unsafe cars ever made) and turned down the entrance ramp to the highway. The road was slippery, and the car immediately started to slide, rotating sideways as it slid. I had never been in a car accident in my life, and I remember wondering, kind of in slow motion, if this was going to be the time. We had been drinking but I was still thinking very clearly. There was an overpass with huge concrete supports, and I remember thinking that we were on track to slide right into those concrete columns, and I was in the passenger seat and that was the side of the car that was going to hit. It was late and there was no other traffic, but we were picking up speed and as we got to the bottom of the ramp, the car started to slide across the highway. I was watching the overpass get closer and closer, and wondering what was going to happen when suddenly there was a series of loud bangs against the side of the car. I realized we were hitting those metal markers on the side of the road as we slid on the ice, and as we bounced from one to the next we started to slow down. I guess the benefit of being in a Pinto was that it is made mostly of plastic and therefore not very heavy, and those markers were just enough to stop the car's momentum before we hit the overpass.

We sat there in silence for several minutes with the snow falling, collecting on the windshield.

"Holy shit" Tim said.

We were just lucky. Sure, we had been drinking and maybe my friend shouldn't have been driving, but it had nothing to do with that. It was just a random thing. As crazy as we were that was the closest I came to a car accident the whole time I lived in the Midwest, which is twice lucky because another thing I learned hanging out with people from Wisconsin – no matter what you do on any given night with a group of people, whether it's a concert, a movie, dinner out at a restaurant, or 4th of July fireworks, you will always either start the night, or end it, in a bar. I was reminded of it later when I did a movie with some Irish guys and the first thing they do when they get to a new city is choose a bar, and that's the bar, for as long or as short a time as they are there and if you don't go there every single night, it's a disturbance in the force.

You really can't understand the Midwest unless you've lived there, pure and simple. People from the East Coast really don't understand the Midwest at all. My parents used to refer to it as the Middle West, which was vaguely quaint, but mostly ridiculous. I know Wisconsin because I went to college there, I've spent a good deal of time in Minneapolis as well, and a lot of time in Detroit because of a car client I had years later as a consultant. I've spent quite a bit of time in Chicago, because I worked for a commercial production company early in my career and we did a ton of work at Leo Burnett, which at that time was a powerhouse and the biggest ad agency in Chicago. It's no accident the legendary comedy show in Chicago is called Second City, because that describes a brand of sarcastic humor that is distinctly midwestern. The producers at Leo Burnett were mostly middle-aged white guys and they had this edgy funny "if you guys from New York think you can come out here and tell us what to do, think again" thing they used to do, which was all about the second city mentality. There is a distinctly dry sense of humor and a skeptical worldview that is distinctively midwestern. And there is the Wisconsin accent, which is distinctly different from a Chicago accent, which is different from a Minnesota accent. People from Wisconsin can be very funny when they imitate their own accents, especially the real old timer Wisconsin accents, where they say, "this aft" for this afternoon, and "shoes" are pronounced "shoo-ahs". There was a bit on the original SNL where Jane Curtin rocked a perfect Wisconsin accent in that skit she used to do with Bill Murray and Gilda Radner, where she played their Wisconsin mom. I think it was called The Nerds. A lot of people totally missed how funny it was. If you've never spent any time in Wisconsin, you just wouldn't know.

When I hear stuff in the media about "flyover states" and political pundits start generalizing about the Midwest, I am glad I lived there so I know how silly it is. I feel the same way about the South. There are right and wrong-thinking people everywhere, and I don't think generalizations and statistics tell a very useful story. I think you can go almost anywhere in America and almost half of the people either agree or disagree with you, so the idea of labeling entire states one way or the other is kind of ridiculous. Wisconsin has a feeling and personality of its own, an edge to the sense of humor, a distinctive accent, a propensity for nicknames, and a special kind of winter, where the cold has a unique quality, a sharpness that you can kind of taste. If you've ever read the book *Smilla's Sense of Snow*, you get it. Scandinavians understand a lot about cold and snow and there's a lot of Scandinavian DNA in Wisconsin.

On the East Coast in the summer of 1973, you couldn't walk down one of the boardwalks in Fire Island without hearing Stevie Wonder or Roberta Flack, but when I arrived at Madison people were listening to Led Zeppelin IV, REO Speedwagon, Wishbone Ash, Boston, Journey, Kansas, Supertramp, and Yes. To me, rock and roll was stoned, drunk, and throwing up in an alley. The only really good rock and roll albums I remember from that whole year are *Dark Side of the Moon* and *All the Young Dudes*. To this day, I want to slip out of the room if *Stairway to Heaven* comes on. I have memories that I can't erase of sitting on lumpy couches with stoned-out Zeppelin fans and fervently wishing I was somewhere else. I have come to think of Jimmy Page as a bit of a genius, but it's all based on the first two albums. I think I and II are landmarks in blues rock but after that, wow, painful.

In the beginning, Rock and Roll was about change, like Punk in the seventies and Hip Hop in the eighties. Once the bonds of the three-minute pop song were broken by FM radio, rock music became an engine of change. The Byrds, Cream, Blind Faith, The Allman Brothers, Buffalo Springfield, The Grateful Dead, The Beatles, Fleetwood Mac (the original Peter Green-led version), Led Zeppelin (early), and a bunch of other bands, even the Stones – took the simple idioms - blues, pop songs, country, skiffle - and expanded them, re-interpreting them, morphing them into something fresh and unexpected.

The Beatles were constantly in motion, always reinventing themselves, doing things in the studio that everybody else had to catch up with, from Sgt. Peppers to the White Album. Are they changing the name of the band? Is it an alter-ego? How did they make that sound? What is a White Album? Why is it called that? People argued about what it all meant, and whether it was good or bad. During that brief time from the mid-sixties to the early seventies, everything was in flux, no one could be sure where things were going, and it was exciting. The music machine hadn't caught up to the music. For a while it was an artists' medium, the labels were not in charge. Cream and Blind Faith, The Dead, and The Allman Brothers pushed the envelope into real substantive improvisational territory. The Byrds hooked up with Gram Parsons and produced Sweetheart of the Rodeo, the first and still the best integration of country and rock and roll; Pink Floyd took strange and psychedelic music to a really interesting place, Bob Dylan went to Nashville to work with Johnny Cash and produced John Wesley Harding. Peter Green, and his band, the original Fleetwood Mac, produced *Then Play On*, still one of the most interesting blues rock concept albums ever made. It started to feel like something that jazz musicians had been doing for years, searching for the original, reinterpreting music structure, embracing discord, adopting new scales, modal structure, free jazz, exposing their fans to things they weren't used to.

And then Miles Davis built the bridge. He was already pushing into the interesting edge of the rock and roll idiom with albums like *Bitches Brew*, and playing the Fillmore East, a jazz musician among all the great rock bands, but the revelation for me, that pulled together the best in rock and roll experimentation and the sophistication of jazz was his album *Tribute to Jack Johnson*, which he made with John McLaughlin in 1971. Miles said, "it's the greatest rock and roll band you have ever heard" and it was. That album for me stands alone, and for a guitar player, it was an epiphany.

Unfortunately, though, by 1973 Duane Allman and Berry Oakley had both died in motorcycle accidents, and the Allman Brothers, once so great, were a shadow of what they had been. After Cream, Blind Faith, and Derek and the Dominos, Eric Clapton slid into mediocrity. The Beatles had split up and proved that the whole was greater than the sum of the parts. Mick Taylor left the Rolling Stones, making them instantly less interesting and Fleetwood Mac, which had been so interesting, morphed into something that was nothing more than fun. The music became entertainment, a product, and the big record companies reasserted control. Bands weren't signing up to do Vegas yet, like Elvis, but that was coming. It was just a matter of time.

Meanwhile, rock music became a wasteland of hair bands and stadium rock, performative but simple and very loud, all show and gesture, lots of glitz, very little substance and not much originality. Kids who take Quaaludes don't demonstrate, they don't want to change anything, their religion is apathy, they just want to party. Country rock was subsumed by bands like the Eagles, with their synchronized guitar riffs and sentimental lyrics, or Pure Prairie League, or Firefall, or America, the idiot stepchildren of Buffalo Springfield and Crosby, Stills, and Nash, devoid of message or depth, crooning whiny songs about tragic relationships and breakups and girlfriends. The Eagles did start to get interesting when success started to eat them up inside and their milieu became regret and loss of innocence and moral bankruptcy, but that came later.

So, we crossed the bridge that Miles created for us and became jazz fans, basically giving up on rock and roll, or so we thought. Miles Davis, Bill Evans, Coltrane, Ahmad Jamal, Keith Jarrett, Gary Burton, Kenny Burrell - suddenly we had a broader universe, a way to expand ourselves, to be better, a music that would teach us new things, new awareness, an art, a history – Louis Armstrong, Sidney Bechet, Django Rhinehart, Lee Morgan, Art Blakey, so many names, so many artists to learn about, to learn from. In the beginning, we had to listen so closely to the music, just to try and make some kind of sense of it, and mostly, other than jazz, we listened to Stevie Wonder and Chaka Kahn and The Brothers Johnson and Marvin Gaye and Earth, Wind, and Fire.

I had a friend, Tim O'Neill, the one I left the bar with who drove a Pinto, who was a big-time high school athlete in Milwaukee, quarterback of the football team, star pitcher on the baseball team. His parents had newspaper clippings of his exploits hanging in frames in their study. I think he had come to Madison on a baseball scholarship. You can get a great education at Wisconsin, but you can also coast and just get by, particularly if you are an athlete. Drinking and getting high, which most of us thought of as recreation, he treated pretty much like a full-time job. But one thing he had was great taste in music, really sophisticated, open-minded taste, which was an intense point of connection between the two of us. And one day he showed up with an album called Countdown to Ecstasy.

"You have to hear this" he says, and he puts on the song *Bodhisattva*.

To be honest I wasn't sure exactly what it was. It was kind of melodramatic, self-conscious, referential, intellectual, sophisticated, original, lyrical, with a distinct sneering undercurrent of sarcasm, not really rock music, or pop either, but song based, no twelve-minute jams or extended solos, but sophisticated and complex. Steely Dan were a studio band and their music was tight and precise and closely related to jazz. Pretty soon they became the hottest band in music. The best studio musicians would line up to play on their albums, including jazz musicians like Wayne Shorter, Tom Scott, Joe Sample, Zoot Sims, Larry Carlton, and the best studio musicians in the industry whose names you don't know. Major musicians would hang out at the studio just to play one solo on a Steely Dan album. Eight different guitarists recorded the solo on Peg before they got what they wanted, and it probably was less than a minute long. It wasn't rock and roll, it was something more, if not jazz, jazz conscious, right from the opening bars of *Rikki Don't Lose That Number*, which mimic the opening bars of Horace Silver's *Song for My Father*. So, there was another bridge, this time from the rock music side, and it led to Aja, again one of the best records ever made.

And then, in 1973 The Harder They Come was released, a cheap little independent Jamaican gangster film and suddenly, everything changed. Everyone was talking about Jimmy Cliff and Toots and the Maytals. Nobody had even heard of Bob Marley yet but that changed in a hurry. Here was a genre of music, kind of a mashup of Calypso, Spouge and American popular music that started in the Caribbean, completely changed the whole popular music scene and paved the way for New Wave, for the Police and The English Beat and Fine Young Cannibals and eventually U2. This music revitalized rock and roll. Imagine the genius of Chris

Blackwell, founding Island Records in Kingston, Jamaica, seeing what that music could be and riding that wave. I saw Bob Marley in Madison in 1975, with the original Wailers band, and it was another epiphany.

I think when we are young, we don't notice other people's addictions. We don't see that the guy who has a problem is the guy or girl who is always available to drink or get high, who bounces from one high to the next, partying with whoever is available. After a while, it's pretty much all they do. Unfortunately, that was Tim. I was fond of him, he had a warm vibe and a nice personality, and he was fun to be around and always up for anything, but after a while, as I came to learn about addicts, the personality becomes a sideshow to the addiction. Of course, I understand it now in retrospect in a way I didn't understand it then, and I still wonder what happened to him, the first friend I lost to his addictions.

Bill:

Pete was a rock during the years after Hank left. I seriously wouldn't have made it through without him.

Pete:

When I went to college, I felt guilty and concerned for Bill because mom was getting worse every year - drinking more, not paying bills, being her horrible mean self - and I left him alone with her. I just tried to block it out, I think.

I just missed the 60s, didn't really tune into Vietnam, then just sort of muddled through the bland '70s. What I remember most was the wage freeze and the gas lines but sort of had the idea in my head "ok, this too shall pass".

When I got to Yale in '77 things were pretty radical there - protests all the time and again, I was thinking "man, calm down". I had a girl spit on me and call me a scab when the workers went on strike, and I attempted to enter the commons for dinner. Her passion struck me as both ignorant and misguided... adding to my disinterest in anything political or controversial.

At that time, mom paid $1300 for my freshman year at Yale and never paid another cent. And here is what she did... one month into my sophomore year I got a notice to go to the Bursar's office. I showed up and they said they were kicking me out of school because the bill wasn't paid (they were already giving me significant financial aid grants and loans, but I think the bill was like $12k). I called mom and she answered, and I said mom the Yale bill isn't paid - she hung up on me and wouldn't answer my calls. I had to go to Darien (took the train and walked from the station to home) and then pushed mom until she found and gave me a copy of her W2. Yale gave me a great financial package for that year and the next 2 years, mainly loans, but when I give to Yale today, I give to financial aid. That school - with all the negatives on the Ivies - really took care of me.

Bill:

Of course, Hank didn't abandon me (or any of us), he left for college. It just felt that way being left behind.

I can't help but focus on what I consider the worst part of living with mom for me which was after he left - partly probably because he left, and Pete too.

Chapter Twelve: One Night Stand

California, tumbles into the sea; that will be the day I go back to Annandale.
(Becker / Fagin)

At the end of my freshman year in Madison I went back to New York. The night before I left I went to a party and I took some speed, what we used to call white crosses, or whites, like in the Little Feat song *Willin'* (weed, whites, and wine) and I drank too much, and ended up curled up on the floor of a bathroom after throwing up violently for a while and then passing out. We used to party very hard but even I knew that wasn't normal, and I knew that the timing was not coincidental, it was something that seemed to happen whenever I made plans to go home. It was meant to be a visit; I wasn't planning on spending the summer in New York. My dad had Crohn's disease, and he was having surgery. They were planning to take out a few feet of his intestines, so not a minor surgery and my plan was to go home and be there for the surgery and the aftermath. It was a serious thing, Crohn's, especially then, potentially life-threatening, but there was no discussion or speculation that he might die from it. My mom was worried about it, but I don't think she thought she was going to lose him.

He went in for the surgery and someone set up a bar in his room at the hospital, which was normal procedure in my family and every evening we would get together for cocktail hour, that was how we did visitation. The hospital always had an ice machine, and my relatives always seemed to have private rooms. My aunt was in a serious car accident when I was in high school and she was at New York Hospital for a while and I used to stop there for cocktail hour on my way home from school every day, it was like a Blum family tradition. The surgery was successful and afterwards, they put my dad on a heavy dose of prednisone with the warning that it might have a negative effect on his personality. The truth is, he wasn't that much fun to be around most of the time anyway, so despite the bar in his room and the cocktail hour, it became pretty clear what they were talking about, the prednisone just upped the ante on the disagreeable side of his personality. One of his first outbursts was directed at me over something to do with my mom, which may have been totally valid for all I can remember, but his anger was totally disproportionate to the event. That behavior was familiar to me anyway. It was something he did to people he was close to, and we had a big blowup about it before I left for college, when he abused a close friend of the family at dinner until she burst into tears, and I called him out on it. Somehow, I just felt like nothing had changed, and it made me wonder what I was there for, who I was helping by being there.

A few years later, there was a weird thing that happened that only my mom and I were present for that gave me some perspective on my experience of him. When he was in his late seventies or early eighties, he took a fall and banged his head. He said he was fine, but he started acting strange. At first, we thought he might be developing dementia, but it came on very quickly, which was weird. It turned out that he had taken a fall in the brook behind their house and hit his head on a rock, which caused a subdural hematoma, which accounted for the strange behavior because there was a blood clot pushing on his brain. The doctors operated on him to remove the pressure, and the surgery went very well, and my mom and I were with him at the hospital in Hartford when he woke up from the anesthesia. Something incredibly strange happened. It was as if the clock had jumped back several decades and suddenly there was this charming, friendly, lovely person there, instead of the grumpy and disagreeable misanthrope I had gotten used to. My mom and I both saw it immediately, standing there talking with him lying on the gurney after the surgery. It only lasted about ten minutes, but he was unquestionably there for that brief moment, really just a memory of the person that he was, at some point in my life, a person I had practically forgotten. It made me sad.

I never intended to stay in New York for the summer, but for some reason, out of inertia maybe, I just didn't go back to Madison as planned. I had two friends, Adam and Jimmy, who were from New York. I had met them in Madison even though we were all from the same New York private school scene. They both went to Riverdale, and they had been best friends since high school. They were a funny pair, kind of like the Odd Couple, because Jimmy was really the only person who could put up with Adam for any length of time. Adam was smart and he could be funny and entertaining to do things with and he was tuned into the zeitgeist, so he had good ideas about things to do but his level of emotional intelligence was very low and he could be really callous and irritating to be around and randomly insulting to waitresses and other people you encountered when you were with him, which was funny sometimes, but mostly it was unpleasant. He left Wisconsin and finished college in California because he wanted to be a movie producer, and I believe those qualities were a pretty good fit for that career path.

Basically, I spent time with my parents, which felt familiar in a depressing sort of way, and I hung out and partied the rest of the time with Adam and Jimmy. One night Adam and I borrowed his dad's car and drove across the river to a Grateful Dead concert at Roosevelt Stadium in Jersey City. If you've seen the Dead a few times you probably know that sometimes they're on and they're amazing, and sometimes they're off and it's nothing. I saw them in Madison at Dane County Coliseum, which was a terrible venue, and they were off, but the night we saw them in Jersey was the perfect night, mid-summer, and they were on. The sky was dark blue in the moonlight and the lights of the Manhattan skyline were just visible from the stadium, magical in their hard beauty. The Dead had recently started Alembic, their sound engineering company, and the sound quality was striking, much better than typical rock concert sound at that time. Sometimes Adam could be fun and easy to hang around with and that night, he was. He had possibly the largest collection of bootleg Dead audio tapes in the country, which was kind of a known thing in the Dead universe and the band definitely knew about it. They were always sending him nastygrams and legal letters, but he paid no attention. I remember he had a recording of the Dead doing Hideaway, the Eric Clapton instrumental from the first Blues Breakers album, which was terrible, embarrassing. If I was Jerry Garcia, I would have wanted to suppress it.

It was the third year of the Newport Jazz Festival in New York and Adam decided we should go to some jazz shows, which was interesting because he wasn't a jazz fan. Keith Jarrett, Gary Burton, and Chick Corea were the new wave in jazz at that time, so it was an exciting time. The music wasn't so challenging that it would defeat you, like Ornette Coleman, or the later John Coltrane. I remember I went out and bought Keith Jarrett and Gary Burton albums after the shows. I had grown up with Louis Armstrong, Ella Fitzgerald, Preservation Hall Jazz Band, and Eartha Kitt and Lena Horne, so I had some instincts about jazz, but this just started to expand my sense of what was new. One night the festival was at Radio City Music Hall. Towards the end of the program something unusual happened, something they used to do at Birdland back in the "battle of the bands" era, but I had never seen it before. They set up four drum kits on the stage. There was a lot of anticipation in the crowd, but we had no idea what was going on. I don't think this was something they had even put on the program. The lights went down and first they called out Elvin Jones and he set himself up and started to play. Even we knew that the guys who had played with Coltrane in his quartet had operated on an exceptional spiritual and musical plane, so we were excited just to see him. If that had been all that happened it would be a memory that I treasured to this day, but then they called out Art Blakey, Buddy Rich, and then Max Roach, three more of the greatest drummers who ever lived. People went crazy over it. They played for about half an hour, first one, then the next, then the next, back and forth, highlighting each of their distinctive styles. Then at the end they all played together in a kind of crescendo. This was the first time I started to understand what a drummer could really do, how complex and interesting it could be and it took me back to seeing Ginger Baker in 1968 and why he was so different from other rock and roll drummers.

I don't think I heard *Stairway to Heaven* once the whole summer.

As my dad recovered, it became obvious to me that I was really accomplishing nothing. I guess I had come to New York to support my mom, but my presence didn't seem to be very important or even relevant. She and my dad had a pretty self-sufficient and exclusive relationship, so it wasn't clear to me once he could function that there was any benefit to my being there. So, I hung out with my friends, went out to the New York bars at night, and the whole experience basically gave me a weird sense of deja vu, as if I was back in high school.

One night Adam and I went out to New Jersey to a party and there was a girl there we knew from Madison. She was a super smart, dark haired, attractive Jersey girl that I had met in the dorms after I first arrived in Madison. She was part of a circle of east coast people that all knew each other. She was looking great and sort of on a whim, during the party, I asked her if she wanted to come into the city and stay over at my house. She looked at me, thought about it for a few beats, and then said,

"Are your parents in town?"

"No," I said.

"Then sure" she said, and she handed me her car keys. We got in her parents' Buick and left. I remember her friend who was having the party was really pissed at me but frankly I didn't care.

"You drive like a taxi driver", she said, which I took as a compliment.

We met Adam and some other people at a bar. She was cool, kind of no affect, making conversation and then it occurred to me, she didn't drive all the way into Manhattan with me to go to a bar. They have bars in New Jersey. So, we went back to my house. My parents had twin beds so there was no luxurious Queen for us to have sex in and then remake so no one would notice, so we ended up in one of the bunk beds in my bedroom upstairs. I remember she said, "I don't like to be teased" and things moved pretty fast after that.

Everything on the surface of the bedside table, including the lamp, ended up crashing on the floor. It was noisy, exciting, and wild. I kind of felt like I was along for the ride, and that was absolutely fine, better in fact. The next morning, she got up, got dressed, hopped in her parents' car and went back to New Jersey. We stayed friends but we never had sex again. And that is absolutely the last thing, and certainly one of the best things I remember about that summer in New York.

Bill:

After Hank and Pete left for college was the worst, the years I spent alone with her. When I left for college, I just wanted to shut the door behind me and forget everything.

A few years ago, an old girlfriend of mine from that time reached out to me to reconnect but I just couldn't do it; I don't want to go back there, I don't want to be reminded of that stuff.

I was still in high school, and Pete and Hank had both left for college. I remember that she was so out of control during this time, and I lived in fear of learning more about how bad her/our situation was financially. When I opened the trunk of the car, I saw literally like 50-100 unopened mail envelopes which mostly looked like unpaid bills. I think the most awful part of seeing this was that she had completely given up. She had no intention of dealing with any of it. I was dumbfounded and scared and ultimately did nothing about it. But the fear consumed me and made me so anxious all the time. I still live with that specific anxiety of being financially broke. It scares me more than death. So strange.

Chapter Thirteen: Too Much Yet Not Enough

Too Much Ain't Enough
(Sign under the giant iguana atop the Lone Star Café in New York @ 61 5th Ave)

The reality of Madison was, we drank too much, we got high a lot, some might say we partied too much altogether. We got in early on the cocaine experiment and even snorted heroin a few times. It's easy to look back and have judgment about it, maybe speculate about what we could have accomplished if we had used our time better, but really what's the point? In the early days of my advertising career, I watched quite a few people trash their careers with cocaine and drinking and I wasn't tempted, there was no mystery in it for me and I think it was because I had gotten it all out of my system already.

One Sunday morning I woke up on the front porch of my house with the pattern of the porch flooring imprinted on the side of my face from lying there all night and it occurred to me that maybe we were spending a little too much time drinking. Bob and Jean's was a bar we used to frequent in Madison, basically one long room with a bar down the front and pool and foosball in the back and a bunch of mismatched furniture. It was short on ambience, and it smelled like hamburgers and beer. We used to get a pitcher and a full glass of 101 proof Wild Turkey and work our way through that and then do it again, passing the Wild Turkey around the table and chasing it with beer. Luckily bar time in Madison was 1:00 AM, so at least no one died of alcohol poisoning or anything. One time one of the bartenders at Bob and Jean's tried refusing to pour me a full glass of 101 proof booze, even though I intended to share it with the table anyway...

"You could die from drinking that" he said, in a no-affect tone of voice, and then he let me convince him to give it to me anyway.

Wisconsin was a hard partying kind of place but at least there wasn't any foolishness with making punch out of grain alcohol or getting dopey college girls drunk who didn't know any better, at least not that I saw. The girls were just as good at drinking as the guys and not all that naïve and if they wanted to have sex with you, they weren't all that coy about it. One cute girl, a nursing student as I remember it, leaned over and whispered in my ear one night,

"Guess what." She said,

"What" I said.

"I never wanted sex this much before" and she wasn't kidding. One of the last times we had sex, she came somewhere between four and six times and believe me, it didn't really occur to me to take credit for it.

Bar time in Madison was 1:00 AM and the TV stations go off then as well, which leaves a pretty good stretch of time to fill before the sun comes up.

I lived for two years in a rundown old 19th century mansion that had been converted into apartments. There were always people coming and going and random people hanging out. One of them was a guy named Tony Brown, a young troubadour kind of guy who used to play gigs around town. His jam was mostly reggae. He covered Bob Marley and Jimmy Cliff songs, and he was always talking about how chill Jamaica was, although I did suspect sometimes that he might have never actually been there.

Based on that extensive background research and the love for reggae music we had developed, my two friends Peter and Steve and I decided to go to Jamaica. It's kind of amazing how non-existent our decision-making process was. We thought Jamaica was cool and we had a week off, so we bought plane tickets to fly from Miami to Montego Bay. Someone told us that Negril was nice, so we figured we would just go there and that was the extent of our plan. To save money we did one of those deals where you hitch a ride with somebody in exchange for helping pay for gas and tolls and stuff. We found an ad in the paper and connected with this guy and his girlfriend, total strangers, who were going to Florida for spring break, and we went with them to Miami to catch our flight to Montego Bay. The plan was for us to meet up again when we got back from Jamaica and drive back to Wisconsin. The three of us crammed into the cramped and uncomfortable back seat of his two door Thunderbird, while the two of them reclined in comfort in the front. Periodically the car would experience some kind of engine knock and he would have to pull over on the freeway, unscrew the air filter and pour gasoline from a glass bottle directly into the carburetor. Pouring gasoline into a hot engine seemed ill-advised to me, but it seemed to work, and we did make it to Miami. The guy was an unbelievable douchebag, and his girlfriend was obviously an idiot, just by virtue of the fact that she was with him. His taste in music ran to insipid country rock bands like Firefall and America and he said so many stupid things during the car ride I lost track of what I was specifically annoyed about and settled into a consistent seething anger. Luckily MAGA hadn't been invented yet or I'm sure we would have been subjected to that. I don't know how we made it to Miami without a fistfight. I remember he called the glove compartment "the glovie". He would ask his girlfriend to "look in the glovie", an expression I have never heard before or since. It occurred to me that if the whole thing went south and we killed them and buried them in the woods it could be a short story by Denis Johnson, or Cormac McCarthy, or Jim Thompson, something that starts out weird and then spirals into something horrifying.

In the universe of seedy motels, the ones around Miami airport are right up there. We had a flight the next morning, so we shared a room. We got stoned before going to sleep but I woke up in the middle of the night and in the eerie greenish light from the mercury vapors out in the parking lot, I saw a palmetto bug on the ceiling, and I swear it was as big as a shoe. I feel like I spent the rest of the night paralyzed, staring at that bug praying that it would not take flight and land on me. I thought about killing it with my shoe but the thought of the volume of its guts that would end up all over me was too disgusting to even imagine. I had never seen an insect that big and I grew up in New York, so that's saying something.

I've heard that Negril Beach these days looks like Tulum or Cancun, with ugly modern hotels and spring breakers on the beach, but back in the mid 70's there was maybe one small hotel and a Club Med somewhere out of town, and it was beautiful and unspoiled. When we arrived at the airport in Montego Bay it was pandemonium, but we found a guy named Sonny who had an old green Chevy Caprice, and we paid him to take us down to Negril. He had worked at a Green Giant factory in Beaver Dam, so we had Wisconsin in common. He took us to a bar called the Tigress, which was on the road close to the beach. There were a few cottages for rent that climbed up the hill behind it and we rented one of those for the week. They were just concrete structures with holes in the walls for windows without glass or screens and minimal furniture, but the price was right.

"You stay here" said Sonny, "and I come back in a week and take you back to Mo Bay" and he drove away.

Almost immediately a young Jamaican guy showed up. He sold us a massive brick of pot, much more than we could ever smoke in a week, but it was cheap, so we bought it anyway and he was pleased. It was like having a pungent ganja aromatherapy candle sitting on your coffee table. You could practically get high just from the smell of it, although all of Jamaica smells like that anyway. Each morning, he would show up and ask us what we wanted to do that day. He had a friend who had a boat so one day we paid a few dollars and went out with him. We did things like that, pretty much whatever he suggested, and it was always cool, and he and his friends were low key. Some days we would just hang out at the beach, which was fine as long as we didn't forget the sunscreen and get fried to a crisp. The Rastafarians would cruise up and down the beach selling beads or ganja or just hanging around. They would sit down next to you and take one of your hands between their calloused palms and talk to you in their musical soft voices about the herb, and Marcus Garvey, and why don't you come up to the mountains and hang with us. Someone had told us to be careful of the Rastas, not that they were scary or violent, but we sort of had the feeling that if we went with them, we probably wouldn't make the plane home at the end of the week, so we prevaricated and appreciatively declined, and they would wander off.

Behind the Tigress there was a tiny kitchen occupied by three large women who cooked in there all day in the sweltering heat. The drill was you would go up to this little window in the morning and they would tell you what they had that was fresh and they would make your choice for dinner that night. There was a dining room, another unfinished concrete structure with no windows or screens or anything, wide open to the night and the sounds of Jamaica, the screeching of the insects and the birds and whatever else was out there in the night. I want to say it was the best food I had ever had, and we would eat there and watch the cats chasing the lizards and crunching them up happily when they caught them. For some reason the tails always went down last.

After dinner we would go down to the bar and hang out, have a few drinks or maybe a Red Stripe, and chat up some

East Coast girls that were there on vacation. They weren't private school girls, they were more the kind of girls you might meet at a bowling alley, or a bar, the kind of girls that had the nerve to go to Jamaica in the seventies unaccompanied. They were nice enough, but clearly not interested in us. Sometimes, at night, one of the Jamaicans would come and say, "come now, man, they're showing the karate movies" and take us to the beach where once or twice a week they would set up lawn chairs and a makeshift screen and show Bruce Lee movies. Sometimes, I think of the time and money I spend now on hotels and fancy restaurants, and somehow, the food is never as good as what those women cooked us for dinner every night, and I haven't slept that well in years.

At the end of the week, we packed our bags and went out in front of the Tigress to go back to the airport, but guess what? No Sonny. Nowadays, something like that would raise my blood pressure. I would be all worried about missing the plane and whether we could get another flight and so on. We weren't all that shocked that Sonny wasn't 100% reliable and we had gotten to know the bus drivers and one of them rolled up, stopped, and asked us what was up. He was like, "jump in, man" and he took us on his route, which wound around all the way up to this big town way up in the mountains with a name we had never heard. There were no tourists, no hotels, just a big market square full of people, milling around, doing business, selling stuff, just locals and not a single tourist or white face in the whole crowd. The bus driver got down from the bus, went off in the crowd and found us a cab driver and negotiated a fare for us. He waved us off and jumped back in the bus and that guy drove us down to the airport. It would have really sucked if we had missed our plane, we would have had all kinds of problems, but we didn't get too excited and people took care of us and the whole thing was chill. By the time we got to the airport it was so hot that the girl in line in front of me fainted and of course all the flights were delayed, anyway. Sometimes if you just slow down, don't get excited and give things time to work out, people take care of you and things turn out alright.

Then, when we were going through customs in Miami, one of the customs agents took me out of the queue and started questioning me about my camera, which he suggested I had bought in Jamaica without paying duty on it. It seemed like a stretch to me since I hadn't seen anything like a camera store the whole week I was there, but he jerked me around for a good hour or more, asking me questions and being clever and tricky. Eventually he gave up and let us through. I was confused about it, until I figured out that he was really looking for dope and trying to make us nervous so he would have an excuse to search us. Ironically, we really had nothing to hide.

Unlike Sonny, the idiot and his girlfriend showed up right on time. As it turned out, the real achievement after a totally chill week in Negril was getting back to Madison in the Thunderbird without beating the two of them senseless and dumping them by the side of the road.

After Jamaica, Madison in March was depressing, what with the cold, the grey skies, the dirty cars, and the road salt. There wasn't any same day New York Times delivery, or internet, or even cable news. In fact, there was no cable at all, and TV went off the air at 1:00 AM, after the final reruns of The Rifleman. There were two newspapers, both published by the same company, one morning and one evening and they were both mediocre. I felt uninformed, out of the loop, and unchallenged, with no way to keep up with what was happening in the world, in art, style, movies, or even politics. We all get that the internet isn't perfect, but the ability to live almost anywhere and still have access to as much information as anyone else changed the world and it probably means that very few people even remember what it's like to feel provincial, to feel like you just don't know what's up.

At any rate, I was starting to get frustrated with Madison, Wisconsin, and it became clear to me that I needed to start figuring out what I was going to do with my life when I graduated. I had always planned on majoring in English Literature, not because I thought it would help me get a job, but because I wanted to be educated and I thought it was important to be a competent writer, and reading is one of my favorite things to do anyway. It amazes me how many people I interact with in business who can't spell or write a competent sentence in the English language and even more who don't have even a basic grasp of American History, or any history, for that matter. Yet I keep hearing that the prevailing wisdom right now is that the humanities are no longer relevant. The only source of knowledge about life, other than living it, is found in books. If you want to get smarter, reading books is how you do it. I read everything that people are saying no one should bother reading anymore: Joyce, Thomas Mann, Milton, Dryden, Spenser, Wyatt, Sydney, pretty much all of Shakespeare, Erasmus, Aquinas, Montaigne, Henry James, Faulkner, Fitzgerald, Hemingway, Richard Wright, Dostoevsky, Tolstoy, Pushkin, Turgenev, Gorky, Leskov. We read Tristram Shandy, and Clarissa, and Faust, both versions, Goethe and Marlowe, and The Inferno. I spent a whole semester on Joyce, another one on just Dostoevsky, one on William Faulkner and Richard Wright. I remember spending a whole night in the basement of the Memorial Library reading Stephen Hero from cover to cover. I studied Jazz, American Popular Song, Race, Sex Roles and Gender Stereotypes, Wildlife Ecology, and I took Business Law, which ended up being one of the most useful courses I took in my whole college career. I can read fast and comprehend and I can write. What more can you ask of your education?

I wrote my term papers in a cloud of cigarette smoke, and they were rarely longer than ten or fifteen pages, but I graduated with a red stole for High Honors in English Literature, which taught me a valuable lesson about brevity in writing. Unless you're Faulkner or Joyce or Dostoevsky or Tolstoy or DFW (a genius, in other words), short is better. My mother used to say that I wrote like a journalist because I wrote my term papers the night before they were due, on deadline, with minimal editing. Often, I felt intimidated handing in an eleven-page paper when the graduate students in my classes were showing up with thirty-page bound versions of theirs, but I found that clarity and brevity count a lot more than volume of words.

I saw David Milch, writer of Deadwood and NYPD Blue, speak once and in the Q&A someone in the audience asked him what books he was reading, and he said he only had time for the classics. I recall he mentioned Dostoevsky. He said that with the limited time that he had he was only interested in reading books he knew were exceptional because there were so many great books, he wanted to re-read and he didn't want to waste time reading anything mediocre. Before the end of my life, I hope to re-read all those books (the ones no one supposedly reads anymore) as well.

I always have sympathy for kids when they graduate from college with no idea what to do with themselves. Of course they're confused, how are you expected to just know what to do with your life when you haven't really done anything? Sure, some people know what they want, but for most of us it has to find us, there's no instruction manual and luck has a lot to do with it.

Another thing you don't notice when you're young is that some of your friends are falling by the wayside, struggling. They are partying too much, drinking too much, taking drugs, taking risks. Maybe they are getting obsessive about relationships and coming unglued when they don't work out, getting stalkerish and weird. The myth is you're going to graduate from college, and everything is just going to work out, the road is just going to rise to meet you and you assume this is true of everybody. But what about people who are having a problem and nobody notices it. What about addiction problems, drinking problems and mental health issues? What about growing up in a ghetto with no prospects? What about bipolar disorder or schizophrenia? These things don't just happen to people you don't know, these are things real people have to cope with, this is the reality of life. It feels disingenuous to me that people act so surprised when bad things happen, as if college kids aren't old enough to have problems, as if some of them don't encounter brutal realities at a very young age.

I think we're foolish if we let ourselves imagine that whatever comes to us is what we're entitled to, as opposed to realizing that we may just be lucky, that our good fortune is not in some way a function of our specialness. At that point in time, when I was getting ready to graduate, my friend Tim had dropped out and disappeared, Adam had gone to Hollywood, Jimmy went to law school, my friend Hugh went back to Boston. My roommate Steve, who I lived with for three years, suddenly, after studying nuclear physics and then majoring in higher math, decided to go to law school. He took the law boards and then he picked up and left. Basically, he drove until he hit Nevada and he's been there ever since. When I look back on it now, it all feels so incredibly random, yet it was a decision point that really affected each of our lives. I had no idea what I was going to do, but as it turned out, all I had to do was wait, because the answer was coming.

Bill:

I have a similar memory to Pete of my Princeton bill not being paid,
I really thought I was going to get kicked out at one point also and same exact thing.
I got mom's W2 and then Princeton just literally just cleared the bill out as paid.

I paid about 1k/year for my education, and I am really thankful for this.

I actually have this weird emotion that I abandoned mom when I went to college. I literally didn't want to know how miserable her life was because I knew I could do nothing about it.

I felt that my only option was to look forward and create a new life separate from her misery which is ultimately what I did.

Chapter Fourteen: Yes, Paris

I would go back there tomorrow, but for the work I've taken on, stoking the star maker machinery.....
(Joni Mitchell)

Before I graduated, I decided to give myself one last shot at musicianship before I completely gave up on my rock and roll dream. I decided to study jazz guitar, and I found myself a teacher in Madison. His name was Mel Jones, which seemed to me like a classic jazz musician name, and he seemed like a nice guy and a serious musician. He came by my apartment for a first lesson, which seemed to go well enough, so I was feeling positive about the enterprise. Next lesson, however, he didn't show up. I called, I left messages, but no Mel and I didn't hear back from him at all for a week or so. Then one night I was watching our battered snowstorm of a black and white TV and there was a story on the TV news about a bank robbery, not exactly an everyday occurrence in Madison, Wisconsin. I wasn't paying very close attention to the story until suddenly the names of the bank robbers appeared on the screen, and lo and behold, one of the guys they arrested turned out to be Mel. I want to say that maybe I took that as a sign that music might not be a great career path for me, at least not in Madison, Wisconsin. I studied jazz guitar for a few years many years later and it was a great experience, but that was long after it had ceased to be any sort of career choice.

I'd like a few words with Malcolm Gladwell about his 10,000 hours, because everything worth being good at is a discipline and you have to do the work and really learn it, and internalize it, but that isn't all it takes. If I had known that, then maybe I would have experienced it differently, but I didn't understand it, so I have the dexterity and I can play, but that doesn't mean I can make a living doing it. I remember teaching myself the pentatonic minor scale by ear, without exactly knowing what it was, something I could have easily learned from a professional in an afternoon and gotten a lot more musical context out of it. Meanwhile, of course, all those free-thinking musicians and rock stars were out in LA driving up and down Laurel Canyon in Bentleys and Porsches and Jaguars and half of them had no more idea than I did what they were doing. But they were doing it. It's possible, in hindsight, that the biggest difference between me and them was that they just did it, they didn't give themselves a choice, but that's all about what could have happened, which is worth exactly nothing.

At that time, people were more open-minded about your career path, which was probably a hangover from the sixties, when it was square to be worried about success or money. Those values were supposed to be secondary to personal happiness and doing something that had meaning or doing something that you loved, at least. The downside, on the other hand, was that you didn't get much direction. You could graduate from college and if you didn't want to be a doctor, or a lawyer, or some kind of businessman, which I didn't, you might not know what to do with yourself. I had no desire to get an MBA and no way I was going back to New York to work for my dad. I wanted to work in movies, or write film criticism, but I didn't have the first idea how to do it. I didn't know any movie producers or studio executives, I was watching Ingmar Bergman movies and reading Film Comment magazine. My roommate's dad was a carpenter, and my dad was in marketing. What I needed to do was get in my car, drive to LA and get myself a job as an assistant or a junior executive at a studio, or write script coverage. I didn't understand that the movie business was a business, like any other, and there were entry level jobs, and that's how you got started. I didn't learn until many years later that there are a lot of jobs in the movie business that don't require creativity or talent, and I was surprised to find out how many studio executives and agents have no love of movies. One of them once told me that she never watches more than the first half hour of a movie, she felt that told her everything she needed to know. Tell that to Martin Scorsese or Francis Ford Coppola, or Ingmar Bergman, for that matter, I'd be interested to hear what they thought about it.

Film schools at that time were about learning to be a filmmaker, not learning how to get a job in the film business. I grew up in New York, which was all about banking, finance, advertising. I had never set foot in LA and I didn't know anyone who worked in the movie business. Nobody was going to call their buddy at a studio and say, "Hey give this kid a PA job". My dad certainly had some bigshot friends, but they worked in New York at magazines, newspapers, in retail and in advertising. Also I had this quaint idea that I was supposed to make it on my own, that it was somehow not worthy of respect to leverage family relationships to get a career.

So, to give credit where credit is due, my dad stepped in with an opportunity even I couldn't refuse, and it was a beautiful thing. He had worked at Unilever for ten years in a high-level executive training program for the top rank of international executives who were trained to run all the global businesses. He knew Unilever bigshots all over the world and when he left Unilever to go back to Macy's they all remained friends. They would come to New York on Unilever business and come up to our house in Connecticut for the weekend. Sometimes they would bring their families. One of them was (Sir) David Orr, from the UK, who ended up Global Chairman of Unilever, another one was the head of Unilever in India. Another was a Frenchman named Phillipe Charmet, and he was the head of the Unilever advertising agency in Paris –

Lintas, Paris. He felt that he owed my dad a favor because his family had spent the summer at our place in Connecticut when things were a bit lively with the leftists in Paris and things were blowing up and catching fire and there were riots in the streets. He decided to return that favor by offering me a job at his agency in Paris and with a push from my dad I had the good sense not to turn it down.

I was determined not to let my father dictate my path in life but only a fool turns down the opportunity at the age of 22 to go live in Paris with a job in an ad agency to go to every day. I wasn't fluent in French, but I had lived with it and studied it my whole life. My father's family was French, and all his family spoke French. We had an au pair for a while who was from Mauritius, and she used to make us speak French with her all the time at home, so it wasn't a big stretch.

Shortly before I left Wisconsin, I was standing in my kitchen having a conversation with my girlfriend, Mary Ann, who ultimately became my first wife. She was funny, sarcastic, and easy to be around. I used to say she was like a club that everyone wants to be a member of, she was fun and up for anything. As I remember it she said to me, "Are we going to get married, or what?" and I said "Sure." and that was it.

So, the plan we made was that she would finish the semester and then she would come to Paris and join me. She decided her parents had to know we were engaged, which led to an awkward conversation between me and her dad, Jim, in which neither of us had the faintest idea what we were supposed to be agreeing on, but he officially endorsed the plan or at least failed to oppose it. He ended up being one of my most favorite people in life and as a father of three girls with a very strong-willed spouse, a model of self-restraint and wisdom to emulate, if not equal.

I left Madison in the dead of winter, when it had been below zero for 45 days in a row, so cold that I put my key in the door of the car I was driving, and it snapped in half in my hand when I tried to unlock the car. I went to New York to get ready for Paris, which included several weeks of training at the ad agency SSC&B, which was part of the same global agency group as Lintas, the agency in Paris where I was going to work. I hung around with Mary Ann's sister Nancy, who was a fashion model and had just come back from Paris before I left, and I ended up inheriting a sublet right near Notre Dame which she had been living in when she was there.

I trained for a few weeks at the agency office in New York, during which I took classes at Berlitz to brush up my conversational French and then I got on an Air France flight and in six hours I was in Paris. It was challenging being thrown into a work environment and having to function in a foreign language, but after a few weeks of confusion and terror it started to get easier. At first, I lived in a hotel on the left bank which was not particularly deluxe, but it was picturesque, and the neighborhood was lively and exciting. I ate dinner alone in restaurants every night, which was pretty brutal, but the people at the agency were nice enough and as I got comfortable things got better and better until one day I cracked a joke in French, and everyone laughed and, in that moment, I knew I was okay. Almost anything that takes place in Paris is going to be better than any other version of that thing somewhere else and Paris is easy to get used to and find your way around. I had only been there once before, when I was in high school, but somehow it still felt familiar. It was winter when I got there, so it was mostly rainy and grey, but Paris is beautiful in any weather. After a few weeks I sublet a tiny apartment on the Rue des Anglais right near Notre Dame. I could walk to work every day along the Seine, as the agency was on the upper floors above the Samaritaine department store, a historic building which is featured in the closing scenes of the Bourne Identity, if you want to look it up.

In the beginning, I hung out with a few aspiring photographers and models who were over there trying to build their portfolios and get started in fashion. It was common for them to go to Paris, or Milan, or Tokyo to jumpstart their careers and build their books. Sometimes they would do good work, and it would happen for them, but only sometimes. I reconnected with a friend from those days recently, who actually did become a professional photographer, but he was the exception, a hard worker and a serious guy and he had some talent. With the girls it was worse. They had to develop a thick skin because there was an exploitive subtext to the whole thing that they were always talking about; which photographers were always trying to get the girls to agree to be photographed naked, "wouldn't you be more comfortable if you took that off?" type stuff. It was the era of softcore "artists" like David Hamilton and Just Jaeckin who specialized in gauzy romantic pictures and films of nubile underaged girls that they called art. Most of the girls were smart enough to go back to wherever they came from after a while, when they figured out it wasn't going to happen for them, hopefully without taking any emotional baggage with them that they couldn't live with or forget about. My sister-in-law, Nancy, was a pretty successful model with a real career. She and her friend Barbara Smith, the famous model and erstwhile restaurateur, had come up together and they were friends, so I knew some successful models. I was subletting my Paris apartment from Linda Tonge, who was a pretty big model at the time, so I used to go over to the modeling agency every month to pay my rent and I often saw the girls hanging around over there who really worked, so I knew it wasn't going to happen for these girls I was hanging around with, but there were plenty of young French guys happy to show up every night and take them out to the clubs, so maybe they felt like it was happening for them in some way.

In the late 70's, you didn't need a lot of money to have fun in Paris, especially in the summer, when it doesn't get dark until 10:00 at night and the streets are full of people until all hours. As it got warmer and closer to the tourist season, the Rive Gauche really came alive, particularly at night when there were fire eaters and performers and freaks of all kinds in the streets. I had a real job, so my life was a little more structured than the people around me, and it was infinitely better to experience it as a working person with somewhere to go every day, rather than as a tourist.

When Phillipe Charmet offered me the job, he was thinking of it as a "stage professionel" which in France is like an internship for students in business school. They put me in one of the account groups working under an overworked and humorless Parisian woman whose name I don't remember and her number two, an English guy, also humorless, who liked to lecture me about how different France was from the U.S. and how I shouldn't expect people to invite me to their houses for a barbecue. I guess he didn't know that we don't have outdoor barbecues in New York any more than they do in Paris.

Rowntree Mackintosh, which was a large candy company based in the UK, was one of the agency's largest clients and they put me to work aggregating a bunch of research into a report for the client. Interestingly, they let me present it myself and the clients seemed pleased, so that was nice, but I didn't really see myself working indefinitely in the role of junior account executive. I didn't have a clear picture of where this job was leading and how long I would be doing it, but for the moment I was in Paris, it was summer and I had a job, so I wasn't looking a gift horse in the mouth.

I had been living in Paris for months when Mary Ann showed up in Paris, from rainy cold Paris winter and early spring to full-on summer tourist season. It was already getting close to the 14 Juillet, Bastille Day, which is the equivalent of July 4th in the United States. She had not had much of an opportunity to get used to being in France, so it occurred to me that we should be doing something special for the long weekend to help her embrace the whole experience. Of course it was the height of tourist season, very late to be making a plan, but word got around the agency and people wanted to help. There was a young woman at the agency whose grandmother ran a travel agency in St. Malo, which is a town on the coast of Brittany, and she set us up to go down there and see her grandmother, who owned a travel agency, and the plan was that she would help us find a place to stay.

The area around St. Malo, in Brittany, and St. Mere Eglise, in Normandy, is where the allies dropped the 88th and the 101st airborne paratroopers behind the German lines to soften up the Germans in advance of the invasion on D-Day. In the end they were dropped all over the place and the whole thing ended up being the site of some of the most vicious fighting in the first few days of the invasion. There were heavy casualties on both sides and many civilians were injured and killed as well and the town of St. Malo was almost completely destroyed. In the seventies there were still many people in France old enough to remember the American boys who bled and died on French soil to free their country, and they had a great fondness in their hearts for those boys and for Americans in general. This old Frenchwoman, Aimee Pansart, straight-backed and thin and very dignified, who met us at the train station in St. Malo had lived through those terrible days and weeks in the middle of the fighting and the carnage and she had many memories. In the end the idea of us finding another place to stay never even came up. We stayed with her at her house in the town of St. Malo for the whole weekend and she told us her story, hours and hours of it, and it was riveting. We were captivated by her dignity and the depth of her feeling and the intensity of her experience. Aimee didn't speak much English, so I translated back and forth between her and Mary Ann, which was much easier than it sounds. I can't do her story justice, but I remember the tears in her eyes when she talked about the paratroopers that died, about the ones that she and her family hid from the Germans, about her relatives in the Resistance that were shot by the Gestapo.

Of course, it wasn't the 4th of July weekend you expect but at heart it was really a lesson in what has made this country great. Sometimes in life we get to touch history directly, without the filter of printed pages, or filmed images, or lectures, or speeches and it is a very rare and special privilege. I'm glad to say that it was obvious to me how lucky we were to hear her story, directly from her, and it gave me a feeling for what it really meant for those American boys to give their lives to drive the Germans out of France. It's not so much the facts of what she said that I remember, but the emotional resonance of it and the intensity of her life experience. All those years later her eyes would fill with tears when she talked about the American paratroopers.

We returned to Paris with much more food for thought than a vacation weekend would normally provide. I corresponded with Aimee Pansart for some time after that, back when people still wrote letters, and then I eventually lost touch with her, but I think her travel agency is still in business in St. Malo today.

Not too long after we got back from St. Malo, out of the blue, I was called to the office of Monsieur Charmet's number two, whose name I don't remember. He and I had barely even spoken before. I wouldn't say I was apprehensive, but I was certainly curious about the purpose of the meeting. As it turned out he simply wanted to check in and see how I was doing, which was nice of him, considering I was just an intern, albeit an intern from the U.S., which I'm sure was a first at the agency. We had a pleasant conversation, and I expressed my appreciation for the opportunity and was otherwise noncommittal, as I had finally learned at this point in my life not to offer too much detail in situations where there might be a subtext that was not evident. After perhaps fifteen or twenty minutes, maybe half an hour max, we wrapped up our conversation and as I stood up to leave, he said,

"Is there anything else I can do for you?"

And I thought to myself……why not?

Some of the most important choices in your life can hinge on the split-second decision to say something or not say it, to play your hand or fold, and this was one of those choices.

My response was, "To tell you the truth, I would really rather be in production", and that answer pretty much determined the rest of my career.

Next thing I knew I moved down the hall to the production department, leaving the account group behind. They taught me, or rather they let me teach myself, how to look at budgets and production schedules and how to use a KEM, which is a flatbed editing machine. I spent a lot of time checking budgets, looking at director's reels and screening rough cuts for people. I attended a big screening where they showed a bunch of American work, mostly P&G spots, to the producers and creatives, and then everybody got to talking about how bad it was, which made me feel a bit defensive, but it showed me how creative work was prioritized in Europe over the US at that time.

We spent most of the summer in production on a big campaign for the Rowntree Mackintosh client. The work was all produced by RSA, out of the Paris office of Ridley Scott's production company, and it was split between three directors, each of whom did a spot for one of the Rowntree brands. At that time creative work from the UK was the gold standard in Europe and pretty much everywhere else in the world, except in the US, where the industry mostly hadn't caught up with what was coming from Europe. A little while later, the "English Invasion" would completely transform advertising creativity when it hit American shores but that hadn't happened yet. A lot of the best work that came out of Paris was produced by British production companies and our Rowntree campaign was one of those projects.

The following year when I was back in New York trying to get started on the production side of the advertising business I was shocked to find that agency people, and even production companies, had barely even heard of the directors we were working with. I remember a creative director from Ogilvy and Mather telling me in a distinctly patronizing tone that the spot I was showing him was "conceptually weak" and "not the kind of work we do here in the States". The director was Ridley Scott and this from a creative director named Jay Jasper who was doing Huggies and Always Pantiliner commercials.

The first film set I ever set foot on was a Ridley Scott production for Smarties, one of the Rowntree brands, kind of the UK equivalent of M&M's except they came in a tube. The commercial was an elaborate fantasy where the Smarties tube transforms into a racing car, a plane and a bunch of other outrageous things that I don't really remember, maybe a rocket ship. I drove out to the shoot with my boss, the agency head of production, an animated, entertaining young woman with bright red hair who had been married to a famous French concert pianist. I think she was English, but she had lived in Paris for so long she seemed like a native to me. We were shooting at an unused airfield outside of Paris. The experience of arriving at the shoot and seeing the production scattered across the shooting location – the crane, the camera car, the helicopter, the lighting and grip equipment, the motor homes and grip trucks, the camera positions, the crew scurrying around like ants feverishly building and re-building the ant hill – is one I have experienced over the course of my career in locations from the Arizona high desert to El Mirage, to the Namib and Death Valley, in cities from New York to fifty other American cities and towns, to London, Paris, Prague, Bratislava, Milan, Rome, Barcelona, Beijing, Tokyo, Hong Kong, and Cape Town, to Pike's Peak and Mt. Hood and a test track in Detroit in the dead of winter, auto plants, test tracks, racetracks, railroad stations, airports, mansions, suburban homes, wheat fields, potato fields, corn fields, the top of towering skyscrapers, construction sites, Army bases, Navy bases, aircraft carriers, Caribbean Islands, and the Isaac Walton Inn, in the middle of a railroad switching yard in Montana north of Glacier Park, where you have to watch out for the grizzly bears when you put out the catering for lunch. Since that first time it has always evoked for me a combination of anticipation, excitement and apprehension, whether I was there as a production assistant, a line producer, a head of production, as the owner of a major commercial production company, or as a movie producer. Of course, I couldn't foresee any of that on that first day but it did become clear to me almost immediately that I preferred to be closer to the "means of production" so if I was going to work in advertising it would be in production and not in another agency.

In addition to Ridley and several other directors who were with Ridley and Tony's company in Paris we worked with Adrian Lyne, who was a big deal in advertising as well and had yet to direct his first film, Foxes, in LA. It was pretty clear that these guys were moving on to feature films and at that time, unlike today, that was a big transition for a commercial director. Howard Zieff, who was from an earlier generation of directors, had directed Private Benjamin with Goldie Hawn; Harold Becker had directed The Onion Field, from one of Joseph Wambaugh's books; and Alan Parker had achieved success with Midnight Express and Fame, but they were the exception, not the rule and commercial directors, for the most part, were still viewed with suspicion by studios. I remember Ridley talking at lunch about his first film, The Duellists, which he had just completed. I don't think it had been released yet but it won best debut film at Cannes in 1977, which I think was just before we shot with him. There was quite a bit of conversation about working with Hollywood studios, which even then was challenging, even for Ridley, who was already top dog in commercials. I don't think anyone doubted that he was going to be a big-time film director, and we found it surprising that the studio would deal with someone like that in a high-handed and dismissive fashion but it became clear to me later how that works.

In the fall I was presented with another one of those go / no go life decisions. Mary Ann and I had made a general plan to get married and she had to go back to finish some degree requirements in Madison, so it was on the table suddenly that it was time to go back. I have always been good at prioritizing and at weighing choices but perhaps not as good at having a long-term vision about what could work for me. It can be valuable to have the ability to set aside your own desires and make good objective decisions, to compartmentalize, but it can also have a downside, which is making apparently sound objective decisions that I nonetheless regretted later. The agency offered to give me a full-time job, not an internship, and a raise, so I had to decide whether or not to stay and I was flattered by their offer and pleased that I had shown enough value that they wanted to keep me on. On the other hand, we had a plan to get married and I had never entertained the idea of staying in Paris indefinitely. I didn't even consider the option of staying there until Mary Ann had finished all her requirements or suggesting that she do that and come back to Paris. In fact, I don't think I showed much imagination about the possibilities at all, and I also didn't want to give her reason to question my commitment to our plan and to her. I had already figured out that I wanted to work on the production side of the business as opposed to working in an ad agency, so I just assumed that the right choice was to wrap it up, go back and get on with the rest of my life.

I try not to regret my decisions, but I would be lying if I said I haven't wondered over the years about what it would have been like if I had stayed on for a while in Paris. Often, especially when you are young, you take the things that are in front of you for granted and you think that the opportunities that you have will come again or that you can recreate what is actually a very unusual set of circumstances and you don't realize that once you move on it will be next to impossible to reverse the course you have chosen and go back, no matter how appealing a prospect it might be. The truth is, I still think about going back and I do have some regrets and if you are going to love a city, Paris is an easy choice.

Pete:

With all the challenges our mom presented and some of the abuse we experienced, she did successfully instill in me/us the need to "be men" – to be successful and make good money to take care of ourselves, families, etc. (later there were issues around "taking care of her" which she was owed because she raised us" but that is another tangent) ... which was definitely a positive thing she did for me. Further, when I graduated, she got my career going in banking by introducing me to a client of hers (she sold real estate) that was a senior executive at the old Chemical Bank, so I have to give mom the credit for helping me get on track to some of my professional successes.

Hank:

It was the 80s in Baltimore; I was in my late 20's and I had just graduated from Johns Hopkins with a master's degree in liberal arts with a Writing Workshop. My focus was Fine Arts, and I was the managing editor of a small press called TROPOS Press; we published a magazine called The Pearl. There was a thriving literary scene in Baltimore at the time, which we called, a little self-consciously "the San Francisco of the East Coast" with a lot of exciting artist efforts, gallery and garden artwork shows, readings at the Baltimore Museum of Art, The Maryland Institute of Art, and City Café (the main spot of poets and artists in Baltimore, which overlapped with a thriving scene in DC.) TROPOS was one of the sponsors of a Workshop that featured luminaries from the Black Mountain "Projective Verse" movement (started by Charles Olson). Robert Creeley, Robert Duncan, Ed Dorn and other big-name poets came to read and teach. It was inspiring.

After the conference one of the professors at the Maryland Institute of Art (MICA), offered me a job teaching, starting as a part-time lit and writing professor with an Assistant Professor title. Within days, I got a second job offer from a guy I worked for at Hopkins teaching Software Application courses and running the IBM and Apple Computer labs for him. He had a consulting firm and subcontracted to an international company called Data Tech, providing trainers to fly into all kinds of US (including Puerto Rico and Guam) and Canadian cities to teach classes of usually about 50 students how to repair IBM and Apple personal computers.

The per course salary for working at MICA was the same as the per day consulting fee that the consulting firm was offering.

Without question, I preferred the prospect of a literary career, but I was also clear I did not want to work in academia. It was my experience that career academia impacts art in an undesirable way – at least undesirable for me, and in thirty-five years, I have not seen much to change my mind. Despite its reputation, I do not think the IOWA Writers Workshop, for example, turns out the best writers. In fact, I'm not sure that art is something you can teach.

I was becoming disillusioned with the literary and art scene in Baltimore. There was a lot of "boy's club" stuff going on, as well as artist egos to contend with and it had all become tedious. Editors that I submitted to and even some that I worked with were sometimes incredibly rude. There was this editors' demeanor at the time that seemed ridiculously autocratic on the one hand, and sometimes obsequious and superficial on the other. Editors, artists, poets I worked with at times lacked even a modicum of decency in their interactions with their peers, and the criteria for publishing and showing artwork seemed so random to me as to be meaningless and ultimately worthless.

So, I had to make a choice between teaching at a liberal arts institution and consulting in computer tech.

I broke the decision down into three possible areas of focus, all three of which had deep existential importance for me.

The first was artistic expression and the actual creation of artworks, which is to say that the pursuit of art was my highest concern, although not at the expense of the love and support of my family.

The second, which was equally important, was my commitment to provide a comfortable life for my family, on a practical and emotional level, which was particularly important because of Jennifer (my wife)'s health issues.

And the third was the pursuit of an artistic career, with the things that might come with that, like wealth, recognition, a PhD, publishing, potential work as an editor, or starting a publishing company or an imprint of some kind.

Once I broke things down this way, the path became obvious, and what has followed is about forty years of supporting my family and producing a lot of art – 12 books of poetry, a book of short stories, hundreds of paintings, drawings, and art for book covers, material in over 50 literary zines and journals, two more books accepted for publication, and an album cover.

Would I be more recognized as an artist if I had pursued it single-mindedly as a career? Probably. Would I be as satisfied with the artwork I have produced? I don't think so. My choice has allowed me to be completely uncompromising. I do not tailor my artwork to an audience, or a venue, or to make a sale. It has cost me publication, recognition, and money, but it is one of the things I am most proud of, that I have stuck to that commitment, that standard, of prioritizing art over everything else, and Jennifer has been supportive of every one of those decisions.

Ultimately, I chose art over making a lot of money and a certain degree of recognition and success. It was tough. We did not buy expensive and beautiful things; we did not buy the Mercedes or take the extended trips to Europe - things family members were starting to be able to afford. Coming from the background of privilege I remember from before my father died, I remember the luxuries – especially the constant travel to beautiful places all over Europe. I wanted those things I had before my father died, but I wanted to pursue artistic expression and creation more, and that has been the difference.

So, I believe that I did choose an artistic vocation in the truest sense of that word.

Chapter Fifteen: Welcome to the Rathole

And the sign said the words of the prophets are written on the subway walls, and tenement halls.
(Paul Simon / Art Garfunkel)

I grew up in Manhattan. I lived there for years. New York has always been an amazing, vibrant place, one of the great cities. I had many of the formative experiences of my life there and I love it, but let's be honest, in the late 70s New York City was a crime-ridden rathole. Now it's a playground for tourists and suburbanites and wealthy foreigners and it is overrun with the super-rich, who seem to be multiplying like rabbits, but in the late 70s and early 80s it was a rathole. The city came within inches of declaring bankruptcy in 1975 and by 1978, when Mary Ann and I moved back, it hadn't really bounced back much. My grandmother died in 1972. She had lived for over twenty years at 1040 Fifth Ave., one of the most prestigious apartment buildings in the city, directly across Fifth Avenue from the Metropolitan Museum. She had a huge two-story apartment with two rows of windows on the 5th and 6th floors overlooking the museum and Central Park with a marble connecting staircase. There was a servants' dining room that was bigger than my first New York apartment. I'm sure that apartment would be worth between thirty and fifty million dollars today, maybe more. When she died, that apartment sat empty for close to two years and eventually sold for around $200,000. It's hard to imagine it now but New York City was on its knees and bleeding out. Mary Ann was held up by a bunch of kids at gunpoint on Central Park West at 11:00 AM on a weekday. Imagine that today. It would be all over social media.

We lived in a one-bedroom apartment in a roach-infested brownstone on the Upper West Side. Even though the city was falling apart it was still expensive and that was all we could afford. There was a private school called Walden at the end of the block on Central Park West, so there were kids around in the morning and the afternoon, but at night it could be a little sketchy. We had a big old hound dog, Travis, who I had gotten as a puppy when I was in college, and the apartment was half a block from the park, so that was good for Travis and no one was going to bother you if you had a dog that size with you, no matter what time of the day or night it was. He never met a male dog he didn't immediately pick a fight with, so that kept things interesting, and he was one of the funniest, most lovable beings you could ever meet. I have never met a man or beast with a bigger heart.

There are things I miss from New York in those days. I miss the chicken teriyaki at the Cherry Restaurant on Columbus Ave. I miss Dobson's and JG Melon's and Peking Duck West. I had a Hungarian aunt, Dorothea, who lived in the fifties on Park Ave. and Mary Ann and I used to have dinner with her and her husband, Nicki, who was some kind of Austrian count. He was very charming, with very classy old school manners and I always thought he looked like Klaus von Bulow, or Kurt Waldheim. I always worried a little that he might also have some similarly unfortunate early history, but I never asked. One night we were at my aunt's apartment for dinner, and she introduced us to a cousin of hers, who turned out to be Tibor Kalman, the famous graphic designer, whose work is in the design collection at MOMA. His wife, Maira, had just written her first children's book, which was quirky and creative but of course it ended up being way more than a sideline and her books are everywhere now. Tibor was doing the design work for a new restaurant that was opening down in the meatpacking district, Florent, which was tucked in between the meatpackers on Gansevoort Street. He gave us one of the matchbooks and sent us to pick our way through the maze of refrigerated loading docks and men in white coats pushing in and out of the rubber curtains carrying whole bloody sides of beef on their shoulders to find our way to the entrance and discover it. Today it's a maze of expensive boutiques and fancy restaurants down there and Florent is gone, but if you want a reminder there's a restaurant scene in Men in Black that was shot there. When I started my commercial production company, Headquarters, I called Tibor for help with the identity work and he turned me on to a couple of his proteges who had a firm called Bureau, which was making a name for itself at the time. I remember Tibor told me that his first job when he came to New York from Hungary was writing fortune cookies for Chinese restaurants. I don't know if it was true but it was a good story and he was a funny guy, one of the best dinner companions you could have. It's unfortunate he died so young. I miss him and I miss Florent as well.

I miss the graffiti.

Terrorism is sometimes defined as a weapon of last resort for the weak against the strong. I interpreted the New York graffiti of the 70s exactly that way. To me it was the disenfranchised and underserved underclass of the city seizing control over their environment, which was dehumanizing and unlivable. Art was their weapon. It was art as violence, as a manifesto, a political statement. I remember standing, sweltering, on hot, smelly subway platforms as the trains clattered into the station covered with huge pieces from end to end, masses of color and weird graphics. There were Dondi White pieces on the subway cars and Seen and Zephyr. Keith Haring and Basquiat were still putting pieces up in the street. Taki 183 was still a thing. The message was: this place is a rathole, but if I have to live this way I'm going to redecorate. It had a message. It expressed frustration. It wanted to tear down the status quo. Now we have Banksy, and thank God for that, and Shadow Man, but the statement is not quite as revolutionary. It's ironic and cerebral, which is thought-provoking and entertaining but it's a little more passive. I think it's a little sad when art becomes disconnected from its original context, when its rebelliousness is made irrelevant by the value it has acquired, and I feel strange when I see Basquiats and Harings in magazine spreads of billionaires' vacation homes. I want to remind people that it was originally for the street and the subway and the artist's squat, and it was diametrically opposed to everything those billionaires stand for.

We went to parties in lofts in commercial buildings in Chelsea and Soho where the photographers used to shoot and live illegally in violation of the building codes. The floors were rough commercial wood or concrete, and the bathrooms were off in the corner behind a curtain. The girls always wanted you to stand guard for them when they had to pee because there wasn't even a door you could close. We had one photographer friend who lived in an abandoned theatre on 14th Street. It was like something from Phantom of the Opera or Hunchback of Notre Dame. You had to stumble through this dark abandoned theatre on creaky walkways, tripping over cables and God knows what else to make your way to this weird little apartment back behind the stage that only had electricity because he had tapped into someone else's power illegally and run an extension cord up the fire escape.

I worked in a Mexican restaurant which was owned by a friend of mine who started it with the money he made working as a male model. A lot of models had money they didn't know what to do with, so they invested in restaurants. People were still paying for things in cash back then and a lot of it just disappeared into black plastic bags and went down to the basement. It eventually found its way back out into circulation in a form of reverse money laundering - before tax investment going in, untaxed cash income coming out. Years later when I sold my brownstone to a guy who owned a restaurant, he showed up with $100K of the purchase price in cash. I know why they have machines that count cash because I can tell you it takes a lot longer than you think from watching TV shows about drug deals to count $100K in ten and twenty-dollar bills.

I spent five months working as a waiter before I found my first work as a production assistant. I had a print directory of all the production companies in New York that was published by one of the trade rags and I went through it, cold calling company after company, week after week, month after month, until it finally paid off. I went for the interview in a blizzard in January. New York was shut down, uncharacteristically quiet from the blanket of falling snow, and the streets were deserted.

The company was called Ampersand, and it was owned by a director named Elbert Budin who specialized in hyper artistic closeup photography of food and product, a genre which was called "tabletop". He invented a camera crane and head combination that allowed him to float the camera over the food in closeup that totally reinvented the way people looked at food, that made it reinterpreted as art. The studio manager was living at the studio, which was a little bit pathetic, but it was lucky for me because he was actually there even though everything was shut down. The company had two whole floors in a huge commercial building way over on West 33 St between ninth and tenth avenues and he had nothing to do because of the blizzard so he told me to come by for an interview. A few days later, I started there as a PA.

If you imagine the Buddha with long grey hair, that's what Elbert looked like. He was thought of as kind of a mad genius. He used to disappear into his office in the middle of the shoot, sometimes for hours, and leave the whole crew, on the clock, and the agency and clients cooling their heels. I don't know if he was thinking, or meditating, or they were just driving him crazy, but he did whatever he felt like doing and he didn't explain himself. At first, I was invisible, but after a few weeks I must have started to look familiar and he started calling me Sonny. There was a girl who had worked there about the same amount of time, and he called her Sissy. She and I used to laugh about it all the time, Sonny and Sissy, but really it spoke to how expendable we were. There's a lot of gallows humor in production. A few weeks later we had a real breakthrough, because he started calling me Jimmy, as if he had learned my name. He seemed kind of proud of himself.

The business in those days was not genteel. Nobody rated the Super Bowl commercials in USA Today. They didn't talk about them on the morning shows or write articles about them in the newspaper. People I met didn't understand what I did for a living. Most of the directors I worked for earned what they had because of their drive and talent and their intensity. The privileges they enjoyed were of their own making so if there was some narcissism that went with it, it also was earned, not inherited. They weren't rich kids who went to NYU Film School or Art Center and graduated with spec reels paid for by their parents. If you scratched the surface, their families owned grocery stores in the Bronx and butcher shops in Brooklyn. Most of them were either Jews or Italians who had fought their way to the top of the ad business by force of will, creativity, and smarts and then transitioned into directing and reinvented themselves. They weren't going to give you anything for nothing. If you wanted their respect, or even their attention, you had to prove your value with your actions and you had to know how to keep your mouth shut. If you were going to talk you better have something smart to say, or at least funny. They had become accustomed to being demanding and often unreasonable and a lot of that behavior filtered down to the people who worked for them as well. We all had bad habits, to varying degrees.

New York was a good place to learn production, because New York was a hard place to do production and that has not changed to this day. It wasn't like LA where the gear turns up in shiny trucks tricked out for production and crew guys invent new stuff every day that makes it easier. In New York you could lose an hour just trying to get a few blocks across town in the summer and you would be sweating and frustrated when you got there. There was no Uber. If you came out of a meeting at 5:00 PM and it was raining there were no cabs and you were going to get soaked before you ever reached the subway, which was guaranteed to be packed and hot. I knew a kid who got stuck in a cube van in a traffic jam in the Holland Tunnel because of an accident on the other side and he was sick for three days from the carbon monoxide. The parking was a nightmare and when you went to do pickups you had to keep an eye out for the tow trucks, because there was no sympathy for the PA whose van got towed away with the props and wardrobe for the next day's shoot in it. When I was a production assistant the line producers would try to save money by sending you with a van to pick up at the equipment houses, but you had to be careful because that was Teamsters Union work and if there were teamsters there, they were going to be pissed about it and take it out on you. When teamsters have a problem, they don't hide their feelings and sometimes PAs learned that the hard way when a light stand "accidentally" fell over on them or something really heavy got dropped on their foot. One time I had a whole camera order and an Elemack Spyder dolly for a pickup shoot day on a Miller Beer job at a bar way out in Long Island and the Hertz van broke down on the Long Island Expressway, right at Kissena Blvd. There were no cell phones back then and of course they had sent me to pick up the whole order by myself, so I had to walk up the exit to find a pay phone, the whole time trying to keep an eye on the van, which had several hundred thousand-dollars-worth of camera and lenses in it which could have been stolen in a heartbeat. The whole crew was waiting at the bar in Glen Cove, and I was stuck on the LIE with all the equipment and no one to send for help.

The crew guys could be fun and some of them were okay, but they were grumpy and quick to find fault with production. If you had Pepsi, they complained because it wasn't Coke, if you had Coke, they wanted Pepsi. It was always something. I remember once getting yelled at, not because the beer wasn't in the refrigerator at the studio at 8:30 AM, but because it wasn't cold yet. But the thing that bugged me the most were the personal errands, the go-pick-up flowers for my girlfriend, buy someone a birthday present, come downtown after the shoot with a couple of the other PA's and move my girlfriend's couch type stuff. The regular work was menial enough and the hours were long, but that was tolerable because it was the only way to get ahead. The personal stuff was annoying.

Conventional wisdom would suggest that most of us are motivated by a desire to get ahead, that we have a goal or a vision for what success looks like. I was motivated, however, especially at first, by the desire to offload all the things that I didn't like and by the conviction that it could be better than it was, that I could have a better experience. I am not one of those people who just loves being on a film set, that gets off on just being part of it all. I have been to a lot of interesting places on production, and I treasure those experiences, but the actual experience of standing around on a film set is not intrinsically fascinating to me.

It didn't occur to me that I didn't particularly like what I was doing, I just figured that I needed to get up the food chain so that things could be less annoying, more interesting, maybe even more fun, and I could make more money. If I became a Line Producer, my PA's could do the annoying stuff; if I became the Head of Production, then I could hire the Line Producers to actually produce the jobs; if I was an Executive Producer, then the Head of Production could handle the details; and finally, if I had my own company, I could make the rules. I never forgot the experience of looking for work as a production assistant and just how universally unpleasant people were. I was sure that it didn't have to be that way and even though production can be stressful and annoying there's still no reason to act like a jerk. It took me a while to work out that the interesting part of the whole thing was working with creative people on interesting work and the rest of it was secondary. I started at Lintas fresh out of college in early 1977. By 1979 I was working as a Head of Production at a major production company in New York. I moved up the food chain very quickly and there were gaps in my knowledge, but I faked it when I had to and learned on the job. When I did that job I supervised the producers, all of whom were older and more experienced than I was. I did the bidding, the estimates and closed all the jobs, on paper, with a calculator. We used to have bike messengers sitting in the reception area, waiting for the bids to come out of the xerox machine for them to rush over to the agencies. To this day I still think I could estimate a production job faster with a pencil than the average bidder today can with a computer.

In 1983 I took a job as Head of Production at Rick Levine, at that time one of the top companies in the business. It was a big step for me, but in 1986 I took a bigger step, becoming the Executive Producer at UK production company Spots Films, running their US operation. In ten years, I went from starting in the business at Lintas, in Paris, to running a major production company.

At the same time, after Paris, Mary Ann and I went from living in a one-bedroom apartment on the Upper West Side, which we shared with our large dog and a pretty large family of hardy New York cockroaches, to having two kids and living in a brownstone which we bought and shared with Mary Ann's sister and her husband in the West Village. New York was bouncing back from near bankruptcy in the mid-70's; it was volatile and crazy, punk and new wave, early hip-hop, Keith Haring and Basquiat. Advertising was big money, big production, and big egos, fueled by a fair amount of cocaine, which we often referred to as "the million-dollar diet".

Barry Myers was my boss and the owner of Spots. Like a lot of commercial directors Barry saw himself as a storyteller and he was desperate to direct feature films. He had reached the top of the commercial business, and he felt he had nothing left to prove, but he had no idea how little tolerance the studio would have for the high-handed behavior that A-level directors in the commercial industry were in the habit of dishing out. It's one thing to run roughshod over a creative director from an ad agency or a brand manager from Coke, it's quite another to try to bully the head of a studio. I know, I've tried it, and it didn't turn out so well for me either.

Martin Amis wrote a book called Money about a British director of commercials aptly named John Self who loses his mind in a fog of drugs and bad behavior while shooting his first movie for a Hollywood studio in New York. I am pretty sure that book is at least tangentially based on Barry, although Martin Amis embellished the story quite a bit, adding in a cocaine problem, which wasn't Barry's vice. The movie was called Skip Tracer, and they fired Barry off it for being difficult about the creative and the movie was a flop, which the studio probably deserved.

Directors like Alan Parker, Adrian Lyne, Ridley Scott, and Tony Scott mastered the art of moving seamlessly back and forth between movies and commercials and making money both ways and they paved the way for all the Michael Bays and even the David Finchers that came later, but there were also a lot of casualties, like Barry, who were sent packing with their tails between their legs. Like a lot of other creative endeavors, talent does not ensure success in the movie business. Other qualities, like people skills, charm, manipulation and ruthlessness can be useful and the closer you get to the top of the creative pyramid, the sharper the elbows you encounter.

I interviewed with Ridley Scott's company several times over the years without ever going to work for him and Tony. One of those times, the first time, I had breakfast with Tony Scott at the Carlyle Hotel in the mid-eighties before I went to work for Barry, interviewing for a job running their commercial division in the U.S. Tony got very excited because Dustin Hoffman was in the restaurant. He was starstruck, which is funny considering Top Gun was about to gross $350M, at that time a stunning amount of money.

I remember he said, "After I did The Hunger, the studios wouldn't touch me with a ten-foot barge pole". The Hunger was his first film and like a lot of directors he was trying to make art his first time out and I guess he learned his lesson from that and from waiting for his second chance.

He was still having a hard time accepting it, even though Hollywood had finally "discovered him", which was going to change his life. When I heard that he committed suicide I immediately thought of that breakfast. He seemed like a genuinely nice person, hugely successful in the hall of mirrors that is Hollywood, but you never know the nature or extent of a person's private pain and success is often as much the problem as the cure. The strange irony was that he jumped from the Vincent Thomas Bridge in San Pedro. Anyone who has spent any time in the production industry in LA knows that bridge because it's the only suspension bridge in LA. Sooner or later, everyone scouts it for a shooting location that is supposed to look like New York. There was a weird irony there. He would have scouted the location years in advance, without realizing its ultimate purpose.

Most of what I learned about judging creative work and bringing creative ideas to life I learned from directors I worked with early in my career. Most of them were arrogant and many of them were a pain in the ass but it forced me to develop a creative point of view, because I wanted to have answers to the creative questions they asked and I found that if I had an opinion they respected that, even if they didn't agree with it, and they started to ask my opinion first before they gave me theirs. Among other things what I learned from them was that creativity isn't just about having a great idea, it's a discipline, and there is a lot of problem-solving involved. Ideas don't usually just present themselves fully formed and perfect. It's about being able to look at an idea or an execution and figure out what's good and what's bad about it. Guys like Barry and Rick Levine, another director I worked with, could look at a creative concept and immediately see what was good about it, what was missing from it, and what it would take to fix it, and they didn't think much of anyone who didn't have the nerve to do whatever was required to make it great, including the client. That commitment to creativity is a gift I have carried with me ever since, although the inability to accept mediocrity can also be a curse, especially when it comes to dealing with movie studios.

Pure creativity, the kind that starts with a blank page or a canvas, is not that common in advertising, or anywhere else, for that matter. I have nothing but respect for the people who have that talent. In advertising agencies, you sometimes find people who have it and working with them can be a rush in itself, even if it's not great art. When I moved on to do feature films, I expected more of that, but in any business true creativity is rare and often mediocrity pays the bills. There is a lot of talk these days about the democratization of creativity, about how everyone can be creative, but real creative talent is just as rare today as it ever was and it's rare.

Real creative people are inconvenient and difficult; it comes with the territory. Easygoing geniuses are rare. It's worth it when they're talented, when they can surprise you with their ideas and their solutions to creative problems. When they're not, the immaturity, the narcissism, and the bad behavior get tiresome, which is probably why I finally gave up my career in the commercial business. I just ran out of patience. I could deal with the talented ones, but the mediocrity became too much to bear.

I read Jeff Tweedy's memoir *Let's Go So We Can Get Back,* and it made me laugh. He expresses surprise and puzzlement that some of his collaborators get fed up and stop working with him and I thought sure, because you're kind of a genius, but you're probably a first-class pain in the ass to deal with as well, and you don't even know it.

Chapter Sixteen: High Stakes

When I was back there in seminary school, there was a person there, who put forth the proposition that you can petition the Lord with prayer……
(Jim Morrison)

There is a photograph of me and my three kids. My youngest son, Mike, who is now thirty-one, is maybe three or four years old in the picture, which makes his sister Laura eight or nine, and his older brother AJ eleven or twelve. Mike is standing in front of me, between my legs, with my hands on his shoulders, laughing, and AJ and Laura are on either side of me, holding on to my arms, smiling. I am wearing a white t-shirt, shorts and sunglasses, and we're on vacation. Even though my expression is not that revealing I know at that moment I was happy. The photograph was taken one sunny summer day in Madison, Wisconsin. I know the picture was taken at the entrance to the zoo in Vilas Park, although you wouldn't necessarily know that from looking at it. One of my father-in-law's favorite activities with the kids, whenever we came to Madison to visit, was taking them to the zoo, so he may have been the one taking the picture, or it may have been my wife, Mary Ann. I look at that picture and I think, "That's what a family looks like, that was a good day. We were together, and we were happy."

When I look at that photograph, that frozen moment in time, I see my best self. I was not confused or preoccupied, I wasn't thinking I should be somewhere else. I knew what my job was. It was to be a good father to my kids, as good as I could possibly be, assuming whatever limitations and lack of training I brought to the job, and I knew it was a gift and I should enjoy it. I knew I was no better or worse than most any other father and I was fine with that, because for the first time in my life I was part of a real family of my own.

This is the thing I have always loved about being a parent, from the moment my first child, my older son, was born. It is perhaps the only thing I know in life that I was in on, one hundred percent, from day one, without having to think about it, without critical detachment or doubt. I'm not one of those people that was always dying to have kids, that imagined they were not complete without kids, that fussed and obsessed over it as a life goal, but once I had my first child, from that moment, I was all in. I'm not suggesting I haven't made mistakes and I'm sure my children each have their own experiences of me, some good, some not so good, or maybe indifferent. I think I had a bit of a temper, but they tell me I have mellowed out a lot since then. I was talking to my son AJ the other day about those trips to the zoo. He remembers another day, the day we took my nephew Buddy with us, when he and my son Mike were little, and he wandered off and we lost him. We eventually found him and now it's a funny story, but there was half an hour or so there when we were alerting security and making announcements on the PA when it was uncomfortable. I wonder if Buddy even remembers it. I'll bet he has a completely different story or maybe he doesn't even remember the day we lost him.

I think memory is all about perspective. The memories you share within families, among friends, with random people, are the stories you agree on, that you tell repeatedly, that you refine, a shared narrative where the discrepancies of perspective are eventually erased. I don't remember anything that happened in the moments, the minutes, hours, or days even, before that picture was taken, or what happened in the five minutes after it and it doesn't matter. I just know the feeling that comes to me when I look at that photograph and that feeling can't be erased or taken away from me. For all I know my kids would say they were thinking about getting ice cream, if they remember that day at all.

To be frank, I have always been a bit suspicious of happiness. Not in the conventional sense of wondering if it's going to last, or if you deserve it, but as a concept. Over the years, starting when I was quite young, people have asked me if I was happy, and I have never known how to answer the question. I always want to ask for clarification. Are you talking about life in general? Do you mean in the sense of am I satisfied, do I feel fortunate, or grateful? Am I happy right now, in this moment? Or is it a larger perspective question? Would I be happier if there had never been a war in Vietnam or if Donald Trump had never been elected? These things are all relative and therefore need to be examined in context, which is something different from happiness. How do you feel about this fact or this situation? Compared to this other thing, do you think this thing is good or bad? Which of these things is better? Bill Nighy was asked in an interview about whether he was happy and he responded that he thought he was better at relief than happiness, which I completely understand.

Happiness is ephemeral, so in a sense you can only experience it in the moment, and appreciate it, before it slips into the past. I have a granddaughter now and she reminds me to be in the moment because at this time in her life, at two years old, that is where she always is, so all I need to do is be there with her and I can't lose. So that's what that photograph says to me and it's no surprise that it's a picture of my kids, they made me feel that way, they were the first.

My oldest son, my first child, AJ, was born in 1983, at New York Hospital, over on the East River in Manhattan. He took his time getting born, so by the time he finally arrived, at 1:30 AM on a Monday morning, we had been back and forth to the hospital multiple times. Mary Ann was wiped out. After she finally managed to deliver him the delivery room was quiet. I think he knew he had the cushiest gig he was ever going to have, and he wasn't interested in giving it up so fast. They had turned the lights down and out the window I could see the East River and the lights over on Roosevelt Island and the 59th St. bridge with the tram going back and forth in front of it. New York City is accommodating that way, it gives you a dramatic background for life's events. They bundled him up and put him in my arms. He was a warm little package, wrapped up tight the size of an artillery shell, just breathing quietly and making little noises. In that moment, I had an epiphany, sudden and vivid. I can still feel the quiet room, the city lights, the warm baby in my arms, almost weightless, like an astronaut in space. I looked at him, and I thought, you are the only living person in this universe that I am connected to by something more powerful than choice, more than circumstances, or intention, or association, or even emotional attachment, by shared DNA. I remember it vividly, the picture in my mind could not possibly be clearer. At that moment, I realized that I had never actually thought consciously about adoption very much, and suddenly it came over me that I had been living with the knowledge that none of the people around me, no matter who they were, or how well I knew them, were literally related to me, that on some fundamental level, I was alone. It was as if something that was buried in my subconscious instantaneously transitioned to my conscious mind. It was an epiphany, there is no other way to describe it.

Having a child actually gave me a sense of security, which was further intensified by the birth of my daughter, Laura, and my younger son, Mike. It seems counterintuitive to get a sense of security from accepting responsibility for a spaceship full of completely helpless little astronauts who cannot possibly survive in the universe unless you make sure their support systems are in working order twenty-four hours a day, but there it was.

Something else came with that sense of security and it was a feeling I thought was fear. It came suddenly and unexpectedly, like a revelation. It was something familiar, but I thought I had packed it away somewhere. I remember thinking 'I didn't think I would ever feel this way again', but it wasn't fear, it was vulnerability, an unavoidable side-effect of love. After making my way through the emotional landscape of my upbringing, which often felt like feeling my way through a dark wet tunnel and finding my way to the light at the other end, I hadn't planned on ever being vulnerable again, and I had no idea that having kids would bring it back, and that I would welcome it.

My daughter was born with something called an intestinal malrotation, which is something that happens during the development of the fetus. At a certain point the intestines are supposed to turn as they develop in the abdomen, and they don't. It is not exactly dangerous in itself, at least in theory, except that it almost always results in the intestines becoming twisted or obstructed and then infected, which can result in septicemia and death. Not everyone who is born this way even knows there is a problem, which means it can strike later in life, but it usually manifests in childhood, and it is often misdiagnosed until it is too late. The child seems to have the flu, and nothing is done and then sepsis sets in and it is too late.

It was obvious during the first few weeks after Laura was born that there was a problem, but we didn't know what it was. It was weird because we were experiencing the happiness of having a new baby, but something just didn't feel right. It wasn't a good situation. The pediatrician in New York totally failed to figure it out and, for some reason, nobody thought to do an x-ray or an MRI or send us to a GI specialist. It felt like they just wanted to get us out of their offices and go back to giving shots and prescribing antibiotics for children with ear infections. Luckily, we flew out to Wisconsin and took her to see a GI specialist in Madison, who diagnosed it immediately and told us she would need surgery to correct it. Our friend Bill was an anesthesiologist at Milwaukee Children's Hospital, and he connected us to a surgeon that he worked with there, Roger Cohen, and we scheduled the surgery with him right away. Bill's wife Sue was one of Mary Ann's best friends and Sue and Bill just came through for us in every way you can imagine. We stayed with them in Milwaukee while Laura was in the hospital and Bill was actually in the operating room administering the anesthesia for Laura's surgery. It would be hard to imagine two people demonstrating any more clearly what real friendship looks like.

It's hard to explain what it feels like to have your child go through something like this, to face the confusion and fear that goes with it, the concern for their safety and the stress of trying to make actual life and death choices under pressure, not knowing for sure if you are doing the right thing. We were lucky. We were surrounded by people we could trust, and the right course of action was clear. We just kept going forward, telling ourselves that it would be okay and in the end it was. We were not prepared to imagine any other outcome. Crisis brings clarity. The adrenaline takes over, the detail falls away and you just do what you have to do, wasting no time on doubt. There is a picture of me, in Sue and Bill's apartment after the surgery, holding Laura. I remember the relief we felt at that moment, the feeling that we could just get on with our life. Little did we know that there was another shoe that was about to drop.

Dr. Cohen, in Milwaukee, referred us to another surgeon in New York, Dr. John Schullinger, at Columbia Presbyterian Hospital, way up on the West Side above Columbia University. Dr. Cohen had studied under Dr.

Schullinger as a medical student, and he recommended him very highly. We took Laura to see him for a follow up exam when we got back to New York, and he examined her, and he was encouraging about her recovery. He had one warning for us, which is something anyone who has had intestinal surgery knows. The most common cause of intestinal blockage is scar tissue from an injury or previous surgery, which can cause lesions and essentially re-obstruct the intestine. He told us to call him if we were concerned for any reason and to keep in touch with him about her progress.

We went back to our life, knowing that there was risk, but feeling like we could put the whole thing behind us. It was a bad scare, but our little daughter had come through it and our family was whole and intact.

Within a week or so, Laura seemed to come down with some sort of cold or flu and we took her to the pediatrician. We were very clear about the risks from the surgery, but the pediatrician seemed quite sure that this was just a run of the mill kid illness, and we believed his assurances that it was nothing to be overly worried about. In hindsight, I'm sure we should have called Dr. Schullinger right then and there, but at that moment, we didn't realize what was happening. After assuring us that we had nothing to fear, suddenly the pediatrician had our daughter admitted to Beth Israel Hospital and within less than twenty-four hours the whole situation went from okay to unbelievable nightmare. One of us, I think it was Mary Ann, had spent the night at the hospital and by early morning it was clear that things were not going well. The Beth Israel surgeon was nowhere to be seen, and no one seemed to be able to tell us what the plan was, but there was green bile coming up out of the tube from her stomach, which is a sure sign of something bad, you don't need a doctor to know that. Somehow, Mary Ann had the presence of mind to call Dr. Schullinger up at Columbia Presbyterian and he was very clear – we needed to get her out of Beth Israel and up to him at Columbia immediately.

To do this we had to sign her out of Beth Israel AMA, which stands for Against Medical Advice, which is what hospitals do to wash their hands of you if you take someone out of their care who is in danger. In this case we were admitting her to another hospital, but that didn't seem to matter. As it turns out, if they sign you out AMA, then they can't send you anywhere in one of their ambulances either, so there we were, literally in a life-or-death situation and I was standing at the nursing station arguing with them about insurance liability, which tells you all you need to know about the health care industry in this country in the late eighties. In all this time, no doctor from the hospital ever showed up to talk to us at all, except for one of the residents, who was an honest young guy, and he told us we were making the right decision to take her out of there. In a stroke of brilliance, one of the nurses suddenly figured out that she could just call us a private ambulance and she did it. She is just one of the people in the situation who I have love for to this day, even though I don't even know her name. We were out of there in a flurry of gurneys and IV's and elevators and out the doors of the hospital and into the ambulance. The pediatrician actually showed up as we were wheeling our baby into the elevator and started shouting to me about septicemia. I really wanted to kill him, but I just didn't have the time.

As we got to the ambulance one of the EMT's opened the back doors and I turned to Mary Ann to see if she needed help getting in and I could see from her face that she had passed the point of what she could stand. She had borne most of the weight of the decision and it had taken everything out of her. She got in the front of the ambulance, and I jumped in the back with Laura on the gurney and one of the EMT's. Meanwhile, in the way that the world is so often surreal when you are experiencing crisis, people were walking by on the sidewalk on their way to work, oblivious, stopping to buy coffee, grabbing a newspaper, each hurrying along their personal path, blissfully unaware as our drama unfolded just adjacent to their everyday lives.

I don't think I know how to pray but I suspect it is a form of bargaining. I crouched in the back of the ambulance looking into my daughter's eyes. She was only eight weeks old, so she couldn't talk to me, she couldn't tell me how she felt, or if she was in pain. Her eyes would start to close, and I was afraid to let her fall asleep. I think it was something I had seen in a movie where some guy has been shot and they're trying to get him to hold on until the medics come or something and they keep trying to keep him conscious. I kept fighting off the cliches that were coming into my mind. They say there are no atheists in foxholes, but I don't know if the guys at Tarawa and Iwo Jima and the Battle of the Bulge were really thinking about God in the middle of that. I think they were bargaining, making promises (if I make it out of here alive, I will never……). I just kept wondering what I could trade for her life, if there was a bargain or a promise I could make and who I could talk to about it.

I just didn't want to lose her. I would have done anything. There was nothing for me to do, except be there and do whatever was asked, so I guess I prayed. I couldn't tell you what I said, or promised, but if the price came due tomorrow, I would gladly pay it, whatever it is, without question. Please don't take my daughter, that was all I had to say, to whoever was listening, to the universe and I feel for anyone who has experienced that kind of loss, because I know, once again, that I was incredibly lucky and I do pretty much give thanks every day, to this day, three plus decades later and I'm sure Mary Ann does as well.

They saved her life. It's not complicated or a matter of opinion or conjecture. They saved her life, Dr. John Schullinger and his team. Sometimes the most important things are simple, and this was one of them. We got there in time, and they were able to save her. She was in intensive care for a week, I think. There was another couple there who had been flown down from Buffalo with their infant in a Medivac helicopter. They didn't make it in time and their child did not survive, it was just too late. So, we were never confused about the stakes.

The human mind is strange, at least I know mine is. We sat there for hours, waiting, while Laura was in surgery, fighting for her life and I just kept thinking about this one scene from the movie A Man for All Seasons. Thomas More goes to see Cardinal Wolsey, who has fallen out of favor with Henry VIII and is dying and Wolsey, played by Orson Welles, says to More,

"If I had served my God half so well as I served my king, he would not have left me to die in this place."

I don't know what that means, but I just kept repeating that line over and over in my head. Go figure. What do you say to someone who has saved your daughter's life? You say thanks and you mean it and you hope that in some way you are worthy of it.

A few weeks later I was back at work, saving the world for advertising, as usual, and one of our commercial directors, an Australian guy, was in town. He came upstairs to my office, and we had a short conversation.

He asked me if things were okay with my daughter, and I told him that she was doing better, and we were feeling like she was going to be okay.

And he said, "Good, I've been feeling like I haven't had your full attention lately."

At first, I laughed, appreciating that he had the nerve to go so dark with his sense of humor, but he looked at me strangely and I realized he wasn't joking.

Chapter Seventeen: From Those to Whom Much Is Given, Everything is Expected

When you invent the ship, you invent the shipwreck.
(Paul Virilio)

When they were building Rockefeller Center the design team engaged Diego Rivera to create a giant mural in the lobby of the RCA building. Diego Rivera was one of the most famous artists in the world at that time and, of course, a communist and champion of the rights of workers. He created an amazing mural paying tribute to the workers of the world with a distinctly socialist theme. John D. Rockefeller, the client, was not shown the mural until it was completed. Needless to say, Rockefeller was not a socialist and he was furious when he saw it and demanded that it be destroyed, sparking one of the most famous scandals in the history of art. Imagine a bunch of guys in hard hats with pickaxes and jackhammers reducing a Diego Rivera mural to dust. This is the fundamental reality of making art for money made large, and versions of it large and small play out in advertising every day. There is a client and he, or she, is signing the check and whatever is created they own, to do with whatever they please. End of story.

No matter how great it is, no matter how much skill and artifice and technique is invested in it, advertising has a shelf life. It's ephemeral. It's not meant to last. A great commercial may get attention and win awards, it may get written up in the trade magazines, and even in the mainstream media. It may not be art, but it can certainly be artful in all kinds of ways. It may jumpstart a director's career, or the reputation of a production company, or an agency creative team, or even get into an advertising Hall of Fame, but the work itself has a short useful life. Over the years I won every award in the business multiple times with the directors and production companies I worked with, from Sharks and Pencils to Cannes Lions and AICP Awards. I worked for practically every major client in the business, from Honda to AT&T, Coke, Pepsi, Visa, GM, Ford, Procter and Gamble, and many, many others. I'm proud of a lot of the work we did but at this point, it's forgotten. A few years ago, Beats made a commercial called *You Love Black Culture, but Do You Love Me*? I think it's one of the most brilliant pieces of advertising ever made, right up there with Apple's *1984*. It makes a statement about our culture and our time and by extension, what the brand stands for. But even so, I think the moment has passed and people have mostly forgotten about it. It's unfortunate but it's true. The message was important but, in the end, it was a commercial.

Phil Dusenberry was without question one of the greatest names in the history of advertising. Over two decades he built BBDO into both a creative powerhouse as well as a profit-making machine, which is uncommon for a big agency, since big agencies are usually driven by account guys who come down on the side of profit. He did it with great work for Pepsi, GE, Visa, and many other BBDO clients, winning a truckload of awards and ending up in the Advertising Hall of Fame. He was a legend. Google him and you will find all that, but what you will also find, in equal measure, is that he co-wrote the screenplay for ***The Natural***. One adapted screenplay for a feature film carries almost the same weight in the Google search of Phil's career as his entire storied career in advertising.

Although I think in principle, I understood this, I didn't apply it. In fact, I failed to treat producing commercials as a business at all. My belief, my credo, if you will, when I was an executive producer and company owner in TV commercials was that good work should speak for itself and if you concentrated on doing good work, the money would come. I didn't believe that making money was the goal. I treated it as an important but secondary byproduct of producing creative work. It was an appealing theory, to me at least, high falutin and easy to feel good about, but in retrospect it was impossibly naïve, and it caused me to overlook the fact that almost everyone around me was hyper focused, in one way or another, on being successful and making money. I tended to underestimate the importance of the desire for money as an influence on people's behavior, especially since it wasn't the primary influence on mine. Also, I didn't think enough about the fact that when you produce advertising, you don't retain any kind of interest or rights in your work, so once you've delivered it your participation ends, regardless of the success or value of the work or the product you are selling. In hindsight, things would have gone a lot more smoothly if I had applied a more dispassionate methodology to the decisions I made, prioritized money and business success over awards and creativity, understood the transitory nature of the work and tried to think of what I was doing as more of a business and less of a cause. Later, when I had the opportunity to produce feature films, I approached it from the same point of view, which was possibly even more naive.

In the commercial production business, it used to be considered almost inevitable that once you achieved a certain level of success, and particularly if you were associated with the right kind of directing talent, you would end up starting your own production company. At the start of the 90s I was running Spots Films, successful, but still the American arm of a British production company. It might have been smart to kick back and enjoy it a little bit, but I didn't trust my bosses in London, and I was concerned that I was investing a lot of personal capital in something I had no control over. I could already foresee that one day things could go sideways in

London, and I might have to start over from scratch, after working hard to build the company into a success in the States, which was a much bigger market than London. We entered into a negotiation over ownership of the American company, which really became a negotiation about control. I should have left the whole thing in the hands of lawyers and accountants and kept it businesslike, but it got personal, and it didn't work out. So inevitably I left Spots. I left with David, who was a director there that I had a close working relationship with, and Tom, who was an experienced sales rep I had hired about two years earlier and we started our own production company which we called Headquarters.

A friend of mine once told me that it is incredibly hard to make a partnership work, harder even than a marriage. At the time I didn't understand what he was talking about. What he said sounded crazy to me, but the truth is, most partnerships are partnerships in name only, not real partnerships where people are truly committed to one another through good times and bad. It's more like parallel play. The reality was that David wanted to be an owner and further maximize his value in the marketplace (read: make more money); Tom wanted to be more important (read: make more money and feel like a bigshot); and I wanted to have the coolest company in the business (tricky to pull off). And if I'm honest, I also harbored a secret desire to produce feature films as well (also tricky to pull off). If your interests are aligned the partnership thrives, but the minute the balance is altered self-interest takes hold and the blinders go on, which leads most often to undesirable outcomes. Our interests were only partially aligned from the start so perhaps it was inevitable that I would never manage to feel satisfied and when the opportunity to become a film producer eventually presented itself, I would jump at it.

In 20/20 hindsight I should have done a lot of things differently, but most importantly I should have given a little more thought to my long-term goals, but somehow I never had time for that. I tended to stay in motion, moving forward, solving problems and experiencing a lot of success, but failing to address a nagging sense of frustration with my career path and often with my partners.

One of the things that is seductive if you are good at managing creative talent is that they come to depend on you, and you often mistake that for friendship and mutual respect. This was a characteristic of my relationships with many of the directors I worked with, particularly my partner, David. They may respect you, but the dependency is seductive and ultimately, it's dysfunctional, so in that sense, it is like a family. I worked with a director once who said that the children of alcoholics make the best producers, skilled at keeping everything under control, keeping the boat from tipping over, keeping everyone calm, distracting everyone while they put out the fire. It was kind of funny, but it made me uncomfortable because it had the unmistakable ring of truth and he was talking about me at the time. It's nice to make good money and drive a nice car and have an assistant, but I came to realize that no matter how good you are, you're being defined in terms of your value to someone else and once you see that, it's hard not to see the relationship in that light. This is the problem with managing creative people. They tend to see you in terms of your value to them and if you start to step outside of that frame, they feel betrayed, and that was something that happened in our partnership. Only one of my partners was a creative person; though the other one was not, he was a handful in other ways, so it was doubly frustrating. When we started, he was crazy and fun to work with, but over time the fun wore off as he became increasingly needy and unreliable.

When we went into business together, I should have put the deal in the hands of lawyers and accountants and let them figure it out, based on shares and numbers and dollars. Instead, I took responsibility for constructing a deal that all three of us could live with, which meant trying to satisfy everyone's needs and desires, and I barely had time to think of what I might want out of the whole situation. There was a lot of happy talk about how great it all was, but it was hard and by the time we got the deal done, I was exhausted by it and annoyed by my partners' laser focus on their own self-interest and blissful lack of concern about whether any of it was going to work for me. Over time we worked hard to make the company successful, and it was, but these issues were never faced, so we built an edifice with cracks in the infrastructure, and those things will always come into play somewhere along the way, just as they will in a marriage if you don't have good communication.

People who work in production love to compare their companies and production teams to families. Actors accepting awards are always talking about "my team" and describing their film as a "family". I brought my son to a commercial shoot in LA once when he was a teenager and after hanging around with me on the set all day, we were in the car driving back to the hotel and he said,

"You guys are like a club – you all know each other and everybody's friends and stuff. It's so fun."

It sounded great and it was sort of true, but it's an easy mistake to make. To work closely with a group of people, to spend a lot of time with them, both working and socializing, you start to imagine that they are your family but they're not, the relationships are situational. I can think of people that I worked closely with, had a lot of laughs, people that I thought would be my friends forever, but when the situation changed, somebody moved on, the relationships just faded away.

When I started producing movies and getting the attention that came with it, it brought all the issues that had been simmering in the partnership to a head, and it just made things worse. I had been head down, handling the day-to-day work of the company, running everything and solving problems, managing the commercial production business. I took on a leadership role in the industry, negotiating union contracts and becoming chairman of the industry trade association. My partners were happy to have me doing all that, but they were not ready for the expansion of my role and the changes in the company structure that came when I got the opportunity to produce my first movie. They felt the balance of power in the company was shifting and they were unable to adjust to it. I saw it as an important expansion of our business model, but it bothered them that my role had expanded and theirs hadn't changed. After years of frustration with the partnership, I didn't try that hard to make them feel okay about it. I probably could have been more understanding, but I was not going to let them hold me back and I didn't bother to sugar coat it. It began to feel like we were in a rowboat in the middle of the ocean pulling in opposite directions.

Throughout my career, I was always convinced there was more I could achieve, that there was a better version of the career I had, that it just wasn't quite good enough. This made it easy to think that transitioning into producing feature films would be the solution, that I would find satisfaction once I had reached that goal and it would be smooth sailing from then on, running a successful production company and producing movies as well. It seemed as if it was the natural progression of things. I took my career in advertising for granted and I failed to sufficiently value what I had achieved. I had experienced a lot of success with very few setbacks, so it was hardwired into my psyche that success was inevitable. I assumed that it was a function of time and effort, that anything

I set my sights on was going to be better, that my career trajectory would always be up. I didn't look back. I thought I could succeed my way through every problem. I assumed that because I had been successful, I would always be successful, that it was some sort of magical quality that I had. And, of course, I didn't attach enough importance to the role that luck plays in success and failure, always. It's one thing to achieve success, and it's another thing to maintain it. The two things require different skills, which was also something I didn't grasp.

There was a parallel path to this as well, a corollary, which was that as my company was coming apart and I was transitioning to producing feature films, my marriage was falling apart as well and, in many ways, it was caused by some of the same behaviors. Mary Ann and I had been married for twenty years. We were good parents, we had great kids, we built a nice family, some would have said a model family. We had made it through some difficult life situations. Unfortunately, what we had never done was create a healthy pattern for communicating with each other, for being open about our thoughts and feelings, for sharing our dreams and fears, for being honest about our problems and listening to each other. Each of us had issues that the other one did not pay attention to. We built our life by getting in lockstep with each other and moving forward and it worked out fine for a while, but the relationship in the center of it never really matured and we stopped communicating. People talk about growing apart and it sounds like a cliché, but it's not, one day you wake up and notice that you're just going through the motions. I looked at my kids, and my oldest was in high school, and his sister was a teenager, and my youngest was eight years old, and I thought I'm going to turn around and in no time you guys are going to grow up and lead your own lives, you're going to leave, and what will I do then? Move to Wisconsin and learn to play golf? Mary Ann was already dropping hints about retirement, but I believed I was just starting to get where I wanted to go and I had zero interest in winding down.

I had a vision that Mary Ann and I were walking together down a long pier, and the pier had ended, and we were still walking anyway, without noticing. I looked down and saw only water and I was sure that if we stayed together, we would drag each other under and we would drown. She didn't do anything wrong; it was the things we didn't do right, the important things we didn't do, the signs we missed, the conversations we never had, and my frustration, that killed our marriage. As it happens sometimes, we got married very young and there were some important lessons we never learned, and it caught up with us.

And then, as if things weren't complicated enough, I fell in love.

I wanted to feel passion and commitment. I wanted to be excited about myself, to feel like there were possibilities in front of me, that I could still achieve things, that I could still become the person I wanted to be. And into the middle of this walked Andrea, smiling and confident, with a plan that made no sense at all and complete faith that it would all work out and I knew she was the key to everything and the only way I was going to get where I wanted to go, wherever it was, the only way I was ever going to become the person I wanted to be, was with her.

I could probably still be sitting behind a desk today, running a successful commercial production company. Maybe I could even have stayed married as well. It was messy. I lost some friends. There were people who thought my choices were irresponsible. At times, I worried that they were. But for me, the door opened, and I walked through it. It wasn't so much a choice as an inevitability. If I had it to do over, even knowing how challenging it was, I would still do the same things. If the universe opens a door, it seems somehow ungrateful, or at least unimaginative, to look the other way. It feels like tempting fate, killing your own spirit. If there's a chance for a great love in your life, you take the risk and you know that if it doesn't work out, there's no one to blame but yourself. Becoming a movie producer was one of those decisions as well. Given a choice I was prepared to deal with the consequences of my decisions. There was no way I was going to deal with regrets. My biggest concern was my kids and thank heaven for them. I think they accepted that I was not perfect, but they stuck with me and let me work my way through all of it.

I never had to do any of this, I saw opportunities and I pursued them.

I became a movie producer, pretty much overnight, and that changed my whole career path. Things were already complicated, and they got a lot more complicated. It's not easy to anticipate when opportunities are going to show up and it's often when you least expect them, and it is challenging to manage the resulting destruction of the status quo. Sometimes all you can do is improvise and hope for the best. I split with my wife of twenty-one years. My partnership of ten years blew up. I felt we had to make major changes to survive but my partners didn't see it. These are things that happened, but they didn't happen to me, I was not the victim of circumstances. I had agency in my life and these things happened because of my choices.

Chapter Eighteen: And Now for Something Completely Different

Millions are to be grabbed out here and your only competition is idiots. Don't let this get around.
(Herman Mankiewicz)

Everything you have ever heard about "Hollywood" and the movie business is true. All the quotes, the anecdotes, the books you've read, the stories you've heard, it's all true. Because of that, when you experience it, it feels strangely familiar. Everything is somehow totally predictable, but it still catches you by surprise. I had a lot of experience and credibility. I was used to being one of the people in a meeting that other people stopped talking and listened to, but I had no idea what it would mean to bring those expectations into a totally new situation with a lot of big egos. I wasn't going to be happy just to be included, so I think I was on a collision course with an immovable object right from the start.

When Sega introduced the Dreamcast console in 1999, the future of their company was pretty much riding on this one product launch. They bought a ninety second block of airtime on the MTV awards, which at that time was basically the Super Bowl for the gamer demographic. The agency had a huge concept, basically a ninety second action film, with all kinds of visual effects and stunts and I knew when it came across my desk that it was one of those career making spots that don't come along very often. They bid three companies, and we all went after it. In the end my director, John Moore, wrote a great treatment and we got it. We shot it up in Vancouver, which was a nightmare. It was busy up there with feature film shoots and there were availability problems with everything, from crew to equipment to locations. It was expensive and frustrating, and we had to throw money at production problems every time we turned around. John dealt with production like a reckless teenage driver. He liked to take every bump and curve at maximum speed with minimum concern for damage to the vehicle. In the end we went close to half a million dollars over budget, which would have sunk a less successful company but losing money on projects like that was a cost of doing business at that time for big companies like ours if the creative was good enough. The other companies we bid against would have done the same.

When the spot aired on the MTV Awards it was a sensation. It won pretty much every award in the business. I expected to sit back and rake in the work from the advertising agencies, which didn't happen right away, but something else did happen that was unexpected. Within a couple of weeks of the spot going on the air, I started to get calls from Hollywood agents and managers and studio executives wanting to know who had directed it. They were trying to find the next Michael Bay or David Fincher, so they were paying a lot of attention to music videos and commercials and the spot we had done fit the action movie template to a tee.

John was essentially shy. He had this "I'm just a regular guy from a small town in Ireland" thing that he did, so he wanted someone else to deal with the Hollywood personalities, which is how I ended up with a producing role on my first movie. We went to a lot of meetings and talked to a lot of agents and managers and studio executives. Movie people are used to gatekeepers, whether you're a manager, a producing partner, or any kind of attachment. They treat you nice and calculate how polite they have to be and how soon they can get rid of you and they don't crack much of a sweat over it. They start by trying to schedule important meetings without you, to see if the director lets them get away with it and from that they measure how much influence you have, whether you are actually important to the process and how soon they can stab you in the back.

We signed with United Talent Agency as a director / producer team and they sent us to a bunch of meetings and we read a bunch of scripts, but the reality was that Fox was looking for someone to direct a movie called Behind Enemy Lines and that was what had really started the ball rolling. The script was about a Navy pilot and his navigator who get shot down in a no-fly zone in Bosnia. The pilot gets shot but the navigator survives. The Navy wants to send in an extraction team to bring him out, but it gets caught up in all kinds of UN politics and he has to use his wits to survive while he waits for them to come and rescue him. At that time very few people in this country had any understanding of what was going on in the Balkans, least of all the executives at the studio and they were looking for a director to jumpstart the project. There were the historical ethnic hatreds, virulent nationalism and war crimes being perpetrated, and basically most people in America had no idea what it was all about. John and I were both knowledgeable about the whole situation, so it was really a no-brainer to put us on the film and let us sort out the story. The project had been set up for a while and they had done a whole series of scripts, but the project was stalled. If we were willing to attach ourselves, they were ready to hire a new writer and restart the whole process, so it sounded good to us, and we agreed. The challenge was to make an entertaining movie about a very serious subject, but we felt like it was worth it and we were naïve enough to be confident we could pull it off.

One of the first things I learned is that in the movie business the only person that gets paid during the development process is the writer and development can go on for a long time. When you attach yourself to a studio film, even if they have had it in development for years and spent tons of money on it, it becomes your film, your responsibility, and your job is to sell it back to the studio. You become the filmmakers and it's your job to get the script to a place where they are prepared to greenlight the film and spend the money to make it. Until you do that, you get paid nothing and all the work you do on it is for free and truth be told, it may never get made. That's why they call it being attached as opposed to being hired.

I found the script writing process baffling. The writer would produce a draft, working with the director, and when they were satisfied, the draft would go to the studio and the studio execs would give notes. The writer was expected to take the notes and go away and do a revision of the script. The process appears to be collaborative because a lot of people are engaged in it. People at all different levels of authority give notes. It is actually part of their job to give notes, so everyone has to come up with some tweak or observation of some kind, no matter how irrelevant and most executives take Robert McKee's famous screenwriting course so they can produce all sorts of verbiage about "second act turning points" and "inciting actions." The writer is expected to synthesize all that feedback into some sort of coherent direction. In advertising everyone defaults to the most senior people in the room and if you don't have something essential to say, you keep your mouth shut. In the development process it was the opposite. Everybody had something to offer, and it was never explicit which notes were important and which ones could be disregarded. The studio didn't consolidate their feedback and speak with one voice, they just expected the writer to sift through all the notes and come up with some sort of solution. After one particularly confusing script meeting, I remember asking our writer at the time, who was an Academy Award nominated writer, what he had taken away from the whole discussion and he just looked at me and rolled his eyes, which at least gave me confidence that I wasn't the only one who found the process confusing.

Finally, one of the writers produced a script that the studio liked, even though he barely knew what continent Bosnia was on and the word came down that they were going to greenlight our movie. I was surprised because they had rejected an earlier script that I thought was better, but either way, suddenly, we had a go movie.

It's not surprising that agents and studio executives lie, lots of people lie. It is surprising, though, how often they lie and then immediately forget about it. When circumstances change and the lie has outlived its usefulness, they carelessly reveal it without realizing that you will notice it and that it will influence the likelihood that you will trust them in the future. William Goldman describes this phenomenon in *Which Lie Did I Tell*? his second memoir about the movie business. This was exemplified for me when they greenlit our movie because suddenly everyone, in their glee over the movie being greenlit, started congratulating us because "The studio never had any intention of making the movie! You guys developed the shit out of it!" and it never occurred to any of them that it was the opposite of everything they had been telling us from day one when we were burning our time and effort on a project that apparently nobody thought was ever going to get made.

From the start our intention was to shoot the film in Eastern Europe, as close to Bosnia as possible. People who do commercials are comfortable shooting all over the place and we had experience in Prague and Budapest, we knew the pros and cons of Romania and Bulgaria, and we knew there was good crew in Croatia, and between all of us we had shot in every one of those locations. The movie business really started in Europe and most of the first wave of great Hollywood directors were European, directors like Victor Sjostrom and Ernst Lubitsch and Erich von Stroheim. At one time there were movie studios in almost every country in Europe. Because of the dampening effect of communism on economic growth in Eastern Europe the remnants of those studios survived as state-owned enterprises under the wet blanket of communism instead of being converted to supermarkets and discount stores, as many were on the East Coast when the movie business migrated to California. They were still there, waiting to be discovered, when the wall came down. This made Eastern Europe an overnight attraction for filmmakers, even though many of the facilities were in varying degrees of disrepair, because the structure was there, and it was cheap. We knew we could pull crew from the UK and Europe, so we were very confident about shooting in the region and we knew it would help us from a budget point of view. Eastern Europe, particularly when you get into the former USSR satellite countries, has a pretty distinctive feel. There is a hard feeling about it, something a little threatening and unpredictable, outside the rule of law, almost as if you scratched the surface, you wouldn't have to go far to encounter things you didn't want to see or know about. It's not so true of Hungary or the Czech Republic anymore but even there you don't have to look too far to find some decaying concrete building, some vestige of institutional brutalism from the former USSR that takes you to a different era and gives you a glimpse of a far more challenging day-to-day existence than we are used to in America. We felt our movie really needed that kind of authenticity, especially considering the brutality underlying the story we were trying to tell, and why not just get as close to the real thing as possible.

There is a practice at movie studios which is generally associated with the film ***Heaven's Gate***, one of the famous financial disasters in movie history. This practice is to put a firewall between development, which involves studio executives and producers, and what they call physical production, which is done by the people who actually do the real production work and hire the line producers and crew and production accountants and so on, that get the movie made. Studios like to put their physical production people in a separate building, that's how much they want to keep them away from the actual decision-making about whether to make a movie or not. This allows marketing, and not production, to drive the bottom line of a movie, and it allows studio executives to feign ignorance to justify unreasonable expectations about budgets. To that end, they like to keep physical production at arm's length until they are ready to greenlight a movie, and then, and only then, fight with them about the price. I don't know what it's like dealing with Netflix or Amazon but I'm guessing it hasn't changed all that much.

When we got on the movie, there was already a big producer on it named John Davis who had a producing deal at the studio and 60 or 70 movies under his belt. His father, Marvin Davis, was the one who had originally sold Fox to Rupert Murdoch and the story we were told was that a condition of the deal was that John had a producing deal for life. He reminded me of a senior account guy at an ad agency. He knew his client and he had an instinct for what they would buy and how to deliver it, and he wasn't too precious about compromising the creative. He wanted to shoot the movie in Vancouver, and he had the physical production guys at the studio on board, but we were dead set against it. He was completely uninterested in the creative arguments for shooting in Eastern Europe. In the end we got our way only because the studio guys figured out what we had recently learned on the Sega shoot, which was that Vancouver was overused, and it had become a nightmare to work there. Nothing was available, so they couldn't get the movie set up and shot on schedule. They had no choice but to circle back and pretend we had convinced them to adopt our choice of location. They assigned the movie to a different physical production executive, who came from an independent film background and immediately packed him off to Eastern Europe to figure out where to shoot our movie. Of course, having decided to greenlight the film after years of development, they were suddenly in a rush to get it made, it had to be done yesterday, so he was under serious pressure to figure the whole thing out. He and I got in sync about all this over a few late-night phone calls spanning multiple time zones and he eventually found the right combination of facilities and price in Slovakia.

This is how I came to spend several months of my life in Bratislava, the capital of Slovakia, where there was a crumbling studio complex called Koliba Studios. The offices and production areas had cracked and broken tiles on the floor and leaks in the roof when it rained but the actual stages were great, as they had been renovated in 1995 when Raffaella De Laurentiis made ***Dragonheart*** there. Outside of town there was an army base, and they gave us the run of the place for a fee that was laughable by American standards and included an actual working missile launcher, miscellaneous military vehicles and several Russian T-72 tanks. I'm pretty sure we could have invaded a country with the stuff they gave us. I remember when I got there, one of the first things I saw was a wrecked MIG fighter plane in the yard outside the studio, looking like a child's toy that has been roughly used and thrown away. Needless to say, it was a far cry from Vancouver and way more authentic.

Once the movie was greenlit, John started scouting locations and casting, doing the logistical stuff you have to do to get the picture made, including a lot of travel back and forth to Eastern Europe and to London for casting sessions. I was still running Headquarters in LA, which was a full-time job and then some, so gradually, I fell out of the loop on the day-to-day progress of the production. I suspect that the studio people and the other producers had decided they had found their opportunity to ease me off the project. Studio executives and producers draw their power from talent relationships, so they were all trying to own the relationship with the "hot young director" who was going to be the next Michael Bay. I figured either John was okay with it, or he wasn't, and there wasn't much that I was going to do about it. I had plenty of other issues to deal with, both professional and personal, so I resigned myself to whatever the result turned out to be. Then, just a few weeks before the start of the shoot, I got a slightly hysterical phone call from John Moore, asking me when I was coming to Bratislava. He was nervous, with the first shoot day of the movie approaching. He had a great crew around him but not much in the way of producer or studio executive experience and John Davis was nowhere to be seen. Basically, I dropped everything, packed my bags, and left for Slovakia. It was a big decision for me and I'm sure it contributed to the erosion of my partnership in Headquarters, but I felt it was my responsibility to support him and the movie. My partners assured me that it was okay, and I believed them, although it would become clear afterwards that it was the beginning of the end of that relationship. There was a production team and a huge crew of very professional people on the movie, so nobody was depending on me to get the movie made. I was just there to help keep everybody calm, run interference between John Moore and the studio, and provide encouragement for him when he needed it. In fact, it was pretty much a babysitting role, which is not my preference, but I was learning how to be a movie producer, and it was really different.

Film sets, movie sets, even commercial sets are all about personality dynamics. Unlike TV, which is about writers, movies and commercials are all about directors, and so the *Sturm und Drang* usually ladders up to the director, or down from the director, one way or the other. But on a film, there is an added element, which is the actors. In commercials, actors are usually pretty much moving props. They are cast according to how they look or speak, whether they are weird, or relatable, big, small, fat, or thin. If the bit calls for a dopey dad, or a sweet old grandmother, it's a type and you cast the guy who looks like a dopey dad or the old lady who has the right grandma look. Directors tend to move commercial actors around like chess pieces and maneuver them into delivering the performance or the gag they need to get the story to work, whether it's an awkward moment, or a poignant exchange, or whatever. If the guy needs to gulp the Coke, you cast somebody who can gulp the Coke, you make sure of it in the casting session. You're not going to have time to teach him how to do it, it's not Method Acting. Clara Peller, the Where's the Beef lady, wasn't an actor, she was a weird old lady that Joe Sedelmaier, the famous comedy director, found somewhere. This is why "real people casting" is such a big deal in commercials. You don't cast Judy Dench and put a wig on her and have her do a special voice and build a weird old lady character, you find a weird old lady and get her to be herself for a few seconds at a time until you have enough footage to cut into a commercial.

I'm sure we've all heard stories about this actor or that actor being unreasonable or acting up, or maybe refusing to do something, or demanding that a script be changed. I'm sure there are times when this is true, but I learned to see it differently when Owen Wilson showed up in Bratislava a few weeks before the shoot and started making recommendations about tweaks to the script. There was some drama going on about it, which seemed reasonable at first because we were so close to the first shoot day, but then I realized that the studio had put script contributions in his deal when they signed him to the movie. He was known for writing scripts with Wes Anderson and the script had gone through some changes from the original version he had signed on for, so what he was doing was really what he thought they expected of him and therefore not strange at all. When I pointed this out to the studio exec, she looked at me like I had lost my mind.

There is no one whose career is more vulnerable to the success or failure of a film than an actor, no one more closely associated with how the public reacts, so it's a big deal when an actor commits to a movie and the more famous they are, the more they have at stake because usually a movie is described in terms of the lead actors that are attached. For instance, it's a Tom Hanks movie or a Denzel Washington movie. Some directors, like Ridley Scott, or Steven Spielberg, or Francis Ford Coppola, or maybe David Fincher, have that kind of name recognition with the public, but that's the exception, not the rule.

People in Hollywood are generally very careless about the things they say when they are trying to get you to do something and very sloppy about living up to their commitments once they have gotten you to agree. Imagine you are an actor, and you have agreed to do a movie six months to a year in advance based on a certain version of the script, and in the ensuing six months you get multiple versions of the script, and each time it loses key elements that you liked about it in the first place. It's not that simple to isolate the point along the way where the script changes so much that you lose interest in the project, but sooner or later, you must take a stand or risk remaining attached to a project that turns out to be a flop. Watching movie box office receipts has become a blood sport, so there is a lot at stake, especially for an actor. Studio heads can (sometimes) lose their jobs, but actors can derail a career, and studio executives are not shy about blaming actors when a movie goes wrong. This is why actors have their own production companies, so they can develop their own projects and, at least theoretically, have some control over their choices.

Watching Owen Wilson, Gene Hackman, and the other actors work on our film was my first in-person experience of watching real actors work and it was eye-opening, totally different from anything I had seen in decades of working in commercials. One day I was watching dailies of a cutaway of Gene's face as he reacts to some bad news on a TV screen. In the shot, there is nothing visible but his face, and there is no dialogue and no music, but I realized I could clearly understand the emotion he was feeling in the scene just by watching his face and he literally doesn't appear to be doing anything. It's magic and that's the thing that real actors have, and it was a revelation to see it in action.

Chapter Nineteen: That Rusty Old Curtain

"So, do you want to give me one, then?"
(Irish girl in bar)
"Do you know what she means by that?"
(Her older friend)

When we made our movie, Western money was flowing into Eastern Europe, but Slovakia was trailing behind countries like the Czech Republic, Hungary and Poland. They were just starting construction of some new hotels in Bratislava but when we were there, there were still only two decent hotels in town, which were next to each other in the center of town, on the Danube. One of them was a typical European hotel, where they put lunch meat out at breakfast and serve runny eggs. Most everyone was staying there but I stayed at the other one, which was called, surprisingly, The Danube. I probably ended up there because production made my reservation at the last minute and the other one was booked. It was nice and clean, the rooms were large, but was also old fashioned and a little weird, as it was a holdover from the Communist Party era. I had visions of grim, unsmiling Soviet officials staying there on diplomatic visits to Bratislava and it functioned the way I imagine the bureaucracy in the USSR worked. If you wanted anything, like getting your laundry done, for instance, or getting your messages and you went to the front desk, the answer was always no. They refused to do anything, they weren't helpful, or even particularly polite. They acted as if they had more important things to do, like a government agency in a Communist country might act, from what I've heard. I didn't know what to make of it. Traipsing around town looking for a laundry or a dry cleaner was not what I imagined the producer of a major Hollywood movie should be doing but at the same time, I had to get my laundry done and I felt foolish going to the production staff and asking them how to do it. Luckily, I discovered the way of underground economies, in this case the housekeepers, who were the answer to everything. They were intimidating, solidly built, serious looking Slavic women but they turned out to be extremely nice, happy to do laundry, stitch up a torn piece of clothing, take stuff to the dry cleaners, or any other errand I could think of, and the room was always immaculately clean. I would drag myself back at the end of a shoot day and find my stuff on hangars on the back of the door, beautifully ironed by hand. All transactions were in cash, and it was incredibly cheap. Once I figured it out, I loved the hotel. The production staff kept asking me if I wanted to move to the other hotel, the more modern one and they could not figure out why I kept turning them down.

Another object lesson in grassroots capitalism were the checkpoints that were set up on the roads, not by the police, but by the military, which existed for the sole purpose of collecting bribes. They would stop your car and ask for ID, registration, etc. and then wait for a bribe and they would keep you there until you handed over some money. It was completely out in the open, and the purpose was universally understood. Mostly we had drivers who were locals, and they handled it, but I couldn't help wondering what it would be like if you didn't speak the language and didn't know what to do, if you were just a tourist driving a rental car through Eastern Europe with your wife and kids.

The world is homogeneous these days. Everywhere you go, there's a Gap, or a Banana Republic, or a Sephora and everyone's driving Nissans and Toyotas and Jeeps. I'll bet there are goatherds in Mongolia with iPhones. I remember going to the UK and Europe when I was a kid and everything was different, especially the cars. I remember learning all the different kinds of cars and how to use the payphones, like in

London, where when you made a call from a payphone, you put in the money after the other person answered. Slovakia still felt like that, different, especially outside of Bratislava, like Kosice, which is a smaller city on the other end of the country, much closer to Russia.

As we approached the end of the shooting schedule in Slovakia I had a series of disturbing phone calls with my partner Tom, who oversaw sales in New York, and Andrew, my Head of Production in LA, and it was immediately apparent to me that something at the company had gone wrong. When I left for Slovakia, they were very sure that they had everything under control, down to insisting that we didn't need to have any status calls or check-ins. I probably should have known that was a bad idea, but still I was shocked to discover how things had deteriorated while I was gone, particularly the director relationships, which are key to the success of any production company. There was bad energy and some of the key talent were confused and disgruntled, but they never brought me in on the situation. When I confronted Andrew, he admitted that things hadn't gone well, and there had been issues with some of the directors, but he said he was told not to involve me. Tom had a pathological need for attention, which I had always tolerated because he was incredibly entertaining and funny and, because he was in sales, it worked. He could pretty much say or do anything he wanted because most people loved him and no one took him seriously. But there was a problem under the surface I wasn't fully aware of; apparently, he had always chafed at being a junior partner in the company, and he thought my going away for a few months was his opportunity to prove that he could replace me. The problem is, if you are good at something you tend to make it look easy; the downside is that, often, people decide that because it looks easy, it is easy, and running a major production company is not easy. Tom was missing the skills and expertise required to do it effectively. The system had always been that when there was a problem or a serious issue, people brought it to me, whether it was clients, agency, directors, or production people, and that formula worked because everyone understood it. I think Tom wanted too much to be liked, and he didn't seem to understand that you can't just act important, sometimes you have to handle the hard stuff and make the right decisions, regardless of the blowback.

My vision was to develop movie projects as an expansion of the profile of our commercial production company, and I had a model to emulate which was Anonymous Content, Steve Golin's company. We had a meeting and my partners signed on to the plan, so I focused on straightening out the issues that had developed while I was in Slovakia, imagining that I had the support I needed to push forward and make this new model successful. I was excited about it. John was in post-production on the movie, so I was going to screenings and meetings at the studio, but I had plenty of time to devote to the company and I was getting attention in the industry for producing the movie. This was good for our business because pretty much every commercial director secretly wants to direct a movie, and it meant that directors were interested in us because they thought I could create those opportunities for them.

As it turned out my partners had a problem that I didn't understand. David's wife, who was a friend, warned me that they were "stuck" but unfortunately, I didn't listen to her. They understood my desire to expand the scope of the company to produce films, but their concern, which David at least was honest about, was that it elevated my role, which they felt made their roles seem less important. As it turned out, they were only paying lip service to the plan I had laid out. They couldn't accept being partners, even in a more successful company, if it meant that their role in it was less important.

David had always wanted a more active role in the management of the company, which I had always deflected, as other directors are always uncomfortable having a director / owner involved in their business. So, they tried to take control and push me out of the way. What resulted was chaos and it started to spin out of control almost immediately.

I was in the middle of getting divorced, which was distracting and emotionally draining, but running the company, dealing with familiar everyday issues, provided a helpful and familiar focus for me outside of my personal life. Navigating my partners' resistance, however, was a challenge I didn't have much headspace for. The worse it got the less patience I had with it, and I made it worse by letting it slide instead of calling them on it right away. I expected them to adhere to the plan; admittedly, I was dismissive and unsympathetic to their insecurities.

I gave them an ultimatum, which was either live up to the commitment they had made or buy me out. They chose the latter, which was a self-destructive choice I didn't foresee. To this day, I hear the voice of my lawyer, Mike Frankfurt, who was a very smart guy with a lot of knowledge and experience in the business, who said to me,

"Why are they buying you out? You should be buying them out."

In hindsight, he was right, but I didn't follow his advice. I didn't have the energy for another fight, so I gave up a successful production company with a great reputation that I had dedicated myself to for ten years. I had a vision for the company's future, but I let them take it away from me. It was unfortunate for me but also for them since they ran it into the ground in just two years and they were left with nothing.

About a year after we negotiated the buyout, I got a call from Tom. Andrea and I were in New York for an industry event, staying at the Mercer Hotel.

"We sure showed you, didn't we?" he said, winning me over immediately by making a joke out of the mess they had made of it.

He asked if we could meet. I had the distinct feeling that this was one of those calls that people make when they are in AA, reaching out to clear the air with people they have history with, or unfinished business. I was happy to hear from him, especially as I felt in hindsight that, as a friend, I had had the sense during the last year of our partnership that he was slipping, and I felt I should have confronted him earlier and told him to get himself into AA and get himself straightened out.

Andrea and I met him for lunch at a restaurant in the meatpacking district. I was looking forward to seeing him; perhaps I was even thinking that we could be friends again, as there were things about our friendship that I missed. Unfortunately, whatever I was expecting, whatever optimism I had indulged in, was misplaced. In the restaurant, there was a woman who had worked for us at one time as a West Coast sales rep. The two of them had never really gotten along, although, or perhaps because, I was a fan. He immediately started an argument with her, from one table to another, in the middle of a crowded New York restaurant. It was embarrassing, but worse than that, it was familiar.

I remember standing at the crosswalk after the lunch was over waiting for the light to change on Gansevoort Street, turning to Andrea and saying,

"Please tell me I didn't manage that for 12 years."

"That's exactly what you did." she said.

"Tell me it wasn't that bad."

And she looked at me and she said, "It was that bad."

Chapter Twenty: Hagiography, or Lives of the Saints

Jolene
I ain't about to go straight
It's too late
I found myself face-down in a ditch
Booze in my hair, blood on my lips
A picture of you, holding a picture of me
In the pocket of my blue jeans
(Ray LaMontagne)

It's a beautiful song, but it's not a love song, it's a song about addiction. Given a choice between the lover and the booze, he's choosing the booze. And you're meant to feel sorry for him.

Hank:

Mom shows up to visit with two suitcases. It seemed strange at first, Jen and I kind of looked at each other, like huh? we wondered if she had planned to just move in, without actually telling us; but then when I took the bags out of the car, I heard the clinking sound of bottles jostling one another in one of the suitcases. That sound is distinctive; it kind of evokes the warmth and friendliness of a familiar bar or restaurant, or of entertaining friends and neighbors at home in the evening; but right away I knew that if I opened the suitcase, there were vodka bottles in there, and not just one. She brought her personal stash, like the risk of going without was far too great to trust us, to trust our hospitality, like there was no way she was going to take a chance or expose herself to us.

Later, the three of us were watching TV. So, at the end of the show, we decided to go to bed, so we ask her if she is coming up, but she wanted to stay put, on the couch, which felt a bit odd. Except when we turned to go, I heard that familiar sound again, of her wedding ring clinking against the vodka bottle stashed between the couch cushions. On some level, I kind of admired her planning skills; she wasn't leaving anything to chance, the concentration she put into it, like managing an illicit love affair, constantly managing a hidden agenda, planning ahead.

I think she always felt like the world was out to screw her, and this was the antidote, the secret weapon; she was just so determined not to let anyone take it away from her. You know some people, they know they have a problem, they know they need to do something, but they feel powerless, whether they need the meetings, or the steps, or the sponsor, or whatever, but they need something, and they know it. That was not her; I don't think she ever had the slightest intention of solving her problem; I think she thought everyone else was her problem.

I respect how hard it is for people who struggle with addiction but it's a personal struggle, and for anyone who is involved in it, especially as a bystander, there's nothing glamorous about it. It's not something you can fix. You're lucky if you can even help. Addiction is held in high regard in our society, it's considered special in some way, and we treat it like a badge of honor, but really, it's a spectator sport. We write songs about it and books and movies. We call it a disease, but it's not a disease. A disease is something you catch, it's contagious, it's a danger you are exposed to, often without your knowledge. Addiction is an illness, which is also serious, but not the same thing. It's an illness that our society invites us to indulge every day of our lives, everywhere we turn. We are addicted to everything, fashion, shopping, food, cars, social media, sugar, sex, pornography, violence, video games, designer clothes, and of course, the foundational ones, drugs and alcohol - prescription, illegal, medicinal, 12-year-old, opiate, manufactured and homegrown, and everything else under the sun.

There's a seductive idea that addiction is something dramatic or formative, and we reinforce that concept by associating it with creativity but in fact, it's borrowed interest. Addiction itself is not that interesting. We glamorize it by making it an essential part of the artist's story, the celebrity story, the biopic, the crucible of suffering that we tell ourselves is the price of talent. We imagine that it's the key to the story, another type of "inciting incident" or character trait. This is the story of Johnny Cash and Jackson Pollack, of Halston, Billie Holliday, Charlie Parker, Lee Morgan, Janis Joplin, Jimi Hendrix and Jim Morrison, about Edgar Allen Poe, Coleridge, Hemingway, Fitzgerald, Chet Baker, and so on, the list is endless. We anchor their stories to their addictions, thereby reducing their talent and their life events to footnotes that come either before or after the second act turning point, which is always about hitting rock bottom. Take *Walk the Line*, for example. There's a point in the film where Johnny Cash gets addicted to pills, and starts acting like a tortured, drunken slob. I want to go to the kitchen and just skip to the part where he shows up at Columbia Records in the black suit and tells them he's going to play Folsom and if they don't like the record, they don't have to pay for it.

As a society, we are addicted to status, money, and success, and often excess and addiction are part of the story, but perhaps we should learn to be a little more suspicious of those glamorous stories. Where did this idea come from that addiction burnishes the greatness of the artist? Perhaps it was Fitzgerald, or Hemingway, or one of the other famous drunks. It's as if the story of an artist doesn't work without addiction to validate the eventual success, without the baptism of fire. Clearly the biopic formula doesn't work without it. But think of the greatness achieved without addiction, like Joyce and Picasso, or despite it, like Miles Davis, or Coltrane, who knew they couldn't fully become themselves until they overcame heroin addiction. Clearly it can be done but it doesn't make a good biopic.

Sometimes the self-abuse becomes the story, not just the addict but others he/she encounters or becomes friends with, and it is frankly horrifying, not enlightening. Sometimes, and this can happen in AA meetings, there is a fine line between the cathartic value of the story, admitting your helplessness, submitting to a higher power, and bragging about your depravity, enjoying the shock value of it, the *Oh man, I was so drunk I fell down the stairs and broke all my front teeth* of it all, the pornography of substance abuse. Unless there is insight that comes with it, I just don't see the point.

From what I have read, Judy Garland got hooked on amphetamines at a young age because the studio pumped her up with diet pills when she was a teenager to keep her from gaining weight. That's the tragedy, pure and simple, the tragedy of how she was abused. She may have been a mess, but the real story is the Hollywood system that crushed her, that made her life a living hell, the reprehensible behavior of influential people, the venal subtext of the entertainment business, the true nexus of exploitive depravity. Billie Holliday is another tragic story, a talented black artist, victim of sexual abuse and racism, persecuted and tortured by society as it devoured her talent. There's meaning in their stories, even tragedy, but the key is the why, not the addiction itself. Behind these stories often are evil, powerful people who know what they are doing is wrong, the exploiters, not the addicts themselves. Addiction for its own sake? Why glamorize it? Who profits?

There were a lot of alcoholics in my family, and my parents had a lot of alcoholic friends. They actively encouraged me and my brother to drink, to join the club, to participate. I had close friends in college who had drinking problems, but we thought they were just partying too much.

The whole thing is just so depressingly familiar, and it took me a long time to see it. And the sad thing about addicts, is that inevitably, they start lying to you and making promises they can't keep, and that becomes exhausting after a while. And at that point, if you don't see what's going on, if you keep buying into it, it's on you, not them.

There is a memory that I share with my brother Jonathan, my adopted brother, from when we were teenagers. My father has gone to bed, and we are up talking to our mom. I don't remember why but we are arguing, and she is frustrated with us. I think her hope was that we would grow up to be reflections of her, to repeat her opinions and her stories back to her, to adopt her mythology, to play along, so she doesn't like it when we are difficult, when we disagree with her, and she can't stand feeling left out. She's a victim of the secret dream of all narcissists, to be surrounded by mirrors. She keeps getting drunker and more frustrated with us until finally she climbs up on the kitchen table and starts waving her arms around and yelling. I feel myself fading backwards, like a contra-zoom in a movie where the background and the foreground seem to go in different directions, detachment washing over me like the salt water when you get knocked over by the surf. The kitchen table was round with a heavy slate top, and I remember hoping the table would collapse and fall crashing to the floor and carry her with it, looking up at her and feeling repulsed by the whole scene but somehow feeling responsible for it as well. My only escape was to disappear inside myself. I remember thinking, how long is it going to be until I can grow up and get the fuck out of here? To everyone else, our parents were Tracy and Hepburn, Bogey and Bacall, Nick and Nora Charles, they bought into the burnished mythology of their charm, glamorous people with drinks in one hand, and a cigarette in the other. For us it was like Stranger Things, living in upside down world. There's a problem when you hide inside yourself. It's very hard to find your way out again.

Hank:

When I was about 14 years old, mom came home cross-eyed and plastered from a night out. I met her at the front door because it was really late (or actually early morning) and I was worried because she had driven home. Though I spoke to her she didn't answer; she just sort of looked at me with a bloodshot and blurry stare and stumbled into her bedroom. She began to wrestle around with her bedclothes in a kind of keystone cops bumbling arms and legs drama, falling on the floor, tangled up in her sheets and blankets like some Benny Hill version of a hobbit, or something porcine snorting around its nest.

I laughed; it was deeply darkly funny, but I also lost a big piece of my innocence, and all of my trust that there was someone looking out for my welfare.

Pete:

As the years moved on, mom's alcoholism and other addiction(s) (she took valium all the time) became worse and worse, but I look back on it and kick myself for never addressing it. For example, she would come visit my family with a bag full of vodka bottles and pill bottles of valium which I discovered but never said anything about. The reason I never did was to avoid the inevitable "flipping out" my mother would do whenever I/we would try to discuss anything of a sensitive nature. It was easier to just get along which I now understand is common with addiction when the addict has no desire or commitment to get better. So, it would likely not have made a difference. But that said, it is what killed her and doing nothing was the decision I made at the time.

I remember when Bill told me about finding all mom's bills unpaid in the trunk of her car. Mom would never even talk to me about what happened and what was going on with the bills for the next 3 years. After graduating I added her to my Amex card, and she spent like a drunken sailor and never paid me what she owed me (when I didn't have any money) was the next money issue.

And finally, years later, she called me saying they were auctioning off her house the next day unless I wired (that day) $20k to her lawyer. I then spoke to the lawyer, asking "is this all there is" and both her and her lawyer lied and told me yes. And then after I paid it I discovered we had two weeks to come up with another $125k. So, we put her house up for sale and bought her a condo to solve her problems. She was never thankful or appreciative and years later we found out that she told her good friend, Laura Kaynor, how her horrible children forced her out of her house and "took her house away from her". Sandy Kaynor was my college roommate and every time I attempted to connect with him when we both lived in New York, he was never available. I now know it was because his mother told him how horrible we were to our mother by forcing her out of her home. Sandy's younger brother even saw Bill years later in San Francisco and berated Bill for how horrible we were for what we did to our mom.

Chapter Twenty-One: You're Gonna Need Somebody

You're gonna need somebody on your bond, you're gonna need somebody on your bond
When it's late, round midnight, and old man death come slipping in the room
You're gonna need somebody on your bond
(Taj Mahal)

Back in 2001, before my company blew up and before my divorce was finalized, but after I did Behind Enemy Lines, my mother told me that she had developed an inoperable, cancerous, tumor. She and her doctor had decided together that any further treatment, whether it was chemo, or radiation, or whatever, would be a waste of time and likely would cause her significant suffering. She decided not to spend the time she had left sacrificing the quality of her life for nothing more than a slim possibility that she was prolonging her life. This was presented to me as a fait accompli after it had been discussed and decided. Atul Gawande, a doctor, wrote a book called Being Mortal about the reasons why doctors often don't give good advice and patients often don't make good choices in these situations, whether because of fear or self-delusion. Patients instead choose to suffer in vain, desperately trying to extend their lives or hold out for a cure, no matter how unlikely that is. She was not that person. Like the ascetic, hard-boiled New England WASP that she was, my mother decided in a dispassionate way that she wanted to live the rest of her life in her own home and preferably die there, and that was that. Her doctor put her on a morphine patch and sent her home and she never spent another day in a hospital. Once the morphine took hold, I don't believe she suffered at all. She used to say to me, "I know I'm dying, but I feel just fine", like she was a little bit puzzled about it and perhaps even pleasantly surprised. I used to say to her, "imagine how lucky you are to choose the manner of your death" and she seemed to agree. At the end of her life, she showed some of her better qualities. She was tough, completely matter of fact, unsentimental and more than willing to find the humor in the situation and laugh about it, determined to enjoy her life right up until the end, even as she declined to share any of her spare morphine patches with me. The remaining months that she lived were some of the best times we ever experienced together, and I believe that she was lucky to see her death approaching in a finite way and have some control over the manner of it.

I was running a profitable production company, I had lots of travel money and AAdvantage Miles, so it was relatively easy for me to fly across the country every two or three weeks to see my mom during the six months before she died and I thought it was a window of opportunity and I shouldn't let it go to waste.

So, there was a runway, and her death was at the end of it and it was relatively short. I was hopeful that the immediacy of it would spur some degree of meaningful relationship clarity but to be honest, it didn't change anything. Our relationship was never instinctive, or emotional, or physical in any way. It was intellectual. She had an unusual sense of humor, she was charismatic and different, iconoclastic, but it was like growing up with Auntie Mame, or Miss Jean Brodie, she was a character. Was it because I was adopted? I have no idea, but my adopted brother wasn't emotionally close to her either. I wanted to find some peace with it, but you don't change the trajectory of a relationship in six months. I struggled to be close to my mother and for a short time we didn't even speak, so the idea that somehow it was going to suddenly change was naive. I imagined, or perhaps just hoped, that she would show me something, that something would be revealed that would fill the void, that would answer some of my questions, but I didn't even know what my questions were. I know now, of course, now that I have some of the answers. It's like Jeopardy, they give you the answer and it's your job to figure out what the question is.

So, mom, did you ever wonder who my birth parents were?

So, mom, were you unable to give birth to your own children? Why?

Did you find it hard to love a baby you didn't give birth to?

Did you ever wonder if you did the right thing?

A thousand questions and I had no idea what they were, so we talked about other things.

My mom was unhappy about my divorce, frustrated with me and of course she didn't hide it. One night I was sitting with her and she was asking about my daughter, obsessing about the divorce going badly and suggesting that it must be hard for Laura to cope. I tried to reassure her, but she wouldn't let go of it. I kept trying to change the subject, until finally I said,

"Look, I'm not going to decide not to get divorced just because you're unhappy about it. I think it's gone a little too far for that, don't you think?"

She seemed not to hear me, and then suddenly I realized that she wasn't talking about Laura at all. She was talking about herself. Memory is an editing process, constantly shifting and rearranging the images and stories in the labyrinth of the mind, reinforcing the familiar, the appealing, the often-repeated stories and events and de-prioritizing the others, until some are almost forgotten, although never completely erased. As she lay there in the darkened room, time faded away and she returned to an earlier version of herself as a child, remembering her parents as they really were, revealing a part of her story she had never even hinted at, her focus subtly morphing from Laura to herself. She told me that her father was unfaithful to her mother, that he had a reputation in town for sleeping around, and that her mother had decided to leave him. She was a young girl caught in the middle of a grown-up situation, like the young boy in the Joseph Losey film *The Go-Between*, bouncing back and forth between her parents as the central drama of their marriage played out. My grandmother had tolerated the situation but finally, inevitably, fallen in love with another man. She had decided to leave my grandfather, which would have been a huge decision for a married woman at that time, scary and completely life changing. Apparently, she literally had her bags packed, ready to go, when, unexpectedly, the other man died. She stayed and their marriage was "saved". That was it, that was all I got and I couldn't get her to elaborate. It was just the skeleton of a story, full of gaps, and I was so surprised I didn't know what to say. I tried to get her to elaborate, but that was it. I couldn't figure out how to get the rest of it. It was like a door that suddenly opened for a moment in time and then slammed shut again.

I grew up with a narrative about my grandparents that came from my mother, who always talked about how long they were together, how they died within six months of each other, she always framed it as a love story, about their distinctive, iconoclastic, bohemian style and non-traditional life and suddenly in that dark room, in the last months of her life, she pulled back the curtain and showed me a completely different picture, a complicated story with her younger self as the central character, a child in the middle of an adult situation she couldn't have clearly understood.

Even though it came so late in the game, the knowledge made me question all the things I didn't know and now would never know, things she had kept to herself for all those years. I wondered if my dad had even heard that story, what it would have meant to know more of it. In some ways, it offered a window into her personality, her narcissistic behavior, her need to be the center of attention. It was easy to imagine how something like that could stunt a person's growth emotionally. I imagined that she had stopped maturing at that moment, that the person I had been dealing with all those years was really that child, stuck in that moment.

There is something I have noticed in the presence of an impending death, in my family and others, which is a form of behavior peculiar to these situations. For some reason when it gets around that somebody is entering their last days, people start acting weird. They can be family members, or just random people, friends, or neighbors, who for some reason decide that they have a role to play in the situation, that they have an agenda that needs to be served. They may start giving advice, unasked, but obtrusively, or being demanding and difficult, and sometimes, even, they steal - jewelry, or money if it's accessible, or they just take random things, artwork, or liquor, things that don't even have significant value. It's as if when death starts to come close societal norms start to crumble and people feel they can do things that they otherwise wouldn't do, as if they are owed something. In our case it took the form of people giving unsolicited advice about my mother's health, even when it was unasked and really none of their business. She certainly wasn't interested in listening to them, so they tended to get frustrated with me or my brother instead, as if we should be acting on their input, which was tiresome.

Often, I would show up from LA, walk into the house, and find people there, hanging out, having drinks, helping themselves to the booze, moving the furniture around, making themselves at home, having whispered conversations or dispensing unsolicited wisdom, and the weird thing was, my mother would be upstairs asleep. They were like vultures, endlessly patient, waiting for a carcass to dismember. It felt like me and my brother were interlopers, strangers in our own house, disrupting the plan. It was creepy and surreal.

There was a good side as well, though, which is that amazing people often do show up in life exactly when you need them, in a way that seems completely random and totally intentional at the same time. It was that way with Faye and Angela, two sisters from Jamaica, who showed up to work as caregivers for my mom and lived with her for the last few months of her life. I don't know who found them, but suddenly they were there, first Faye and then Angela, and once they showed up, everything seemed to fall into place. The hangers-on went away, things calmed down and nothing got past them. They were relentlessly protective of my mom and they would call the minute anything happened they thought I should know about. My niece wrote a poem about them called Two Angels after my mom died which I kind of dismissed at the time as immature and sentimental but now I'm inclined to think was absolutely on point.

They had a baby monitor so they could hear from the bedroom if my mom needed anything, and they used to sit downstairs with it on. My mom didn't have a TV, so many nights I sat by her bed and read poetry to her, mostly Robert Frost. I wish I had known Rilke at the time, I think his sensibility would have been more resonant for the moment, more focused on the inevitable, but Frost was okay and familiar. I remember coming downstairs one night after she fell asleep, and they were making fun of me about how sexy it was listening to me read poetry on the baby monitor.

She ended her life in a world of her own, that reached back through the generations to her great, great grandfather, who built the place just after the Revolutionary War, in a house full of history and of myths. When she married my father, it was literally falling down. Half of it had burned to the ground in 1942 and her dream was to restore it one day and that dream came true, thanks to my father. She gave tours, the house was in magazines, it became like a museum, a monument to her family, her ancestors, her place, the history and eventually a kind of mausoleum. She grew up surrounded by six hundred acres of forest that had once been farmland and the ghosts of her ancestors, whose presence she undeniably felt. She thought of herself as the last in her bloodline and although I didn't really understand at first why my brother and I were not really her descendants, of course it was true. In the end she died in the solipsistic universe of her history, preceded, a few years earlier, by my father, whose determination to drive nine miles each way to get the newspaper at the age of eighty-three was revealed to have been ill-advised when he died in his car.

Something I learned about that house, that land, from all that history, is that things are just things. The emotional value that we attach to them is purely a function of the lens through which we see them, it's like the gauzy diffusion filter on the lens in an old glamor photograph. Inanimate things have no intrinsic emotional content, no matter how old they are or how much history is attached to them. The Hummel figurine that somebody's grandmother loved that she got in Germany on her honeymoon, that she dusted carefully once a week and put back in the cabinet for fifty years, is just a little piece of china. When you see it on the table at a tag sale the only value it has is what someone is willing to pay for it, despite what you can imagine about its history, how special it was to someone. If you buy it, it has a new life, with a story of how you found it at a tag sale one Sunday and snatched it up and paid for it and brought it home. The old life is forgotten, it no longer exists. It has no intrinsic emotional life no matter how much that old lady loved it.

This home, this place, with all its history, all its significance, when my mother died it became just a big old grey house and the history that was attached to it is just whatever anyone remembers or writes down somewhere. I felt that loss of emotional resonance when my mother died, that the emotional attachment was evaporating, slipping through my fingers, leaving only my memories of good times I had with my kids there, or things that happened when I was a kid many years before. I thought it would feel good to take it on, to make it my own. I tried to keep it, to keep it going, but eventually I had to sell it and when the time came, I turned the key in my heart, closed the door on it and left it in the past.

My parents died within a few years of each other. In both cases, I would have to say I had mixed feelings. When my father died, it was the family accountant that called to give me the news. I still think it's weird that my mom didn't call. It felt transactional, like a formal notification of some kind. I was in my office in LA talking to some people when I got the call. It was not unexpected; my parents were in their eighties. In my mother's case, of course, there was a runway, so theoretically I had time to prepare myself. My life was in so much turmoil I'm not sure how much bandwidth I had for grief, or sadness, anyway, and if I'm honest, I didn't have a strong or sudden emotional reaction. I don't know if there is a way you're supposed to feel, or act, and my relationships with both my parents were complicated. In both cases there was no funeral, we had a party, a remembrance, a kind of service, and that was completely true to who they were, no more no less.

I think it's possible that regardless of how fortunate the circumstances of your adoption, at heart, you still feel abandoned in some unspoken, fundamental way, so when you lose your adopted parents, it feels like an experience that's being repeated. Once again you find yourself alone, torn out of context. In her book, *A Living Remedy*, Nicole Chung describes telling someone, "It's like being unadopted." There is a quality of familiarity that is deeply unsatisfying. It lacks the purity of grief, the satisfaction, the catharsis. I felt outside myself, as if I was watching everyone else having the experience, the poignant moment, playing my part until it was over. That was my experience and I'm guessing that Jonathan, my adopted brother, the person I lived through it all with, felt the same.

I think critical detachment is the miracle and the curse of being human. I have adopted two dogs in the last fifteen years or so and I believe that they both have loved me with all their hearts. They knew, in whatever way dogs have conscious thought, that where they came from was bad and they were happy with us and I want to say that canine self-awareness stops at that, but even dogs have separation anxiety. They didn't wonder how it happened, or how they came to be where they were, or ask themselves why we adopted them, or what was in it for us. They didn't wonder if maybe they would have been better off somewhere else, and they didn't wonder at how lucky they were either. Maybe they had a dim memory of another place, maybe the distinctive sound of a car engine, or a person's voice, would jog them back, Proustian, to their beginnings, or remind them of what it felt like to be lost, abandoned, terrified, bereft.

I was four months old when I was adopted. I discovered that in some papers I found in my parents' study after they died. I can't even imagine what it would be like if I had missed the first four months of my children's lives. It feels like it would have been a lifetime. I feel for people in the military who have that experience on a regular basis. I can't help but wonder where I processed those four months, where that memory is, because all I feel there is an abyss, and I see nothing.

Hank:

When mom finally died, I felt relief from the torment that living with her over time meant to Pete, Bill, and me. So, I was relieved for the three of us then and there but also relieved for our younger selves who had experienced the trauma and relieved for our future selves who would not have to accommodate her disruptive agony anymore. I also felt relief for her that she had been delivered from all that pain, torment, and agony herself.

I don't remember grief.

I have cried only once in a therapy session, but I don't think it was for losing her. I think it was about the pain and suffering all of us endured.

Bill:

My emotions when mom died were definitely relief and sadness at her life and the situation overall.

I remember spending those days going back and forth to the hospital and being with her in the hospital was torture. She was delirious and irritable all the time. It was just awful.

For the first couple of years, I used to have a recurring dream that she was still alive, and I'd wake up and not be sure if she was alive or dead. It was so weird and so disconcerting.

I wish I had more emotion to share around this but It's hard for me to remember how I felt. I used to go running in between the visits to the hospital and listen to Joe Henry tunes, I have such a vivid memory of that for some reason.

Pete:

When mom died, my feeling – honestly and unfortunately – was one of relief – both for her and me/us. Being with her was nothing but stress and pins and needles. She was a tortured soul and never happy so her dying, in a sense, was her release from a tortured life. The night she died – in the ICU – the nurse shared a powerful story. She was in the ICU for about 3 weeks, agitated and miserable the whole time. At like 3 am the nurse went into her room; she had taken all the tubes out and was sitting up in bed. The nurse said, "you seem very calm, are you ok?" ... my mom responded "yes, my husband is coming to get me" ... she passed a bit later.

Chapter Twenty-Two: Gulliver's Travels

"I think you are another of these desert-loving English. No Arab loves the desert. We love water and green trees. There is nothing in the desert."
Prince Faisal (from Lawrence of Arabia)

I had a dream once and, in my dream, I was lying on the ground and I couldn't move because I was tied down with little ropes connected to stakes in the ground and I was surrounded by a crowd of little people, and they were all talking and gesticulating and pointing at me, just like in Gulliver's Travels. But here's the strange part. The whole thing was taking place on the beach in Malibu, and the people were all studio executives and agents and managers and lawyers. So, let's be honest, I'm not sure if I really dreamed that but looking back, I do feel like I lived it.

Our movie was successful. We were sandwiched between Spy Game, Tony Scott's movie, and Ridley Scott's Black Hawk Down, so it was a competitive landscape, to say the least, but we won our first weekend and the studio was happy. It did well in theatres and in DVD release as well and we made it for a very reasonable budget, so it was good news all around.

What came next should have been fun and exciting but mostly it was a dispiriting trip through a minefield of mendacity that eventually ended for me alone at the sushi bar at Nobu in New York, down in Tribeca, drinking cold sake in the middle of the day. Here, try this. Sure.

I was friendly with a few studio executives and agents, and they encouraged me to give up the commercial business and produce movies full time. In hindsight maybe I should have thought more about it but, of course, it was exactly what I wanted to hear, there was confirmation bias weighing heavily in my decision-making process. Things were going south with my partners so the idea of walking away to do something I wanted to do anyway was appealing, if not seductive. In retrospect, I am amazed by how little thought I gave to the risks, considering what a major life decision it was, but I guess I had already decided to do it, so it was a foregone conclusion. I really didn't do the math. It was going to take several movies to get my producer fee up to the range where it would make sense and John was likely to only do a film every two or three years. Producers don't make any money until a film gets greenlit and into production, so I probably should have realized that I needed to concentrate on being friends with the studio to ensure a steady stream of work. I had no idea how long it would take to get a greenlight on our next movie and get it made, so if my hearing had been more acute, I should have been able to hear some of those little stakes being hammered into the ground already and felt those ropes starting to tie me down.

Andrea was friendly with a screenwriter she had met at my stepson's grade school. He and his wife were a writing team, and Paramount had just approved the final draft of their screenplay for The Italian Job, which was a remake of a caper film released in 1969 starring Michael Caine, primarily known for an exceptional car chase involving multiple Mini Coopers. The new Mini had just been released so it was an ideal tie-in for the studio. They had Mark Walberg and Edward Norton attached and they were looking for a director. Behind Enemy Lines had been released in the fall and on New Year's Day, 2001, the writer came over to see us with the approved final script. It was Andrea that made it happen; no agents or studio executives were involved. I read it and immediately gave it to John with my recommendation that we do it. Shortly after, we had lunch at Drago with the writers, and we told them we were in. John and I had dinner with Donald DeLine, the producer who had developed it at Paramount and we all got along, so it looked to me like it was going to be our next project. I liked the original film, and I thought Mark Wahlberg and Edward Norton were great choices for the story, so I was excited about it. John got on the phone with Sherry Lansing, who was running Paramount at that time, and she said she was ready to give it a greenlight. It felt magical the way the pieces were falling into place, like it was meant to be.

This is when I learned about something called "options".

It was common practice at the time for studios to require new talent, both directors and actors, to commit to giving the studio three pictures, something that is often erroneously referred to as a "three picture deal". In fact, those pictures are "optional pictures", which means they are optional for the studio, but not for you; you give them to the studio in exchange for getting your first picture. You commit to doing two more pictures for them, whenever they choose to exercise the option, and the obligation lasts as long as it takes them to collect on it. Your agents and lawyers tell you to agree to it and because you are new to the game, you go along with it because you don't know any better. When I read our contracts for Behind Enemy Lines, I questioned the options clause, but the agents and lawyers didn't want to hear it, it was non-negotiable, "everybody does it." At that time, there were only half a dozen studios in Hollywood and since they all play by the same rules, the agents and lawyers have a lot more invested in their relationships with the studio than they do in protecting you, so the deck is stacked against you. These people are basically all in the same club so people who are willing to rock the boat are few and far between. I have worked with quite a few lawyers in my career, and I have never met a group of lawyers as averse to conflict and as oblivious to legal ethics or conflict of interest as Hollywood lawyers. The few who stand up to the studios, like Bert Fields, or Mike Adler, are legendary, and there's a good reason for that, there are so few of them.

I accepted the fact that we had agreed to options in our deal with the studio because the agents said it wouldn't be a problem. Don't worry about it, everybody does it, is the way the agents sell it to you, even though it is clearly not in your best interest. Next thing I knew we were in a meeting with the heads of the studio, the first and only time that ever happened, and they were saying they wanted us to make Flight of the Phoenix. They were "exercising their option" and they weren't going to let us do The Italian Job at Paramount, even though Paramount was willing to give them half the movie. I remember noticing there were no agents or lawyers in the room to speak for us, it was just the two of us and these two guys. I pointed out that Paramount was greenlighting the movie and making us pay or play and that just seemed to make them angry, but they agreed to release some money so we could start prepping Flight of the Phoenix while the script was being written. That was the kind of leverage I was used to exercising in the commercial business, but I could tell they weren't used to being addressed that way and they didn't like being put on the spot. Italian Job was a go movie, whereas Flight of the Phoenix didn't even have an approved script or a schedule. They had a deal with Scott Frank to write the script, which was great, he's a great writer, but it can take a long time to get to an approved script on a major studio film, even with a writer as good as Scott Frank attached to it and sometimes, you never get there. As it turned out we could have easily done The Italian Job and been in post-production long before there was a final approved script on Flight of the Phoenix, but the decision was being driven by the egos in the room and egos often count for a lot more in Hollywood than logic or ethics.

Sherry Lansing was furious. John took the call from her in my car, and I could distinctly hear her screaming at him, even though it really wasn't our fault. Our agents and lawyers were useless, exactly when we needed them to be useful. Andrea, who was my girlfriend at the time, had created this opportunity for us with no help from anybody. It was a good script. F. Gary Gray ended up directing it and it turned out pretty well. It would have solved a lot of problems for me to jump right on another go movie and we would have had some real momentum, but the Fox executives felt like they had discovered John and they just didn't feel like letting him make a movie at another studio; the bottom line was they had the power to bully us into submission. It felt like indentured servitude in fancy clothes, pointless and arbitrary, and that was just the beginning.

"At the end of the day, these people forgive themselves everything" John said.

The Italian Job was released in May of 2003; Flight of the Phoenix was released a full year and a half later, in December of 2004. Because of what was said in the meeting the studio had to prove they were serious about Flight of the Phoenix, so they released production money for scouting and prep and sent us off to travel around the world. The movie was about the crew from a decommissioned oil rig whose plane gets caught in a dust storm and crashes in the Gobi Desert. Therefore, not surprisingly, it became our job to talk to people who knew things about airplanes and dust storms and oil rigs and deserts. We flew something like 25,000 miles in a little less than a month, from California to Paris to Casablanca to London to Johannesburg to Namibia to Cape Town, and then to Beijing, and back to California. At some point in a trip like that, everyone gets to the point where they want to kill each other, and this one was no exception.

I had noticed that John tended to lose his temper at times, but I considered that standard director behavior, and I took it in stride, figuring it was just the stress of the project and the pressure he felt to get the movie made. However, as the trip went on, I started to notice that even when a solution was found for whatever problem he had, he was never satisfied; he seemed to want to hold on to his anger. Once I noticed that, it was hard to "unsee" it, it was a pattern that repeated itself, his anger was performative, and that was something I hadn't dealt with before, and it made me wonder about our relationship. As a producer, part of my job was staying calm and dealing with problems as they presented themselves, but this felt pointless to me, and the possibility that as his producer I was facing a future of this worried me; I had sacrificed a lot and taken a lot of risks to go down this road with him and I wasn't sure this was a pattern I could live with. But I stayed on the project anyway.

I love the desert. It's vast, like the ocean, unchanging, then suddenly changeable. Dust storm or hurricane, the scale and fury are the same, transformative, you wake up the next day, and the landscape is completely changed. The desert is quiet and calm, yet dangerous, still, like a predator waiting to strike, quiet, indifferent. Like the ocean it makes you feel a certain way, not wet, of course, but dry in the same tactile way, something you feel all over your body. It doesn't care about you. And our movie was all about the desert.

There are four or five different kinds of deserts on the planet, depending on how you classify them, ranging from subtropical, to coastal, semiarid (meaning cold in winter), polar, and so on. Interestingly, the two Polar Deserts, Arctic and Antarctic, are the two largest deserts in the world, both larger than the Sahara, but nobody thinks of them as deserts. We needed an unbroken landscape of sand dunes, as far as the eye could see, which narrowed the field considerably, and it needed to be a place which was relatively safe and accessible as well, which narrowed the field even more. John wanted to shoot in the Gobi, since that was where the story was set, but that required approval from the Chinese government and the chances of that were slim. It would have been extremely difficult to mount the production in Mongolia, but John didn't care about that, so production was quietly rooting for the Chinese government to turn us down. We focused our efforts on Morocco and Namibia while we waited to see if there was any chance we could get permission to even scout the Gobi, let alone shoot there.

Most Americans think of the desert, if they think of it at all, as a place to either stick an oil well, dig a mine of some kind, or roar around in a four wheeled vehicle carving up the landscape, all of which are extremely destructive from an environmental point of view. They look at the desert and see nothing. The desert is an ocean, vast, and alive with all sorts of life that is not immediately visible to the naked eye, a place that is beautiful and perilous, where one mistake, one miscalculation, can easily become fatal. I find it relaxing in its inevitability, and I think it's tragic that people look at it and miss the life that it contains.

If you have ever been to White Sands, in New Mexico, or the Sahara, or you have seen the Sonoran Desert in the spring after a little bit of winter rain, or Joshua Tree, you know the desert can be one of the most surprising and beautiful places in the world. The Namib Desert is the oldest desert in the world and one of the most beautiful.

We went to the Sahara first and the sand dunes there are astonishing when you experience them up close, much larger than you expect, and so much more interesting in their form, so exact, mathematical in their perfection, with lines perfect as a knife edge, but organic at the same time, since they are shaped by wind. The dunes have geography, they are an identifiable landscape and many of them have names, which was a surprise to me. I think this is one of the reasons why sandstorms are so fearsome, because they are not only destructive to anything living, but they can also completely alter the landscape, like a tornado or a hurricane.

We flew out into the desert in a Moroccan Army helicopter and landed in a small flat plain between several large dunes, not far from a large Bedouin tent, which was black and showed no signs of life at any time while we were there. It may have been occupied but I suspect that Bedouins are not all that interested in socializing with tourists or film crews. I was struck by how yellow the dunes were and how deep the depressions between them and how hard it is to make any progress walking in the sand, which makes it very easy to understand the value of a camel.

After the scout we stopped at an Inn at the edge of the desert, which was basically a beautiful swimming pool and a bunch of huge tents. I wish I could remember the name of it or even exactly where it was. We drove away from the sand dunes into a flat plain of hardscrabble gravelly desert and then suddenly, there was this beautiful place, like an oasis. I dream about spending time there, in the desert, doing nothing, being nowhere, in the heat of the sun in the daytime, taking camel trips into the dunes in the cool of night, diving into the blue of that swimming pool, eating food that does not require utensils made of stainless steel. I wanted to just stay there and forget about the movie and all the rest of the drama - my career, my partners, the movie business, the commercial production business, all of it. I wanted to just think of nothing for a while.

The Namib Desert is like a giant sea of sand dunes, some of them close to 1000 feet high and it is a coastal desert, which means that the desert literally runs right into the sea. Because of the dangerous waters it is called the Skeleton Coast and there are ships buried in the desert, eerie shipwrecks that have been swallowed up by the sand. The dunes are an amazing orange color, different from any sand I have seen anywhere else and there are black skeletons of dead trees sticking up out of the ground. I have heard stories from people of seeing lions in the surf, grabbing fish from the water, like bears in a stream in Alaska. It is a strange and beautiful place, relatively unspoiled and surprisingly accessible and close to production support from South Africa. When we got there, we knew it was the place.

It's hard to travel around the world and it's particularly hard to travel in Africa, without being conscious of the vestiges of colonialism, like crop circles which are so graphic when seen from above but difficult to see clearly up close. The world is shaped by hundreds of years of colonialism and exploitation, which is obvious in varying degrees, but there are some places where it is inescapable, like Africa and Central America and the Caribbean. Southern Africa has a particularly tragic history, and Namibia is part of it, having been exploited and carved up by the Germans and Afrikaners, who managed to wipe out most of the indigenous people, particularly the Herero, in a series of wars and tribal conflicts.

Today Namibia is a beautiful and peaceful place. There are even vacation homes on the coast, but it's hard to be completely oblivious to the history, just as it is in other places that have been raped and savaged by colonialism.

It was clear to us that Namibia was the best place to shoot the movie, and the only challenge was to get the studio on board, since they were not familiar with it and kept referring to it as "Nambia" and asking where it was and if there was terrorism there.

Even though we had our location we had to go on to China, as John was holding out for the Gobi, no matter how unrealistic it was. As a result, we spent three or four days hanging around in a hotel in Beijing, waiting for approval from the government to scout the Gobi, which was not forthcoming. I hadn't been in China since 1997, right after Deng died, and I was stunned by how much it had changed in five years, from a grey monolithic metropolis into an international city full of nightlife and restaurants and excitement. There were other film crews in the bar at night, and it felt alive and awake. I wonder if it's still like that or if that was a brief moment in time.

Every night we would meet in the bar at the hotel so that John could torture our line producer and her Chinese production contact about the approval for Mongolia, acting like they were failing to come through, which of course was patently unfair, and losing his temper, pointlessly, since we all knew it wasn't going to happen. Predictably, it didn't.

Eventually, we convinced John it was time to go back to LA and sell Namibia to the studio. They bought into it, although for some reason they never learned how to pronounce it, or figured out what time zone it was in. Physical production got busy putting the budget together, and it felt like we were in production, like it was a go movie, but we had spent too much time in the desert and what we were seeing was a mirage.

Chapter Twenty-Three – Whatever You Do, Don't Turn a Go Movie into a Development Deal

I'm only happy when it rains
I'm only happy when it's complicated
I know you don't appreciate it
I'm only happy when it rains
Garbage (1995)

It was never a go movie; it was a development deal masquerading as a go movie. Once we got back to LA it stopped being about prepping a movie and turned back into trying to get a script the studio was prepared to greenlight, a Sisyphean task, or in plain language, something that makes you want to shoot yourself in the head. The studio started to choke off the money supply, which is something they do to force you to give them what they want. The group of people who were working on the movie got really small. The only thing the studio was willing to spend money on was writers and we went through a few of those, all good ones, and none of them seemed to be able to deliver the story the studio wanted. In the absence of a strong creative point of view the default on a big studio movie when development is stalled is to throw money at a new writer and hope for magic. Months passed and more months, but no magic. John would spend a few weeks in LA, have a bunch of meetings and then go back to Ireland and hide. He wouldn't even pay attention to projects that we had set up in development, so he would have meetings and promise to do things and then leave me to take the phone calls and try to explain why nothing was happening.

While we struggled along with our feet in quicksand trying to get an approved script, other opportunities came and went. The movie was moving at a snail's pace. We lost our production designer to a Christopher Nolan Batman movie.

Agents and other producers would call me with projects and tell me the studio was putting our movie in turnaround. I had an opportunity to write a script on a project we were attached to, the studio was on board, but John vetoed it, out of some vague suspicion or jealousy I never understood. I had other projects I wanted to set up, but the studio was indifferent. Finally, there was a project with Robert Redford. We had two meetings with him. The first meeting he walked into the room, and I remember thinking, Holy shit, it's Robert Redford. I was legitimately starstruck. Better yet it was life-affirming to have him turn out to be exactly as cool as I had always thought he would be. The script was good, and it felt like we were getting a shot at making up for the Italian Job disaster. We still didn't have an approved script or a greenlight on Phoenix and once again here was a project we really wanted to do.

I was frustrated after a year or more of getting nowhere. I wasn't making money, and I wasn't having fun either, so I figured this time around, rather than just give up a good project and go quietly, we should make a fuss and maybe the outcome would be different. We still had time to make another movie. I thought John and I were on the same page. I felt like we could push back, and I thought our agents would help. It turned out that all three assumptions were laughably naïve. The studio threatened that if we did the Redford movie, they would give Phoenix to another director. I thought they were bluffing, and I said so, but it turned out that I was the guy with no picture cards in his hand.

It was around June of 2003, and I was in New York with Andrea. We were staying at the Mercer Hotel, which at that time was our favorite hotel, still affordable enough that you didn't have to rob a bank to pay for it. We had been at an industry event the night before where I had received a lifetime achievement award from the commercial industry trade association, which was exciting, and it was the first time we had been to an industry event as a couple so the whole thing was a real high point for us and we had seen a lot of old friends from the commercial production industry as well. Andrea was somewhere at a meeting, and I was at the hotel. The studio, amid all the drama, had finally decided to greenlight Flight of the Phoenix and signed off on the budget, which was sudden and a little surprising. My assistant gave me a heads up that John was going over to the studio for a meeting, which I assumed was a handshake and a pep talk about starting production. I remember it occurred to me that it was a bit strange that this had suddenly happened while I was out of town, but I didn't have time to think it through and I was still feeling the buzz from receiving the award the night before and all the positive feedback we had gotten from the industry friends we had seen. My cell phone rang, and I saw it was the assistant to Hutch Parker, the Head of Production at Fox. When I answered, she immediately put me through to him, and literally, without preamble, the first thing he said was they were taking me off the movie, they didn't want me to go on location in Namibia. My first thought was, comically, wow, why would they do that?

"It's just too difficult to get him to do what we want with you in the way" he said, "I'm protecting your credit and your fee, but we're firing you off the movie."

I remember thinking *isn't it the producer's job to protect the movie? Why would you want to work with a director who does everything you tell him to do, where's the creative integrity in that?* Years of fighting with agencies and clients over creative, protecting the director's vision, flashed through my mind and I thought, this is how bad movies get made, because you guys can do stuff like this and get away with it.

It turned out that making a fuss about the Redford project was the end of a road, the final excuse they needed to get me out of the way, not the solution to a problem, or fighting for an opportunity. John failed to back me up, which was all the permission they needed. Now they had John where they wanted, with no buffer, taking instructions from them and rather than fight it, he embraced it. They ended up with a flop on their hands, but studios are used to that, it's part of their business model, like private equity charging all the failures to the one unicorn and calling it a business model. As for John, I think the movies he's made since speak for themselves.

I went over to Nobu, in Tribeca, and sat at the sushi bar by myself. Michael Wimer, our agent at CAA, called and tried to act concerned but it was clear that he was just checking a box. He was in the meeting, he obviously knew about the whole plan in advance, so his first concern was the agency, particularly the agency's relationship with the studio, his own relationship with the studio, and then John's relationship with the studio; my situation wasn't even on the radar. Whatever it meant for me to be fired off the movie was irrelevant, whether I was his client or not. Several senior people at the studio, including the head of physical production, went out of their way to let me know they didn't have a problem with me, and they weren't involved in kicking me off the movie, which was nice, but also irrelevant.

John didn't call me. My experience when I got back to LA was surreal. John was grumpy and resentful, as if I had let him down, as if I had it coming. He even brought out a small dose of the performative anger, but when I called him on it, he seemed to get confused and unable to explain himself. He said he was going to call the studio and demand they put me back on the movie; I took that as bluster and posturing, which it was. His indignation petered out very quickly, and he and the production crew just went on preparing to leave for Namibia. I kept showing up at the office; the story was that I would stay in LA and work on other projects we had in development. I went along with it, as the studio was still paying our expenses under our production deal, and frankly, I didn't know what else to do and I figured maybe I had some time to get another project going. People say that you're not a producer until you've been fired off a movie for the first time, but it was the first time in my career I had ever been fired from anything, and I was completely unprepared.

They say in golf that you should play the course one shot at a time, and I tried to apply that rule to my situation. You can succeed again, and you can fail again, but you can't un-fail. No matter how many birdies you have, the bogey stays on the scorecard. The antidote for failure is not success, it's acceptance. To achieve it you have to stop and think and gain perspective. I've read all the self-help stuff about failing fast, but it's wrong. You don't fail fast, that's giving up, which is not at all the same. When you really fail, you give everything you have to something you care about, something you believe in and hold out until you run out of options and you are forced to give up, and then you give up. Then you fold up your tent, move on, and accept that whatever it is, no matter how great, it isn't going to happen. When you experience that, you're entitled to the wisdom that comes with it, but still, it often doesn't come right away and it's hard to accept. I put everything I had into being a movie producer and I had way too much attached to the outcome, and it was all pulled out from under me in a heartbeat.

My life was like a favorite sweater. There was a lot to love about it but I also felt like it was falling apart. I kept pulling on the loose threads, fussing with them, trying to fix it one thread at a time, but after a while, I realized that I wasn't fixing it, I was just pulling it apart. The more I tried, the less it worked, until the whole thing, career, partnerships, marriage, things that I had spent years building, were all pulled apart. I knew there were consequences, and I was prepared for that, but here's something I learned. It's one thing to know that something isn't working and have the courage to change it. It's another thing entirely to figure out how to start over. Starting over is hard.

The beauty of it, though, was that Andrea was all in. She believed in me, and she believed we would get through it and sometimes one person that believes in you is enough.

Chapter Twenty-Four: A Desperate Cry for Help? Really?

Everybody has a plan until they get hit in the face.
(Iron Mike Tyson)

In the early 2000's, we were living in the shadow of 9/11, the country was nervous and in shock. Bush Jr. was president, and we were working ourselves up to the invasion of Iraq. I had experienced a lot of change, and I was trying to figure out where to go next, particularly with my career. Both my parents had died, I was divorced, I had split with my partners, I had produced my second movie, finished my production deal with the studio and my director partnership was over. It was clear to me that I didn't have a future as a studio producer. It felt like being an account executive at an ad agency - you spend your time keeping the client happy and they're paying, so they get to be right almost all the time, even when they're wrong. I was pretty sure I hadn't walked away from a successful career in the advertising industry to do that job. I wanted to produce projects of my own, to pursue my own ideas, but the reality of it was I was naïve about the real job of a producer, which is to put enough pieces in place that everybody wants so that eventually they make your movie, they can't help themselves. It's very rare that the material gets a movie made, it's all the attachments that make the deal, it's the context that matters.

So, I chose a path which was essentially delusional, which was to write a few screenplays and jump start my own projects. I read Syd Field, and I took Robert McKee's class a few times. I read a bunch of books and as a producer I had already read a lot of screenplays and sat through a lot of script meetings. At one point the studio had even agreed to let me do a pass on a project we had set up there. The project was stalled and none of the writers were getting it, and I had a take everyone liked, so they decided to let me take a pass at writing the script. I figured maybe I could get them to do it again. I got the idea originally from a friend of mine who was a successful screenwriter. I had a book I was trying to get set up and I was trying to get him to write it, so I could go back to the studio with him attached to it and he said, "why don't you just write a draft yourself and use that to set it up, and then they can hire me to re-write it?" I'm sure he was just being nice, trying to say no and stay friends, but I thought, right, why not? I can just write a producer pass and that will get the ball rolling. I had almost done it once already, so I thought I could probably do it again.

I did write the script, but it didn't jumpstart anything. It was, however, one of the most satisfying things I had done in years, and it got me excited about the idea that I could do the kind of interesting movies I had wanted to do all along. I wrote several scripts after that, including a script about a journalist in Baghdad during the invasion of lraq, which I wrote in the moment, while it was happening. There was a universe of like-minded people who had researched and read what the arms inspectors in Baghdad were saying, which was that there were no WMD's in Iraq, and there was no threat to American security at all, but the country was really aligning behind Bush, and I felt like we were in a distinct minority. I remember noticing all the Support Our Troops signs sprouting up around our neighborhood in Santa Monica and realizing that the facts were no longer important, the country had decided it was time to start a war in the Middle East, that there was some sort of strategic advantage in that, and people were prepared to buy into whatever lame justification the Bush administration came up with. I finished my script and revised it and rewrote it several times, but I think it could have been Chinatown, and it still wasn't going to get made.

In the end, I had made some friends and worked with some talented people in Hollywood, but no one was going to stick their neck out to do a project with me. I had nothing they wanted. I had ideas, but studios don't buy ideas, they buy names with ideas attached to them. A bad idea with a name attached to it will outsell a great idea on its own in Hollywood 100 % of the time.

I enjoyed writing screenplays, and I was working on the kind of projects that interested me, so for a while I convinced myself I could make it work, that it was a path to somewhere. I had a lot of interesting meetings with agents and managers and studio executives, drinking bottled water and listening to encouraging vagueness. Hollywood is a kind of desert, but you'll never die of dehydration there. Lots of encouraging and complementary things were said, lots of good coverage was written, but what I finally came to understand was that if you're not hearing it directly from a Russell, or a Denzel, or a Leo, whoever it is whose name is being thrown around, or if you don't have somebody attached with a big deal somewhere, it means exactly nothing.

The bottom line is I don't know how close I came to success with my projects; you never know that unless you succeed. In the end I spent several years and a lot of money supporting my writing habit, trying to get my projects made, while I was supporting my kids, my future step-kids, paying lawyers, paying LA private school tuitions, and so on and so on, and there were more than a few people who let me know that the likelihood the path I was on would lead to success was very small.

I like to think of it now as a gift I gave myself, and in some way, it restored my sanity, but one day, I woke up and thought, this is a hobby, not a career, and I realized I had people and a life to support, and this just wasn't getting it done. Maybe that realization should have come a few years earlier before the price tag got so high, but if you have ever tried to achieve anything difficult, anything that you can't be sure of succeeding at, one thing you learn is that you never know how close you are to either success or failure and there is an endless supply of stories, advice, anecdotes, Ted Talks, valuable insights or just plain foolishness that support any decision or choice you face, whether to call it and move on, or hang on because your dream is right around the next corner. Stories like Matt Leblanc having $11 in the bank when he got the part on Friends and Silvester Stallone having $104 in the bank when he sold the Rocky script and Chrissy Metz having .81 cents in the bank when she got the part on This is Us, actors who had no money and no prospects at the moment they were offered the role that defined their careers. Or writers working at Starbucks when they sold their script and so on, including the inescapable Van Gogh never sold a painting in his life, the ultimate cliché that people never stop repeating.

If I had approached the opportunity to do movies as just a way to change careers and make more money I think it would have worked out, but my lack of detachment caused me to make some bad decisions and draw attention to myself in ways that made me a target and the people I met on the studio side of the business were happy to punish me for my arrogance. I had a dream of achieving something in the movie business, of changing my life, of traveling in a different circle, and for a while I achieved it. I achieved some success at something that not very many people get to do, and it was exciting, but my responsibilities caught up with me and they took precedence over my movie career.

The truth of that came to me in a strange way. Predictably I got into a writer's group with a bunch of other unsuccessful, or at least aspirational, screenwriters. Writers' groups are a phenomenon that are about as common in LA as a Tupperware party in Stepford, kind of a cross between a support group and a wake. Half of the people in the group are sure they are about to be successful, and half are sure they are going to be waiting tables for life, and who makes up each group changes from week to week. Every week you show up with a piece of writing you're prepared to share; it could be part of a script you're working on, or a treatment, it can be pretty much anything, but you must read some of it out loud and listen to everybody's feedback.

Earlier in the week I had been driving around in my car, thinking about running out of things, like time and money, thinking that I had made some career choices that weren't working out, feeling like the engineer in an old silent movie on the train that is steaming along and around the corner, it's going to run out of track. I had no idea what that was going to look like, which was really the worst part of the experience. I have always suspected that considering the state of the world, the basic randomness of existence, anyone who doesn't think about suicide, at least in an intellectual or conceptual fashion, once a week is a damn fool, so I was wondering, academically, what it would take. If it's a relief to just step off the train, if maybe you can do it and somehow nobody would notice, speculating about what kind of magic it would take for everybody to just continue with their lives without noticing that you had disappeared from the scene.

When you live in LA you spend a lot of time in your car and you think a lot of weird thoughts, everyone does. This is why you see people sitting in their cars crying, laughing, yelling, arguing, practicing foreign languages, putting on their makeup, tweezing their chin hairs (gross) and no one finds it strange. So I built a story around it, about a guy who realizes, randomly, that he is in a place in his life where everyone that he cares about is reasonably well taken care of and happy, that no one is depending on him for their survival, or even their happiness, and that this situation is a form of stasis, which is unlikely to occur again in his life. He sees that it is like a door that will only be open for a short time, if he only has the guts to just walk through it. At the point where the story starts, he's just trying to figure out a preferred method. Hanging himself in the garage? Pills in the bathtub at the Beverly Wilshire?

So, I showed up at the writers' group and read the story.

When I finished, I looked around the room and realized immediately from the concern on people's faces that I had made a mistake. I spent the next fifteen minutes attempting to reassure everyone that it wasn't a cry for help, that I wasn't trying to get their attention. I felt like I had done something thoughtless, or at least careless, that these were nice people, and I had abused their kindness. When it was time to leave, I think that some of them were still a little unsure whether they should let me go, or whether some sort of intervention was called for. In truth, what had happened was that I had asked myself a question and answered it. I made a quick journey into existentialism and came out the other side. What I discovered was that no matter how bad things looked, there was no acceptable way to give up on the people in my life, that it would be inexcusable, that it was offensive to even think about it and that was the end of that line of philosophical exploration. Also, I learned that the whole thought process was a waste of time. I did learn something useful though, which is that even when good things happen, when you get things you want, or achieve things that really matter to you, it doesn't necessarily make everything else that is going on in your life easier. In fact, it often makes everything much harder.

So, around this time I was talking to divorce lawyers a lot, both mine and the other side, and they were all saying *hey buddy you better go back to making money in the commercial production business because the court isn't going to buy this career change story and you are going to be paying a lot of alimony and child support.* And they were right, there may be a money tree in Hollywood, but it was not bearing fruit for me and there was a whole lot more going out than coming in. I felt like my best move was to go back to the industry where I had had my greatest financial success. If my original plan to keep my production company and broaden the focus into doing films at the same time had worked out, circumstances would have been different, but the split with my partners had killed that option and I didn't have a platform, so I had to start over again. I had just enough money and enough of a reputation, and just enough friends, that I was able to start a new production company. I had some interesting young directors and a sales rep I partnered with in New York. Andrea had taken a few years off to look after her special needs daughter and she came back to work with me, so it was starting to work out, things were starting to get interesting. We had a nice little company, we did a few interesting jobs and that's when the financial crisis hit, in 2008. If we had had a little more time and a few more projects under our belt, we might have squeaked through, but we just didn't have the wherewithal to survive it. So, Andrea and I went from having a lovely wedding in Mexico in 2007, with our family, our kids, and a few close friends, looking forward to building our life together, to facing, a few short years later, a mountain of debt.

To be honest, I think there were more than a few people who were happy to see us struggle. When you have a big profile, and you are successful and well known in an industry and people feel like you turned your back and walked away from it, or them, my experience is they hold it against you, whether they admit it or not. Some just turn their backs on you because they can, because they no longer feel like they have something to gain from knowing you, and some are actively rooting for you to have the comeuppance they think you richly deserve. And finally, our relationship had caused some gossip in the industry when we first got together, so there were a few people that had an attitude about that as well. I discovered that people were happy to have a meeting or a lunch with me to pick my brain, to get some free advice, but it turned out to be worth exactly nothing to me in dollars and cents. My good friends at Radical Media made me a really good offer to come in with them, but I couldn't accept it because it had to be in New York, and I couldn't leave my kids and move all the way across the country after getting divorced from their mother, especially after I had made them all move to LA a few years earlier, so that one great opportunity was out of my reach.

I have generally found it to be simpler to have integrity in business. I'm not saying I'm a better person, it just makes the decision-making process a lot simpler because you can decide not to do things you don't think are right without taking expediency too much into the equation. Unfortunately, though, necessity will force you do things you don't want to do, and I found myself working with, or for, a series of people that I really didn't respect. We didn't see eye to eye and I'm not good at disguising my feelings when I'm not down with whatever is going on. I don't apologize for it, I had a family to support, and I needed the money, but it hurt my reputation, and it made me crazy. Predictably, again, those relationships did not last, and I felt tarnished by them.

For the first time in my life, I was really worried about money, because ours was running out and that is something that demands your attention. Like a baby crying in the other room, it's hard to ignore. According to Dave Chappelle, the fear of poverty is a treadmill, and he is right about that. I know that being poor and being broke are not at all the same thing, but still, the fear and the constant stress were exhausting. With the possible exception of Las Vegas, LA has more people driving around in fancy cars they can't afford, living in mansions they can't afford, going out to extravagant dinners in fancy restaurants they can't afford, sending their kids to expensive private schools they can't afford, buying jewelry they can't afford, flashing Rolex watches they can't afford, shopping in designer boutiques they can't afford, than any other city I know of. On some level, based on my personal experience, most of these people are living with a constant nagging fear that it's all going to end somewhere that isn't going to be good and they don't really know what that looks like, but they are afraid of it, and they are pretty sure that whatever it is, they have it coming. Because the thing is, no one knows how much is enough and on some level we probably all have it coming in one way or another.

It is tempting to assign higher intention to the events that happen in our lives, to imagine that there is a higher power that is acting on us, fulfilling our dreams, or visiting retribution on us for our sins, good karma, bad karma, schadenfreude. We've certainly seen enough athletes thanking the Lord as if they are certain that he / she has taken a personal interest in their success, that winning that championship is a direct result of their personal relationship with the almighty. But I ask myself, would a deity really have the time and patience to get personally involved in the outcome of a sports event? I give myself credit for the things I've done right and I fully accept responsibility for the mistakes I've made and the things I've done wrong, but I try not to take too much credit, or accept too much blame either way, because at that point, it's your ego and then you're not thinking straight. There were decisions and consequences, actions and reactions, outcomes and hindsight; There was good and bad luck and I suspect that's it, the universe gives and it takes away. I'm not inclined to assign intention, to ask myself why something did or did not happen. At this point in my life, I have to answer only one question, which is simple.

Was there something I should have done differently and more importantly, could I have done it differently? Once I have dealt with that, I'm good, I'm not crying in my car, or begging forgiveness, or cursing my fate.

Andrea and I fell in love. It was an all-consuming passion, and it changed our lives. There was no turning away from it, or denying it, and I can't imagine who I would be or what my life would look like if we were not together. It was complicated and challenging, and our children were compelled to come on the journey which was not always easy for them, or us, but there was no other way. They showed a lot of character, and I think in a way, we're better for it, or at least more resilient, tougher, more empathetic.

We were at couples therapy one day, something we started because our relationship began with so many challenges, we figured why not just try to get it right from the start instead of waiting for it to get complicated and trying to untangle it. I was going through a litany of all the scary things that might happen if we went broke, for real, something which can test a relationship more than almost anything else. Our therapist, who was a pretty insightful person, kind of let me wear myself out reciting the list and when I stopped to take a breath, she said, "Yes, all of those things could happen" and she paused and I thought okay......and then she finished the sentence, "but not today".

And we did go broke, in classic LA fashion, and I learned that even that was something we could survive. I have a picture in my mind that kind of symbolizes the whole experience. The scene is the two of us pulling up in our Lexus at one of those dealers that buys gold and silver and pulling some silver platters out of the back of the car - Andrea's grandmother's sterling flatware, her mother's sterling brazier that she got as a wedding gift and a bunch of other what-not to sell for cash so we could go to Vicente Foods in Brentwood to buy groceries to make dinner for the family, who were theoretically at home doing homework, but were most likely playing World of Warcraft. The boys were anyway, and their sister was watching TV, all of them blissfully unaware of what was going on. I sold my guitars and Andrea sold some of her jewelry, but not her engagement ring, which somehow, we had the sense to know would be a mistake. I remember calling Peter Norman, the jeweler who made her rings for us, and he said, "you don't want to do that" and he was right. That would have been hard to forget, so I'm thankful to him for that.

Andrea figured out, before it was a thing, before Poshmark, that designer labels have resale value, and she figured out where to go and what to do to turn those expensive clothes into cash. She got by for a year on free samples of the beauty products she was used to buying and I sold my vintage Rolex, which was painful because it was a gift from my father-in-law. But in the end, it was her attitude and devotion to our life together that got us through it and our determination not to let anyone down, especially not each other or our family.

It was a bit of a horror show, and we really couldn't share it with anyone, because in LA, people tend to behave as if financial problems are contagious, like a virus or a rash, or bedbugs, and they want to avoid you, for fear of catching it; and what they are most afraid of is that you will ask for help. There was an unexpected benefit, though, because it brought us closer. There was a "you and me against the world" quality to it. We were always clear we were in it together; we didn't blame each other and there was comfort in that. We had devoted all of ourselves to each other and our blended family and, in some ways, we had paid a high price for it, so there was no way we were going to allow ourselves to be defeated.

Every night, no matter what happened, when we got into bed, Andrea would say *this is the best part of the day* and every morning she would wake up happy. It makes it so much easier to believe in yourself when you're with someone like that, and if that's not love, I don't know what is.

In the end, we started our own consulting business and at one point, in a perfect intersection of the sublime and the ridiculous, we found out we had closed a new client, which was great news, but we had to fly half way across the country to kick off the project and we only had enough cash in our bank account to buy one-way tickets and our credit cards were maxed out. We couldn't rent a car because Budget doesn't accept debit cards unless you can show them your return ticket and we didn't have one. We had to take Ubers the whole time we were there, and I had to borrow money from my cousin so that we could buy our tickets home at the end of the week. We knew the fees from the client were coming but large corporations don't always pay so fast, and in the moment, it was stressful in the extreme.

Even while it was happening, though, it was hard not to appreciate the absurdity of it.

It was a dark time, but it was also exciting and great in a lot of ways. Andrea was my lifeline and her love and belief in us carried me through the times when otherwise, frankly, I might have given up, and there were a few people, notably my cousin, Hugh Burns, who came through for us when it mattered, with a loan that got us through.

"You're good for it, right?" he said.

I promise you, whoever you are, here's the thing, an experience like this is just something that happened to you, it's not who you are. How you deal with it is who you are. Sometimes the best lesson you can learn is to find out you can survive something, even though you are so afraid of it that it wakes you up in a cold sweat in the dead of night.

Pete:

Money is nothing more than a point in time... sometimes you have it, sometimes you don't. It never determines who you are as a person and tying your own self-worth to your money/possessions is a dangerous thing, but a lot of people do it.

I left the corporate world around 2006/2007 and started my own business at the same time I was getting divorced. The business I was starting was a consulting and recruiting business for the financial industry, basically taking my talents to those that needed it in the industry. I had a ton of business lined up and I had a financial position that was supportive of my moving in this direction.

Then 2008 hit... I lost all my net worth – more than half in the divorce but all my net worth was in financial industry stocks that went almost to zero, so I lost the rest of it – plus, all the business I had lined up completely dried up... basically, I had no assets and a lot of debt. For the next several years I was able to create enough business to pay the monthly rent and bills but that was about it.

And other things happened. Probably because of everything that happened, and things not going according to plan, my new wife and I were constantly fighting, and my former wife sued me, so I owed her more money. Much of the business I was trying to do was falling on deaf ears – meaning, per the above, people totally blew me off constantly.

Professionally my experience is that when you are in a position of authority/power – perceived or otherwise – everybody is your best friend. If you lose that position – everyone disappears, including if you "need/want" them, or you reach out for whatever reason during your down time, they completely ignore you... but when you "come back into power", all of a sudden they are reaching back to you like you are their best friend, basically because now they think you can do something for them. There's no point in even getting upset about it – it's a simple fact.

I owe a big debt of gratitude to my brothers who both gave me money and employed me in businesses for income, plus my college roommate and two other work colleagues who loaned me money to pay off my ex-wife. Yes, I ultimately paid everyone back...except for my brother who refused to accept the money back. Long story short, when you're down, you really come to learn who your true friends and family are.

Chapter Twenty-Five: The Sacred and the Profane

"You know why I quit playing ballads? Cause I love playing ballads." (Miles Davis)

In my experience, the correlation between success and contentment is not direct or consistent. Notice we're talking about contentment here, not happiness. The idea that success and contentment are closely associated is a fantasy. Successful people tend to be driven, which is not a quality that often leads to contentment, because of the tyranny of expectations. It turns out contentment is harder to achieve than success. It's possible only the laser focus, and self-abnegation of the serious Buddhist can achieve it. We have no way of knowing if our expectations are the grail, or the mirage, so we are tortured as much by our success as our lack of it. We are preoccupied with coherence, we build structures to bring order to our lives, religion, government, society, civilization, law, morality. Contentment is not easy, it's hard, and happiness? That's something you just catch yourself at, perhaps you sneak up and surprise yourself in a moment of happiness.

Look at really great artists, musicians, writers – Coltrane, Miles, Pollock, Rothko, Joyce, Van Gogh, Dylan. The great ones don't repeat themselves. They don't settle into the pocket and churn out the same familiar stuff, endlessly ringing the cash register. They don't do tribute tours or accept residencies in Vegas. Sometimes they lose their way, but they keep moving forward, challenging, changing, breaking the mold that they themselves have created. If they stop pushing, they die inside. For true artists, what they have achieved is behind them, it's history, and often their fans turn against them, resentful when their expectations are not fulfilled.

I think of Michael Jordan after he won his first championship, stretched out on the floor of the Bulls locker room with the trophy in his arms, sobbing. That wasn't happiness, it was relief. *I gave them what they want, now maybe they'll leave me alone.* But he didn't stop, he just raised the ante every year, pushing everyone around him even harder, collecting championships. Look at Michael Schumacher, when he won his first Formula One World Championship for Ferrari, same thing.

Most of the time I think we do things not because we think them through and decide on a rational course of action, but suddenly, and often irrationally. Mostly, we make the most important decisions of our lives impulsively, we do the things we feel compelled to do, we do them because we must. How they turn out is more often a function of luck than anything else. As Daniel Kahneman, the Nobel Prize winning behavioral scientist says, people tend to grossly underestimate the role that luck plays in their lives and he's done a ton of research on the subject, his point of view is based on math, on analysis, on facts. Often, things happen and we go back and rewrite the story into a form that we can understand, that makes it make sense, and sometimes we even decide we knew in advance what was going to happen, but we didn't.

And what about the power of passion and how it becomes a force in your life, how life can suddenly become a drama, a tragicomedy, a romance, and suddenly irrational impulses become serious life decisions, and mythology kicks in? Helen, purportedly the most beautiful woman in all of Greece, turned down legions of rich and influential suitors and finally chose Menelaus, king of Sparta, for a husband. Yet when Menelaus was away, she met another man, Paris, fell in love, and ran off with him, literally causing the Trojan War. Thousands of people died in the war and Troy, a great city, was destroyed, so totally eradicated that historians didn't believe it had even existed, until Heinrich Schliemann unearthed it in 1870, 3000 years later. She and Paris must have known Menelaus would retaliate for what they had done and that he would come after them, but they did it anyway. And in the end, Paris died, their children died, pretty much everyone in Troy was killed, and she ended up back in Sparta with Menelaus. I wonder, what is the lesson, the moral of the story? Did she ever regret it? I suspect she didn't. It wasn't a rational process. The gods may have been involved, but the story is really about the power of the profane, and really, between the sacred and the profane, what is the difference? Between true religious fervor and human passion, what is the difference?

Sometimes you find something, or you meet someone, and it changes your life. It's not rational. You might have an exceptionally organized and successful life and suddenly something happens, and it changes you completely and all your plans and everything you have built is blowing in the wind, like leaves before the storm.

I think how overengineered passion and love and lust are, in a purely evolutionary sense, for humanity to have survived at all. How easy it would have been for mankind to have been wiped off the face of the earth if not for the drive to reproduce and the capacity for suffering, both fueled by passion, sacred or profane, religious or temporal. Consider that we have feelings so intense we are prepared to suffer and die for them, things that are not even concrete or measurable; human beings make decisions this way all the time, and although it's counterintuitive, it's probably one of the reasons the species survives.

I felt like I was stalled, that my life was stuck, and it had to change. What I discovered was that when you have dreams, and unexpected things happen, there are challenges that come that you couldn't possibly have foreseen. They say that the universe gives you the challenges you can handle, and that was my experience, because they were also the challenges I needed, and they were a gift, even if it wasn't always obvious. I had certainly created a lot of challenges for myself, and inevitably there were a lot of challenges that came with trying to blend a family as well.

Our lives are entropic, constantly falling apart even as we are planning and building and bringing our dreams to life, the perfect ice cube that comes out of the freezer ends up a puddle of water and drips off the side of the table. So many things I had achieved, my marriage, my career, my partnerships, my success in business, and many of my friendships, just blew up, and no one was responsible for it but me, and it was messy, and people got hurt, but if I had left well enough alone, it might have been worse. Sometimes, inaction is just as dangerous as action, and more often than not, it brings regret as well, which is poison. Once I opened the door to change, there was no turning back, I had made my decisions, and there was no way I was going to be able to collect the water and turn it back into ice cubes. I know at times it was hard for my kids, and I think there is nothing on earth as powerful as your children's ability to love you despite the things you do and forgive you, or at least cut you some slack, for the moments you're not proud of. And there aren't many things as valuable as a few good friends.

When they threw me out of Choate, the headmaster, Seymour St. John, took me aside, because after all, it wasn't enough to throw me out, he had to have the last word as well, and he said,

"What is it with a kid like you, who has all the chances, and you just blow it." And in that moment, I thought of Holden Caulfield, and Salinger, maybe, and I decided I was okay with it.

In some ways, perhaps he had a point. Maybe I could have been chairman of a bank, or president of a studio, or maybe I could have been a congressman, or a senator. However, it's also true that pursuing big goals like that can force you to accept a lot of mediocrity from yourself, a lot of expedient decisions masquerading as realism. You can make ugly compromises and questionable moral choices and still not end up as the person you imagined or hoped to become, so I'll stand by my choices, accept the challenges that came with them, and live with the consequences. And maybe if everything hadn't blown up, if Andrea and I hadn't had to start over, if we hadn't had to do the hard work, the door wouldn't have opened, and the most miraculous thing wouldn't have happened, which is what came next...

Chapter Twenty-Six: Synchronicity

Ain't we walking down the same street together on the very same day? (Paul Simon)

Pete:
She told us that we had an older brother who died in childbirth. She said it so often that one time I heard her mention having three children, and I corrected her.
I said "Four, Mom" without thinking about it.
We never knew what to believe, or if anything she said was the truth, and a lot of it definitely wasn't the truth.
I think what saved us was that we tried to stick together and get through it as best we could.
But the story about the fourth brother really stuck with us, and of course, now we know why.

A few years ago, I put a conference call on my calendar with three guys I didn't know. At that point, I had been on 23andMe for years and I had close to fifteen hundred "relatives", none of whom shared more than three percent DNA with me which, I'm pretty sure, means they could be anything from a second or third cousin to almost anyone on earth. I had resigned myself to the idea that my birth parents were either already dead, or I would never find them, and I hadn't thought very much beyond that. I had read the story about Steve Jobs, who was adopted, finding out that Mona Simpson, the writer, was his sister, which I thought was sort of cool, but hardly something that was likely to happen to me. I was paying less and less attention to the emails from 23andMe breathlessly announcing *new DNA relatives!* After sixty years of knowing only that I was adopted and nothing more, knowing next to nothing was the norm, just a birth certificate with my adopted name on it and the hospital I was born in, so I imagined I was comfortable with the likelihood that it would stay that way.

Then, one day, out of the blue, I got a message through 23andMe from a woman who turned out to be my niece, Brook. I looked her up and it turned out that we shared over twenty percent DNA, which is the percentage of shared DNA for a niece or a grandchild and since she is about the same age as my children, she clearly wasn't my granddaughter. I don't know who was more surprised, her or me.

People ask me how it felt to suddenly discover that I had three brothers, what I felt in the moment, and the answer sometimes surprises them. I was in my forties when a therapist told me that studies have shown that people who are adopted often have a pervasive and unshakeable feeling that they don't belong, like spectators in life. I had never heard anything like that before, and it was the first time I had a label for a kind of empty feeling that I had known for years without understanding it or even being fully aware of it. I felt like I was lost, and I didn't really know why. I wasn't even conscious of the weight of it until it was lifted off my shoulders. What I felt was relief; there was a past, an explanation.

What Andrea says, is that in that moment, everything changed and nothing changed, and she is correct. I have found that life-changing moments can be like that. Things slow down; detail recedes. Things get simple, not dramatic so much as the opposite, devoid of drama. Those moments, whether joyful, challenging, scary, possess a kind of quality that is compelling in its clarity, and this moment was certainly one of those.

I had no idea what was coming. We came home from our end-of-summer vacation. I sat down at my computer Monday morning and there was a message there from a young woman I did not know (that was Brook) that would change my life and the next thing I knew I was the oldest of four full brothers. From the moment I got on the phone with them, they were not strangers. Nature versus nurture may always be a scientific debate without a resolution, but what I do know is that connecting with my brothers brought me three best friends I never expected to have. My experience, which I think is shared by a lot of men, is that once you reach a certain age, you are unlikely to make very many new friendships that are close and intimate, where you feel free to share your thoughts and feelings openly, but whatever the obstacles are, they seemed to be absent from my relationship with my brothers from the start.

When I hung up the phone, we had been talking for an hour and a half. I turned to Andrea and I said, "I love these guys!"

And she said, with a hint of sarcasm, "Of course you do, they're just like you."

On the day I got that message from Brook, my niece, I received a gift that I had always hoped for, but did not expect, a gift from the universe, the product of chance and luck. I used to think that if I had family out there, it was probably a waste of time to search for them. If it was going to happen, they would find me, which was in some way just a fatalistic rationale. I didn't think that having intention, or expending energy or resources to make it happen would have contributed to the outcome at all. But Andrea signed me up for 23andMe, and sure enough, they found me. I think it's important to understand how incredibly lucky it was that this happened at all.

I am beyond grateful for my (extended) family, my three brothers and their wives and my six nieces. And at the same time, I am supremely cognizant of how important the role of luck and coincidence has been in this.

Experience is a matrix of overlapping stories and each of those stories is colored by the perspective of the teller and the perceptions of the receivers of those stories. The truth is an energy that travels through it, but it's ephemeral. It can't all be captured in any one single moment or story and when you try to hold onto it, to nail it down and remember it, it fractures and slips away. The story is a moving target. It's constantly being refined and improved. With every telling, it changes ever so slightly.

When I look at my parents, and when I say my parents, I mean both sets of parents, my adopted parents and my birth parents, it strikes me that they are all ultimately unknowable, and the more they fade into the past, the more I try to focus on them, the more they fade into each other – the parents I knew, and the parents I never met – as if they are in the process of completely fading into each other, so that in some way, my brothers and I are actually products of a common experience. It feels as if we did grow up together, even though we only met a few short years ago. As Hank says, I feel as if you were there, it's just that you were temporarily absent or something, and I get what he means. I feel that same way, like I missed the specific events, but somehow, I was there anyway.

Without being reunited with my brothers, with my "first" family, I could never close the circle. It would have remained a mystery to me, and I would have taken that puzzle with me to my grave, along with the weight I was only marginally conscious I was carrying.

I'm not necessarily an authority on adoption, I just know my own story and the other stories I've heard, and read, but I have spoken to other people who share versions of my experience, and there are a lot of them, and they are all different. One thing I have noticed is that adoption seems to be mostly talked about from the perspective of the mother who gives up the child, not from the perspective of the child who was given up. It's like a prison of silence, because you have no experience to remember, you have nothing to contribute to the story, it's as mysterious to you as it is to anyone else. You were there and yet you have nothing to contribute. The story always seems to start many years later with a search, a discovery, a perspective that looks back on the event and attempts to interpret it based on whatever information is available.

When you are adopted, especially if you are adopted into comfortable circumstances, you are constantly told how lucky you are, how great it is, how loved you are because you were "chosen", what wonderful people your adoptive parents must be and you are constantly reminded that you should be grateful, in general, but especially to them. The corollary of this is that if you have any other feelings about it, if you are ambivalent, if you feel abandoned, if you are even confused, if you feel anything other than "lucky" and "grateful" you feel guilty, ungrateful, and unworthy of the advantages you have been "given" and the effect this has on your self-esteem is significant. There is nothing worse than growing up with parents who are perfect, whose faults are off-limits, not open for discussion, whose failures are your failures. If there is nothing wrong with them and you are not 100% happy and fine, then, there is something wrong with you. And what's worse, you don't even know what it is.

One of the strange things about adoption is the element of choice, which is inherent in the process. It takes a foundational phenomenon that takes place in nature and turns it into a transaction. Prospective parents fill out applications, they make choices, they show up on a given day to take possession. But childbirth and genetics in nature is random in the extreme. It's a process you set in motion either by accident or on purpose and you know from the outset that you have no control over it, nature is doing its job, the universe is in control, and you wait for the result. When that child is born you know that it has a random collection of traits determined by the incredible mathematics of DNA and the magical calculus of chance, and the next thing you know you are recognizing yourself and your spouse in the random characteristics of that child and sometimes, you are taking responsibility for them. So, adoption and birth are nothing like each other, except for one thing – everyone's life is an accident of birth, but adoption attempts to bypass the natural randomness of the universe, it defeats the chaos, and for that, I suspect there is a price to be paid. And despite the intention, the positiveness, the assumed generosity of the act, adoption stories are often complicated and not necessarily happy.

I often say that I experience life as a puzzle, as something I am constantly trying to figure out and now I know why. At the center of my experience there was always a blank space, like a document with important parts redacted. I had the feeling that there was always part of the story that I didn't have, that other people knew what was going on and I was just outside of everything, trying to figure out what the rules were, what I needed to know to find my way through life. Eventually I figured out that everyone lives their own story, there really aren't any rules, that I needed to find the answer myself, rather than expecting someone else to give it to me. I wonder if it's just me or are there others that have this exact same feeling, being an outsider in the world.

My brother Hank told me that he thinks I was there with him and Pete and Bill when they were growing up, just out of the room, temporarily not around, for some reason, and I understand what he means by that, as if I was just older and away at college or something. It feels as if we have a lifetime of shared history, or that our lives are visions of each other through a looking glass. I grew up living in a brownstone on the east side of Manhattan with a country house to go to on the weekends and trips to England and Europe, Mexico, Bermuda, the Caribbean, going to restaurants and the theatre;

they did too, but they were elbowed out of that life by chance at a young age. They grew up in Darien, Ct., arguably an upper-class suburb, but on the wrong side of the tracks, with a mother who was an unreliable, unpredictable, narcissistic alcoholic. My experience was objectively privileged, theirs was not, but strangely, when we compare our memories, we find ourselves in some way telling the same stories, comparing the same notes, revealing the same emotional landscape, the childhood you survive, and somehow, ending up with objectively similar lives. Both of my mothers, Lee and Nancy, were proud of their New England family history, proud of being a ship or two after the Mayflower, direct descendants from the original thirteen colonies, land grants from George the Third or the Massachusetts colony, all regularly lubricated with alcohol and delusion. Both fathers, both named John, one I never met, and one, who to this day is still a mystery to me in many ways.

We grew up in the same part of the country, in similar environments, and it's entirely possible that our paths crossed, without us ever realizing it. I tease myself with this. I remember in grade school going to visit a family in the suburbs in Connecticut somewhere that my parents knew, but I don't remember who they were and I only remember going there once. They had three boys, three brothers, and we played baseball out in the street, and they asked me if I could play on their Little League team, and we went to McDonalds, the first time for me. I wonder if those boys could have been my brothers. Of course they weren't, but coincidence is a powerful force in human experience, and, in this case, the difference between perception and reality is amorphous. I feel as if in that moment I might have outstretched my hand across the randomness of experience and touched their existence and how much my life would have changed if it were true, if I had only known, if it had been them, it gives me chills just thinking about it.

I was told that it was common practice at adoption agencies to try to match adoptees with families that were as much of a match as possible from the standpoint of factors like ethnicity, religion, locale, and so on. I'm not sure how that policy was communicated, or if it was even official or presumed to be scientific in some way. Maybe it's a function of 1950's naivete, but there are a lot of similarities between their memories and mine and the net effect of it is that we are able to understand each other's experiences innately, both on a practical and emotional level.

It's eerie how easily the four of us have settled into a rhythm, as if we have known each other all our lives. I can't explain it. It's just a function of the familiar nature versus nurture debate, which I suspect isn't going to get resolved for generations into the future. We share mannerisms and attitudes. We are just very similar. Everyone sees it, it's unmistakable. Andrea says the first time Pete walked into the room she gasped, not that we are exactly alike, but something about the immediacy of it, or the physicality, something she has a hard time explaining.

I know that not all stories of adoptees who are reunited with their siblings or parents are happy stories. In this, I know we are incredibly fortunate, and I am cognizant of the randomness of the entire event and the role that luck has played in the story. Brook was not looking for lost relatives. She went on 23andMe because she had ordered a kit for her husband and Amazon sent her an extra one by mistake. Brook is not a fearful or risk-averse person, so she just figured why not? I'm sure she never even thought about what might happen or imagined anything like what actually did happen.

I have a friend who spent time and money tracking down her birth mother and eventually found her and a half-sister she didn't know she had, but in the end, it wasn't that successful. They were not open to the connection with her, they didn't embrace the relationship or open their lives to her, and she is not particularly close to them.

I also know that there are many tragic stories of mothers who gave up their children, forcibly, unwillingly. I wonder if Lee had still been alive when this happened, would it have eased her pain, or made it worse? And if my adopted parents had still been alive, how would they have reacted? Would they have experienced it as disloyal? We will never know, and frankly, I am relieved. Some things are better left alone.

Think of the course of Lee's life. Suppose I was never put up for adoption, but everything else was the same. Her husband still dies on vacation in Italy, but now she has four boys to raise, not just three. Imagine she doesn't bear the guilt of giving up her child, does she still become an alcoholic? Maybe she was one already. Suppose John Stanton hadn't died and the two of them had raised a family of four boys together, but she was still an alcoholic. Suppose they stayed together. Suppose they didn't. So many paths, so many possible stories.

Pete:

I was always perplexed by how mom continued to discuss the "stillborn child she lost at childbirth". I kept thinking "you've had three additional sons since then, haven't you come to terms with it after all these years" ... but, more accurately, I kept thinking – even in my youth – that there was something more to the story. When Brook found Alex on 23 and Me, I immediately knew it was our brother – and that it was the child mom was tortured by giving up – that she had been calling her "first son/still born child". It was like the tumblers all fell in place. That was it – and meeting Alex and coming together after all these years as the four brothers seemed easy – like we'd known each other forever and that the "sins of the past" were somehow at least addressed in the end. I do wonder what would have happened if we had discovered this when our mom was still alive – i.e., how would she have reacted?

It's hard to find a connection to someone you've never met, to reconstruct a person out of the fragmented images and stories you've heard, the hall of mirrors, the information you're given, the assumptions that have been made, the narrative that has developed over the years. How do you accept what you are told and try to own it, look for the nuance behind the stories? I search inside myself for a memory of my mother, or my father, even though I know it isn't there.

I think the answer is you don't. Four people, each one had a story, each one was my mother or my father, who were they, what did they want, what kind of lives did they live, what does it all mean? Two of them I never knew, and the two I knew are mysterious to me as well.

I have my brothers, I have a family, an extended family now, I have my story, my life, finally I can embrace it. It's enough.

I felt that there was something missing from my life, I felt it instinctively more than consciously, and if this hadn't happened, I would never have known why, I would never have experienced the relief that went through me when it happened. I would have never understood the question at the center of it all, let alone the answer. My life is better because of it, somehow simpler and clearer, and certainly for the people that have come into it, the family I suddenly have. And something else is apparent as well. Whatever their qualities, their faults, their private pain, my parents, both sets, were just people, and maybe it's time to forgive them all, and let them rest.

In our first conversation as brothers, the four of us, Bill said, "Maybe we can fix the past" and I thought, no, that's not how it works, you can't fix the past, but now I'm not so sure. I think maybe he was right. Maybe you can.

Epilogue

"Sometimes you have to play a long time to be able to play like yourself."
(Miles Davis)

My brothers and I are baby boomers, there's no denying that, and we are probably unexceptional. We weren't separated by war, or famine, or holocaust; we didn't cross an ocean in a rubber raft, we are not victims of oppression. Our story is simply the result of decisions that normal people made in stressful situations, decisions that carried emotional weight for everyone involved, that were made with good intentions and the best information available at the time. And still, they were monumental decisions that determined, in great or lesser degrees, the course of our lives, and we were exceptionally lucky to experience the resolution that came for us, too late for our parents, but just in time for us. And that is a story that should give people hope. Amazing things do happen, in unpredictable ways, and all of us are lucky, at least sometimes. Nothing is predetermined. There are no certainties; good things are no less likely to happen than bad ones.

These days nobody likes to be called a baby boomer. It conjures up images of aging, overprivileged, me-generation narcissists depleting the Social Security and Medicare trust funds and playing pickleball in Boca and Sun City. This goes hand in hand with a pervasive commercialization and trivialization of the sixties into tie-dye t-shirts and bell bottoms, Tiffany peace signs and nostalgic images of naked kids frolicking in the mud at Woodstock, the irresponsible progeny of the serious generation that grew up during the war.

But it's not that simple.

I was born halfway through the two decades that frame the baby boomer generation; technically I am a part of what is often referred to as the second wave baby boomers, the group whose lives were defined by a period of massive upheaval and change. I was a teenager in 1968, an impressionable age at an impressionable time, my world view irreparably formed by the late sixties, by the decade from the release of Meet the Beatles, in 1963, to the end of the Vietnam War, in 1973. During that time, President John F. Kennedy, Robert Kennedy, Malcolm X, and Martin Luther King, Jr. were assassinated; Fred Hampton and Mark Clark were murdered by the FBI and the Chicago Police Department, and there was no investigation, and no one did anything. Jimi Hendrix, Janis Joplin, Duane Allman, Jim Morrison, and countless others flamed out and four student demonstrators were shot and killed by the National Guard on their own college campus at Kent State University in Ohio.

When Lyndon Johnson, isolated by criticism of his escalation of the Vietnam War, announced that he would not run for re-election, we thought it was the beginning of something, people talked about revolution, one that would bring radical change – the end of the Vietnam War, the dismantling of the military industrial complex, the triumph of the civil rights movement, the success of the environmental movement, and more besides. Eugene McCarthy won the New Hampshire primary, politicians in suits and ties were coming out against the war, the South was being desegregated; everything seemed possible. Then, implausibly, in January of 1969, came a vicious backlash, more like whiplash, Richard Nixon was sworn in as president, restoring "law and order" became the word of the day, and although we didn't know it right away, it was all over. We thought it was the beginning, but it was the beginning of the end. To say it was surreal is an understatement.

I think it has largely been forgotten that there was a moment in time when we might have transformed the country and the world into a more peaceful, more ethical, livable place, peacefully, without violence or exploitation. The great problems were all on the table - racism, poverty, abuse of power, colonialism, imperialism, destruction of the environment, even global warming – but the overwhelming inertia of the status quo, the power structure - threw out the anchor and stopped progress in its tracks. The backlash was sudden, driven by the personal and corporate interests of a bunch of old white men who couldn't let go of the privileges they believed they were entitled to, even for the sake of their own children, regardless of the cost to the country and the planet. So, we have all the same problems today, but far worse, calcified by years of inaction, protected by lies and corporate self-interest, perpetuated by the self-serving personality cults of Wall Street and Washington D.C. and the for-profit news industry.

If you think it's the baby boomers who created the mess we are in now, think again. We inherited the mess, and we imagined we could fix it. Think where the country might be today if we had spent the last 50 years solving these problems, instead of investing in fantasies of empire and American exceptionalism. This is the tragedy of the sixties, not the things that happened, but how close we came, the revolution that, in the end, didn't happen.

I prefer not to think of myself as old, but once you get into your sixties, you're not middle aged anymore, so where does that leave you? It's like being in a kind of limbo, not clearly defined, where there are unfortunate signposts that you start to recognize, things you heard your parents say when you were young, things that sounded ridiculous, but now you understand what they meant. My mother used to complain constantly about getting old, about the indignity of it, now I know what she was talking about.

It all seems so predictable, the medications you start taking, the issues that come up, it all makes you feel like a cliché. The other day, I was filling out a questionnaire at some doctor's office, and they ask you what medications you're taking, and I said to the assistant, or the tech, whoever it was asking the questions, "I'm a sixty-five-year-old white guy. What medications do you think I'm taking? Losartan, Atorvastatin, Cialis, Xanax. And I'm healthy, and when I talk to my doctor about it, he says, "It's just a function of the aging process, it's how old you are, there's nothing wrong with you."

I feel like a stereotype. They ask me what my health goals are. More hair, fewer pounds, and a harder dick, what do you think they are? And they just look at you like you're being difficult. There's a questionnaire now where they want to figure out if you're depressed, or suicidal, where you rate the questions on a number scale, and then they add it up and decide if there's a need for intervention. They're tricky about it, like you're not going to figure out what they're getting at. Are you kidding me? What thinking person goes through their day without wondering if it might be time to end it all, proactively, before things get any worse? Read the newspaper, look at the world, you can't refuse to acknowledge at least some of the time that it's hard to be optimistic about the future. But you can't be honest, you have to manage their expectations because if you open the door to that conversation, you'll never get it closed again, you'll be labelled as an old person with depression, instead of a wise person with experience.

Again, it's something we've all heard before, but you reach a certain point in your life where you realize you must come to terms with your own death, when it becomes a fact, not something you can push out of your consciousness, like the end of the world. I'm starting to ask myself am I going to save enough money by the time I can't work anymore so that my kids don't have to spend their money taking care of me; are the people around me going to have to remind themselves of the person I used to be because I have lost the plot and become old and angry and confused? Will I be able to fade gracefully back into the universe, into the heart of the mystery, without causing struggle, and pain, to the people I love? Is there a way to ensure that Andrea and I can die together so that neither one of us will have to learn, after all these years, how to be alone?

I remember as a child, reading that the sun was eventually going to burn itself out, or explode, and the earth would be destroyed and life as we know it would come to an end, experiencing existential fear and despair for the first time, asking my mom if it was true; and she told me not to worry about it, it wasn't going to happen for millions of years, and I believed her, and found other things to worry about.

But now, it's not so easy.

My real fear is that we have missed the window, that the movement that was crushed in the sixties and seventies, the issues that were put in a box and stuffed into the closet, global warming, the environment, racism, poverty, and endless wars, the solutions that remain unimplemented have now become a Pandora's Box of existential threats that it may be impossible to solve; that because of the power of capitalism, of big business, of money and monopoly, the backlash that started under Nixon, consolidated under Ford, rendered Carter, a truly ethical man, politically impotent, and powered its way right up through Reagan, Clinton, both Bushes and up to the nightmare of the present day. From Nixon's war on drugs, to Reagan's war on the poor, to Clinton's regrettable dishonesty, and Bush's war on intellectualism, knowledge, and truth, to Trump's war on democracy, our chance to build a healthy society that values everyone equally has been lost.

I hope for the sake of my children and grandchildren, that it isn't so.

Sea levels are rising, the earth is warming, mankind has acquired the power to alter the planet to the point where we have put our own existence in danger, and people who should know better, instead of responding to it as a crisis to be faced and dealt with, people who actually have the means to do something about it, instead are making ridiculous plans to colonize outer space, and buying islands, and freezing themselves so that they can wake up when it's over. We used to laugh about people like that, and say they had more money than sense, but it's not so funny anymore.

Frankly, nature may just decide that mankind has outlived its usefulness, that we have failed to care for this miraculous world we have been given and come up with a virus or send us a meteor that will kill us all, leaving the planet to repair itself without our venal, selfish, interference.

All these things, and many more besides, could happen.

But you know what?

Not today....

Pete, Bill, Lee, Hank

Birth Mother
Emily *"Lee"* Adams Heart

Birth Father
John Stanton

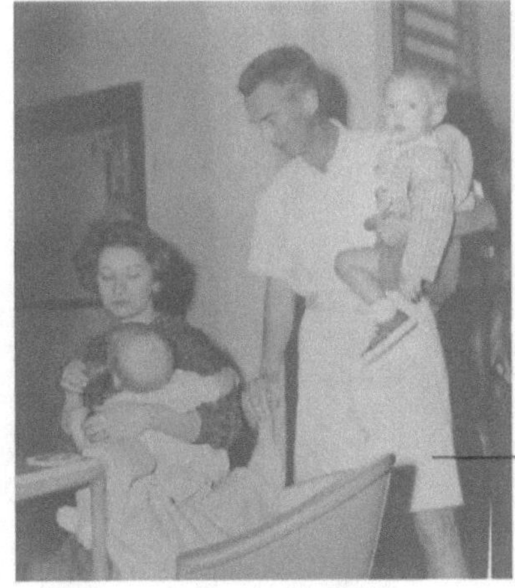

Lee & John Stanton

Adoptive Mother
Nancy Pierce Phelps
Phelps Corners

Alex

Adoptive Brother
Jonathan & Alex

Adoptive Parents
Nancy Pierce Phelps
John A. Blum

Alex

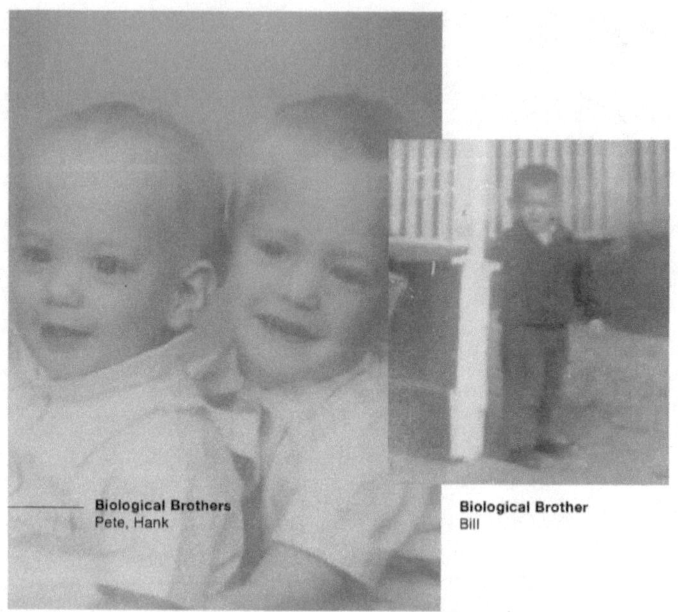

Biological Brothers
Pete, Hank

Biological Brother
Bill

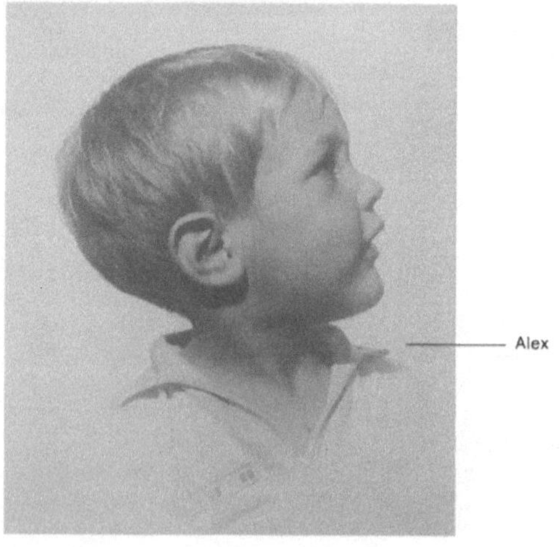

Alex

Alex and Bill

Alex and Pete

Alex and Hank

Acknowledgments

My thanks go out to a lot of people who contributed to this book:

First, to Hank, Pete, and Bill, my brothers, for their openness and support, and for their testimony. And to Hank, my publisher, for his guidance.

To my adopted brother, Jonathan, for sharing those years with me, whose unique understanding helped me believe I wasn't crazy.

To my niece, Brook Stanton Zaengle, who set the whole process in motion, and to Jamie Stanton, her sister, and my editor, who made many insightful contributions to the final manuscript.

To Richard Posell, a longtime friend and for many years my lawyer, for his comprehensive notes and informed perspective. Also, to Carolyn Hill, an adoptee with a far more complicated story than mine, for her interest and insight.

To Ed Zier, who read an early draft of the complete manuscript, gave me my first impartial notes, and offered sound advice, and to Randy Croy, for his interest and support.

My lifelong friend, Chip Koch, deserves special mention—not just for reading the manuscript (more than once) and offering support, but for teaching me, back in 3rd or 4th grade, how to swallow pills without choking, thereby saving my life—or at least sparing my mother a significant source of irritation.

Margot Ellis contributed her thoughtful comments, and vivid memory of my "terrifying" father. Hugh Starkey, an old friend and, unexpectedly, one of my mother's admirers, asked me why—and that turned out to be one of the harder questions I had to answer.

Lacey Ruskin, my sister-in-law, told me she heard my voice on every page—as if that were a good thing, and Melissa Shiel, Scotty Ruane, and Lisa Lane—Andrea's lifelong friends, offered interest, comments, and encouragement. I hope for them it was worth the wait.

Andrea read it repeatedly through every iteration, always re-directing me when I lost my way. Every reader, however many there are, owe her their gratitude, because without her there would be a lot more overly clever, annoying nonsense in this book.

My children, A.J. and Laura Blum, encouraged and supported me throughout this journey, and many other journeys as well. I hope I deserve them.

My son Mike made me see that sometimes it's just not about me, that perhaps I am less deserving of both blame and praise than I think.

My stepdaughter, Rachel, set an example that challenged me to be more generous, and less judgmental.

Alex, my stepson, took the good with the not-so-good and chose to focus on the good. My world is better with him in it.

Rebecca Whitney consistently brought her creative support, imagination, and friendship to this project, as did Calvin Lyte Sr. our head creative guru.

Nikki Hainstock, shaman, adviser, and friend, for her insightful reading of the manuscript, understanding everything.

I am grateful to Steven Reiter, Ph.D., Walter Slote, Ph.D., and Josie Kelly,MFT., all of whom, decades apart, kept me from losing hope.

And to Sophie Caminiti, my friend and book consultant, Michelle Blankenship, my tireless publicist, and to Morgan Messing and Samantha Dockser, my excellent social media team.

Thank you.

"Happiness is the sweetness of desiring what you have, fully aware of its fragility, its brevity and its limits."

Stephen Grosz

www.ingramcontent.com/pod-product-compliance
Lightning Source LLC
LaVergne TN
LVHW100517110826
845146LV00002B/672